THE LONDON HOSPITAL
MEDICAL COLLEGE LIBRARY
TURNER STREET, LONDON E1 2AD

Books are to be returned on or before the last date below,
otherwise fines may be charged. Overdue books cannot be renewed.

Dramatherapy with children and adolescents

The development of the dramatic imagination is the means by which we can consider the implications of our actions. Failure to provide dramatic structure for the dramatic imagination can result in chaos, and confusion and imagination out of control leads to chaos in the community. Thus the role of drama in the healthy development of every individual is increasingly recognized, and especially its importance in working with children and adolescents. *Dramatherapy with Children and Adolescents* addresses in practical ways direct approaches to work with both individuals and groups and provides firm guidelines and theoretical frameworks for therapeutic intervention.

The first three chapters are concerned with the play of young children from contrasting approaches. The next three look at the context of dramatherapy work and some specific issues of theory and practice. These are followed by three chapters describing specific applications of dramatherapy with different groups of adolescents. The book closes with three chapters which look at the development processes of the dramatherapist and the family, and the themes of psychopathology and creativity.

The contributors – from Britain, Denmark, Greece, Israel, the Netherlands and the USA – draw on a wide background of experience in using drama with children.

Dramatherapy with Children and Adolescents will be invaluable to all professionals who work with children, including social workers, probation officers, nurses and teachers, as well as dramatherapists and playtherapists.

Sue Jennings is Senior Research Fellow at the London Hospital Medical College and a dramatherapy consultant to courses in Israel, Norway, Denmark and Greece.

Dramatherapy with children and adolescents

Edited by Sue Jennings

London and New York

First published 1995
by Routledge
11 New Fetter Lane, London EC4P 4EE

Simultaneously published in the USA and Canada
by Routledge
29 West 35th Street, New York, NY 10001

Typeset in Times by J&L Composition Ltd, Filey, North Yorkshire

Printed and bound in Great Britain by
Biddles Ltd, Guildford and King's Lynn

British Library Cataloguing in Publication Data
A catalogue record for this book is available from the British Library.

Library of Congress Cataloguing in Publication Data
A catalogue record for this book has been requested.

ISBN 0–415–11040–8 (hbk)
ISBN 0–415–11041–6 (pbk)

*This book is dedicated to
Sophie and Harry*

Contents

List of illustrations   ix
Notes on contributors   xi
Acknowledgements   xiii
Introduction   1

Part I The play of young children   5

1 The dramatic world view: reflections on the roles taken and
     played by young children   7
     Robert J. Landy

2 Fear and tension in children's games   28
     Iona Opie

3 Dramatherapy with children who are trapped in their
     spontaneous play   40
     Galila Oren

Part II The context of dramatherapy work   61

4 The role a role-play may play: dramatherapy and the
     externalization of the problem   63
     Torben Marner

5 How individual is individual therapy? The use of contextual
     therapy principles in the treatment of children and
     adolescents in dramatherapy   75
     Jan-Berend van der Wijk

6 Dramatherapy for survival: some thoughts on transitions and
     choices for children and adolescents   90
     Sue Jennings

Part III Dramatherapy with adolescents   107

7 Pinocchio – a handicapped brother: working with healthy
     siblings through dramatherapy   109
  Pamela Mond

8 From adolescent trauma to adolescent drama: group drama
     therapy with emotionally disturbed youth   150
  Renée Emunah

9 Images and action: dramatherapy and psychodrama with
     sexually abused adolescents   169
  Anne Bannister

Part IV Developmental framework   187

10 Shall I be mother? The development of the role of the
      dramatherapist and reflections on transference/
      countertransference   189
   Di Grimshaw

11 Families and the story of change   210
   Simon Dermody

12 The labyrinth dance of adolescence: journey through darkness
      and light   233
   Yiorgos Polos

Name index   243
Subject index   245

Illustrations

FIGURES

4.1	Graph plotting the power of the Troll between the fifth and sixth sessions	71
6.1	Integration of the person	92
6.2	Integration of society	92
6.3	Integration of person in relation to the world	93
6.4	Integration of preventive and curative theatre through the mask	93
6.5	Integration of historical facts with the dramatic 'as if' principle	94
6.6	How medicine, theatre and religion were intertwined	96
6.7	Relationship of the dramatic development of the child through Embodiment, Projection and Role (EPR), leading to character formation	97
6.8	Relationship of the two realities through dramatic playing and games	98
6.9	The relationship between development stages in the maturational process	100
6.10	The relationship of 'staying or going' or 'settling and wandering'	102
6.11	Integration of the dramatic processes of theatre art	105
7.1	Drawing by a 12-year-old girl showing her sister (lying on a sofa-bed) and herself	117
7.2	Drawing by a 10-year-old girl showing herself and two sibs in relation to their handicapped baby sister	119
7.3	Pictures used for creative writing activity in relation to issues arising from the Pinocchio story	131
7.4	'Before' and 'after' work on the Pinocchio story	137
7.5	'Before' and 'after' figure drawings	143
7.6–7.7	'Before' and 'after' family drawings	144/145
11.1	Family spectogram of a 7-year-old boy	220

TABLES

7.1 Common issues of sibs   112
7.2 Description of fifteen six-piece stories   122
7.3 Comparison of scores of fifteen sibs according to Basic
    Ph.   124
7.4 Development of work with sibs   127
11.1 The stages of the family life cycle   229

Contributors

Anne Bannister manages Child Sexual Abuse Consultancy for the NSPCC and is a dramatherapist, psychodramatist and social worker.

Simon Dermody is a theatre graduate and psychiatric nurse who trained as a dramatherapist, play therapist and family therapist. During ten years of therapeutic practice within the NHS he specialized in child, adolescent and family work. He now practises independently and is currently studying for his Ph.D in the specialist field of work with families.

Renée Emunah is founder/director of the drama therapy programme at California Institute of Integral Studies and past president of the National Association of Drama Therapy. She has worked with emotionally disturbed adolescents for over sixteen years.

Di Grimshaw is a registered dramatherapist working in the NHS with people with learning difficulties. Her earlier work was as a residential social worker and drama teacher of young people. She is on the executive committee of the British Association for Dramatherapists.

Sue Jennings has taught and practised dramatherapy in a variety of settings including adolescent units and family centres. Her doctoral research with the Temiar people of Malaysia looked at the socialization of children and young people through dramatic rituals. She is a senior research fellow at the University of London, as well as an actress and broadcaster.

Robert Landy is assistant professor at New York University and director of the masters program in drama therapy. He has pioneered drama therapy in the USA and is a prolific writer on the subject. He has written and researched a new model of drama therapy application known as the 'role taxonomy'.

Torben Marner is head of the department of child psychiatry at Hilleroed Hospital, Denmark, and works as a court consultant for young people and families. He works predominantly as a family therapist, inspired by systemic theory and practice, and integrates dramatherapy methods into his approach. He teaches family therapy in Oslo, Iceland, Prague and Moscow as well as contributing to the Institute of Dramatherapy's courses in the UK.

Pamela Mond is a clinical dramatherapist working at Zvat Hospital, Israel. She specializes in work with children and also teaches and supervises dramatherapy trainees.

Iona Opie is an international expert on children's games and stories and the author, with her late husband, Peter Opie, of many books.

Galila Oren graduated in acting at Bel Zvi in Israel and then completed an MA in drama therapy at New York University. She now works as a child and family dramatherapist in mental-health centres and special-education programmes in Israel. She is a teacher and supervisor on the Tel Hai dramatherapy training programme and also teaches social workers at the Institute of Social Work Training in Tel Aviv.

Yiorgos Polos is a dramatherapist, theatre director and social worker who lives and works in Athens. He has worked with young people with disabilities, mental-health problems and social difficulties, and teaches a variety of students and professionals. He is currently working in the psychiatric department of Agia Sofia as well as having a private practice and responsibility for the organization Aiwpa (Swing) for the research and study of artistic expression and creativity.

Jan-Berend van der Wijk works as a dramatherapist at a clinic for children and adolescents with mental-health problems in Smilde (The Ruyterstee). He works mainly with individuals and also with groups. He teaches dramatherapy at Leeuwarden and also supervises students on placement.

Acknowledgements

As editor, I should like to thank all the contributors for working so hard within the time-scale, and for their flexibility in making changes to their chapters. All of their ideas have helped me clarify my own ideas. Special thanks must also go to Audrey Hillyar and Pauline Sands for their help in the preparation of this manuscript. I should also like to thank Mooli Lahad, Alida Gersie, Derek Steinberg, Gordon Wiseman, Ann Cattanach, Steve Mitchell and Elizabeth Newson for their stimulating discussions on the nature of dramatherapy as well as the nature of childhood which have been immensely helpful to me in formulating my own thoughts and reflections.

Sue Jennings

Introduction

Sue Jennings

As I sit and reflect on the introduction to this book on dramatherapy, I am reminded of the many changes that have taken place since writing my first book, *Remedial Drama*, over twenty years ago: language has changed, education and health-care provision have changed – and I would have liked to have said that negative attitudes towards children and young people have changed, but I fear not. Although they are one of the most vulnerable groups in our society, they carry the burden of all our projections and ideals and dreams. Children should grow up being good and useful and kind to animals, contributing to the economy and helping old ladies. Many people think that children who do not conform to this fantasy image are bad and wicked and must have been born that way, and therefore they must be denied support or therapy or even life.

We need to be able to explain and blame; so, for example, young people are blamed for not contributing to the economy (just as old people are blamed for not being useful). However, both young and old alike need nurture, care and support, as well as stimulus, imaginative education and that curious combination of stability and excitement. If we do not have a balance between the two, then we grab more of one: the child who feels rootless will often go out to get more kicks, and the child who is stifled can go into depression.

As parents and families feel more isolated, and social and cultural groups break down and extended families disperse, young people more and more are having to fend for themselves. No longer are they able to stay with Nan for a time until things calm down – she may well be in a home by now.

Birth to adulthood is a time of development, growth and change, which is most influenced by the context in which we grow up – both family and society – together with our biological birthright. Whatever our physical endowment, it matures in relation to the world around us. Hence, the very nature of this book is to look at ways in which the dramatic intervention through dramatherapy can be helpful to troubled children and adolescents.

If we understand that the development of the dramatic imagination is the means by which we can consider the implications of our actions, we can see the importance of the drama in development. Infants are born into the human race as dramatic people who commence dramatized interactions at days rather than months old, and strive after mimicry and innovation both physically and vocally. Even as I write this piece it is suggested that the great geniuses of science needed a highly developed imagination with which to hypothesize before commencing their scientific investigations. For example, the *Daily Telegraph* reported on 19 February 1994 that: 'Dr Roger Shephard of Stanford University . . . suggested that the most revolutionary scientific insights were performed in the imagination in advance of collecting any hard evidence.'

Some time earlier I myself had written that:

> The infant is born with creative potential and the capacity to symbolize: indeed it is the very capacity of human beings to pretend or make-believe which enables them to survive. We cannot envisage a life within which we could not imagine how things are – how they were, or how they might be. The creative imagination is the most important attribute that we can foster in children, and it is the basis of creative playfulness.
>
> (Jennings 1993: 20)

This book illustrates from different perspectives and practitioners how dramatherapy with children and adolescents can both be an important therapeutic intervention as well as working preventively to develop healthy individuals.

The first three chapters are concerned with the play of young children in contrasting approaches. Robert Landy (Chapter 1) emphasizes the importance of understanding 'children's logic' and takes us into a new theory of role which illuminates very strongly our understanding of early child development. Iona Opie (Chapter 2) shares her extensive experience of children's games and folklore in looking at the intrinsic fear and tension in children's games. This understanding is important for play and dramatherapists, providing a greater insight into children and their needs. Galila Oren (Chapter 3) presents case histories in which she looks at how some children become trapped in their spontaneous play and, paradoxically, how dramatic play can resolve these issues. The next three chapters look at the context of dramatherapy work and some specific issues of theory and practice. Torben Marner (Chapter 4) has brought together systemic family therapy and dramatherapy, and looks at how problems may be diminished or resolved through externalization methods such as role-play, role-reversal, storytelling, letter-writing, drawing and so on. Jan-Berend van der Wijk (Chapter 5) looks at the 'contextual principles' applicable to dramatherapists who are working with individuals. In Chapter 6 I consider the basis of the dramatic imagination for healthy survival and the importance of being able to 'wander' as well as 'settle'. The following chapters all deal with specific applications of dramatherapy with contrasting groups of adolescents. Pamela Mond (Chapter 7) presents evaluated research in working with the neglected area of siblings who have brothers or sisters with disabilities. Renée Emunah (Chapter 8) describes her practice of group dramatherapy as a container for the safe exploration of adolescent turmoil or trauma. Anne Bannister (Chapter 9) describes her use of both psychodrama and dramatherapy with sexually abused adolescents in relation to client 'images' and related 'action'. The final three chapters lead us into developmental frameworks for looking at the processes of the dramatherapist, the family and the images of 'light and dark'. Di Grimshaw (Chapter 10) shares her own development as a dramatherapist alongside her professional work with young client groups, and addresses the issues of transference. Simon Dermody (Chapter 11) looks at the emergence of the 'therapeutic milieu' through the integration of dramatherapy and play therapy with family therapy principles. To close, Yiorgos Polos (Chapter 12) looks at the themes of 'darkness and light' in relation to his work with adolescents and, more generally, in psychopathology and creativity.

Most of these chapters have been written by dramatherapists or by contributors to the greater understanding of dramatherapy and its therapeutic practice. I hope it will stimulate both those readers involved in demanding work with children and adolescents, as well as those seeking to further their own imaginative development.[1]

Sue Jennings
Stratford-upon-Avon

NOTE

1 Caution: Many dramatherapy techniques and methods are highly stimulating and evocative and could result in extreme client distress if applied inappropriately. They can also become the tools of manipulation and control of clients and become anti-therapeutic. Dramatherapists are professionally trained at a postgraduate/ professional level and adhere to a Code of Ethics and practice. No dramatherapy methods should be used without appropriate training and supervision.

REFERENCE

Jennings, S. (1993) *Playtherapy with Children: a practitioner's guide*. Oxford: Blackwell Scientific.

Part I

The play of young children

Chapter 1

The dramatic world view
Reflections on the roles taken and played by young children

Robert J. Landy

INTRODUCTION

During a thunderstorm late at night, Georgie, age 4, woke up and cried. She was frightened by the noise and the flashes of lightning. Her brother, Mackey, age 2, slept through it all. In the morning, the two spoke:

> *Georgie*: Mack, are you afraid of storms?
> *Mackey*: Yes.
> *Georgie*: But you didn't wake up last night.
> *Mackey*: I wasn't outside.

Overhearing the conversation, I thought of Alice's adventures in Wonderland and through the looking glass (see Green 1965) where logic is turned on its head. Or, perhaps more apt, a different logic is at work. Alice's fictional adventures are reflective of the world view of many young children, whose sense of reality is quite different from that of grown-ups. Although I eschew Lewis Carroll's romantic conception of childhood, I agree with him that the early years in one's life are highly dramatic and imaginative. I also believe that one way of understanding early childhood development is to accept the unique logic of children on its own terms. As one who conceptualizes personality as a system of interrelated roles and social life as an interplay of character types, I offer a dramatic conception of childhood.

The dramatic world view implies that:

1 In everyday life, as in drama/theatre, persons or actors take on and play out personae or roles in order to express a sense of who they are and what they want. Role-taking is an imaginative process of identifying with a role-model and internalizing several of its qualities. For example, if I see my father as a victim, I might take on his propensity to feel victimized and begin to view myself as a victim. Role-playing is an external process of enactment where, for example, I enact the role of victim in relation to some real or imagined victimizer in my life.

2 Each role taken or played represents one part of the person, rather than a total personality.

3 There is a paradoxical relationship between an actor and a role, a person and a persona (Landy 1993). When an actor, such as Vivien Leigh, takes on a role, such as Scarlett O'Hara, she is both herself (Leigh) and not herself (Scarlett) at the same time. In a like manner, a child playing doctor is both the child (not doctor) and the doctor (not child) at the same time.

4 When in balance, the relationship and tension between actor and role promotes creativity, spontaneity, and healthy development. When the actor is too merged with a role or too distant from a role, a sense of confusion as to one's identity subsists.

5 Roles exist in relationship to one another. Each one taken or played often implies the possibility of the role not taken. Thus, each time one chooses (or is chosen) to be a victim, the possibility also exists of becoming a victor (survivor) or victimizer.

6 People make sense of themselves (and others) by taking on and playing out roles and communicating that sense to others through stories. Each story contains views of individual people or generalized groups of people as told from the perspective of a particular storyteller.

This chapter, applying the dramatic world view, attempts to examine primarily the early development of roles. The cast of characters to be explored is small, including the two introduced at the beginning, Georgie and Mackey, my children.

To allow myself the appropriate aesthetic distance, I needed to confront certain methodological problems. Certainly my objectivity would be impaired. Unlike Piaget, who formulated some of his developmental theory through observation of his children, I was studying my children in a non-scientific way. I engage with my children in an often random, imaginative fashion, telling stories and playing roles with them as a way of building my sense of father and of participant observer. My years of notes do not add up to a scientific understanding of role-development. They read more like a diary written by a novelist or poet or painter, noting striking observations about phenomena. (For an application of such an approach, see Hillman 1983.)

Furthermore, as I was taking notes, I was in the process of developing observational criteria regarding role-taking and role-playing, a process that is still developing. I still raise the same questions that I asked four years ago: is it possible to know when one has taken on a role? What is the relationship between role-taking and role-playing? Although one can see a role as it is played, how does one know what to call it? What do we call, for example, the 4-year-old who is afraid of storms – the fearful one? the coward? Is there some system of roles or role-types to refer to? When observing role-play, what aspects does one need to look at? And on a larger, philosophical plane, where do roles come from? Are they inherited? taken on from the social world? generated through an individual creative act?

These and many related questions guided my research process for the past several years. My methodology is, in many ways, a work in progress. As such, I cannot claim that my findings are either reliable or generalizable in a scientific sense. Their value will lie in their uncovering of individual moments that, if well described and substantiated, touch on a more universal experience. This is the method of art.

My research findings also added to a theoretical understanding of role-development. In an earlier publication (Landy 1993), I devised a system of understanding role in terms of role-type or universal form, similar to Jung's notion of archetype; role-quality or descriptive aspects of role; role-function or the reason that one plays a role; and style of role-playing, or degree of affect and cognition, verisimilitude and abstraction. Also, I devised a taxonomy of roles identifying and categorizing role-types that subsist throughout theatre history and in everyday life. The taxonomy includes eighty-four role-types organized into six domains: somatic, cognitive, affective, social, spiritual, and aesthetic.

In looking at the early development of roles, reference will be made to these recent conceptual findings. My primary approach, however, will be anecdotal and interpretive. As such, I offer a number of stories about Georgie and Mackey and examples of their expressive activities, both visual and verbal. This information should provide a view of how and when roles are taken on and played out. I offer a way of knowing about roles that is quite different from the cognitive schemes presented by Piaget and his colleagues. This is a dramatic method, a story method, a way of knowing through telling. It differs from a more scientific method not in its rigour and intention, but in its vision of who we are as human beings and how we make sense of our existence.

GEORGIE

As early as 1 year old, Georgie was eager for stories. She would ask that each story told by her mother or father be repeated endlessly. By 2, she would do the same, although she preferred that they read picture books to her. Georgie was a wonderful audience to their stories but would rarely venture out into the storyteller role herself. At least, that's how it appeared to her parents.

The other side of her social reticence was the fact that she seemed to have a rich imaginative life. By 1, she would gather her stuffed animals and other soft objects and arrange them in various pleasing tableaux. They would appear to be audience to her storyteller role. In that role she would talk to them at length in an apparently nonsensical, sing-song fashion. Even though she was unwilling to 'perform' for parents and friends, she had nonetheless taken on the role of storyteller as a 1-year-old and practised it within her arranged world.

Georgie told her stories in many ways – by 'speaking' to her dolls; by setting up tableaux, which in themselves embodied a story; and, as she became older, pushing 3, by drawing pictures. Her pictures revealed a complex narrative that often helped her make sense of real or imaginary experiences.

For example, at 3, Georgie drew a picture which she characterized as a faraway place where people are different. She noted the following characters in the picture: two gypsies, a bride and groom, a baby, and a faraway house.

This picture was quite clear to both her parents as it depicted not only several basic role-types that Georgie took on at an early age, but also a significant experience in her young life. When Georgie was 8 months old, she and her parents moved to Portugal for half a year, where her father was a Fulbright lecturer at the University of Lisbon. The experience of being in a foreign culture where babies are treated reverently and playfully by nearly everyone, including passers-by on the street, left a strong impression upon Georgie. To be a baby meant to be unconditionally lovable and desirable. Even though her actual memory of Portugal was limited, she continued to look at photographs and request 'Olà stories', tales of her adventures in a faraway land where babies rule the roost, the sun always shines, and playground and beach are a five-minute jaunt from the apartment.

Each day out, whether to the city, the beach, or the market, the family would see gypsies and Georgie's attention was often drawn to them. The gypsies were pariah figures who looked and behaved differently from the others. Some dressed flamboyantly and exuded an air of fierce independence and sensuality. Sometimes the gypsy women were beggars and would be dressed in rags and would carry babies who appeared equally ragged and desperate. Other times, they would coach their young children, like the Peachums in *The Threepenny Opera*, to look pathetic and beg for small change. There were many rumours, told everywhere, of how the gypsies would intentionally maim their children so they would appear even more pitiful on the streets. Georgie's parents were used to aggressive homeless people on the streets of New York, but this was more exotic, more primal. Who were these people and where did they come from? What dark rituals did they practise? Were they actors wearing elaborate disguises or were they simply as they appeared – poor, oppressed outcasts whom no one really wanted. Did they choose to be pariahs or did others cast them in this role?

At 8 months Georgie was, of course, oblivious of these questions. But she was well attuned to her parents' reactions to this faraway culture. She came to know gypsies through her parents' eyes. In many ways her parents were gauging their own sense of rootlessness, alienation, and strangeness through their attention to the gypsies. So, too, were they weighing their own sense as parents who needed to guard against any impulse to use or abuse their children. They were wrestling with two images of parents and children – the first, observed in this faraway culture, unconditionally loving parents exceedingly attentive to their radiant children; the second, the distant or absent father and pariah-like mother, imposing an attitude of mendacity upon their oppressed children.

It was curious that Georgie drew two gypsies. When asked why, she had no explanation. Maybe they were mother and child, as they so often appeared on the streets. Maybe they were simply another variation on mother and father, a prominent theme in Georgie's drawings at 3 years old.

Where did Georgie's sense of gypsies come from? There were no photographs of gypsies at home nor did her parents speak of them in the house. At 3, it was hard to imagine that Georgie remembered seeing them or hearing talk about them when she was barely 1. Could it be that Georgie had internalized a gypsy role? If this were so, it might not be based on her memory of actual gypsies but on the part of her parents that identified with the rootlessness and romance of the gypsies.

The fact that gypsies appear in Georgie's picture of _____ significant. It could be that each expressive act of _____ more roles. We can assume that the gypsy role _____ an early cultural experience as filtered _____ parents. If this is so, then Georgie _____ qualities, as mentioned above. S_____ purposes, e.g. to express he_____ the age of 2 she has tak_____ dolls, and in danc_____ disconnection _____ frequently _____ an on_____ re'_____

as a_____ pleas_____ where a_____

The br_____ since she was 1, whe_____ and respond intently to a_____ day life. Generally, the roles of b_____ with those of Mommy and Daddy. These, very clearly, were two of the earliest roles she had taken on.

I give the example elsewhere (Landy 1993) of behaviour at 17 months when Georgie moved back and forth between her parents, touching each one and chanting: 'Mommy, Mommy, Mommy,' and 'Daddy, Daddy, Daddy.' Then she retreated to her dolls and spoke to them, as if to tell a story of who she was in relationship to her parents. Through her play, Georgie was not only taking on the roles of mother and father, but also staking out her own territory as child in relation to them.

In a faraway land, the parents as bride and groom are a foil for the gypsies. The parents must be stable, married, and connected, unconditionally nurturing, unlike their counterparts who are strangers in a strange land and who might mistreat their children in order to feed themselves.

Even at 8 months old, Georgie made distinctions between the bride/mother and the groom/father. The father had clearer boundaries. He worked in the house and was not to be disturbed when working. The mother, however, was less clear. She wanted to be unconditionally available but could not, due both to circumstances, e.g. illness and work, and temperament, in that she felt ill-equipped to amuse an infant twelve hours a day. That ambivalence often caused her anxiety and guilt. Georgie could not and would not leave her mother alone. She constantly tested her, demanding extra feedings of breast milk, refusing to eat much solid food, denying her privacy or time alone.

Role-theory tells a story of family legacies. Role-types and qualities seem to be passed on from one generation to another. The Jungians take the idea much further in suggesting that archetypes which are unconscious, collective forms of being embedded in the psyche, are ubiquitous not only in families over generations, but also across cultures throughout history. Although there appears to be much validity in this point of view, it doesn't address the specific ways that children take on and play out the roles of mother and father. Georgie's conception of mother appears to be that of one who wishes to be unconditionally loving but cannot always be so. The mother role that Georgie takes on well reflects her mother Katherine's reality as she attempts to be a 'good enough' mother for her daughter. In truth, Katherine has taken on her conception of mother from her own narcissistic mother. Through therapy and years of reflection, she has become aware that she was mothered by a person who always put her own needs before her children's and demanded to be mothered by others, e.g. husband and children, to protect her from maternal responsibilities.

The narcissistic mother breeds children who are unclear as to how they are to play out their child roles (should they mother their mothers?) and how they are to take on the mother role. When they are young, their children will play out these confusions in relationship to their dolls, friends, and others in their social world. When they are grown and become mothers themselves, they are often faced with the kind of ambivalence experienced by Georgie's mother.

Of the two parents, the mother is the most significant for Georgie. She is the first one she goes to when hurt or sad or lonely or needy. She is the primary feeder, teacher, moral figure, and punisher. In Georgie's imagination she takes on many incarnations as bride, fairy godmother, queen. As bride, she is endlessly hopeful, a fairytale figure who may well live happily ever after.

This image of the bride is reflected in many of the stories read and films watched by Georgie at 3 years old. The figures of Cinderella, Ariel (from the Disney film *The Little Mermaid*), and Belle (from the Disney film *Beauty and the Beast*) all become brides and as brides will be endlessly happy. This is the mother Georgie so very much wants to have and to become. Less than this, which is reality, is often unacceptable and cause for disappointment, resistance, and anger. In taking on the romantic role of bride, Georgie plays with her fantasies. She tells her dolls and stuffed animals that she will marry the prince, that this is what grown-ups do. Georgie also sees that these female figures have to endure hardship before their transformation into bride. Cinderella, for example, is endlessly humiliated by her step sisters and step mother, that is, until she meets her saviour in the figure of the fairy godmother, a perfect helper who will allow her to transcend her squalour and find the perfect life of brides.

In playing out the bride, dressed in a yellow gown at 4 or an Afghan at 3 or a ragged towel at 2, Georgie enacts the ritual of trial, transformation, and perfection. While in role there is a clear end in sight and that vision steers her through the hardships of biting brothers and scolding, demanding parents. The function of the bride role, then, is to provide a sense not only of romance, but also of a happy ending to the difficulties of living among demanding and self-involved people.

As I am writing about the bride role, I notice that with each attempt to write the word 'bride', I instead write down (in longhand) 'bridge'. In fact, it happened so often that I could not dismiss it as a typographical error. How then, I ask myself, is the 'bride' a 'bridge'? It seems to me that, for Georgie, the bride is a bridge between the drudgery of everyday life, as in Cinderella's burden of virtual slavery, and the fantasy of a perfect relationship or marriage with a saviour figure, whether mother, as in fairy godmother, or father/husband, as in prince. The wish for a perfect mother, father, and husband, all of whom can magically fulfil her needs, is a very comforting one for a child who has not too long ago lost her mother's breast and her mother's body as an endless supply of sustenance and identity.

In standing alone at 2 years old, Georgie, like other children, needs bridges or, in D. W. Winnicott's terms, transitional objects (Winnicot 1971), to help her cross the dangerous waters of separation and individuation (see

Mahler 1975). In this deeper sense, the bridge serves as a transition between a merged identity with the mother and a separate identity as a girl who will grow up and 'marry' other roles, that is, take on those roles that are needed to further her developmental journey.

In normal development, the roles taken will further the process of individuation and allow for effective marriages with others in their complementary roles. In abnormal development, the individual unable to separate from the mother will seek others with whom to merge or to mother. Thus, one's own identity will become submerged in another and one will use the other as a kind of skin to enter in order to feel whole. For this kind of woman, the husband would be seen as a romantic figure, a prince whose function is to save her from both the drudgery of everyday life and the need to become an independent human being in her own right. While it is normal for a 3-year-old girl to wish for a prince on a white horse to whisk her away, it is not so for a 30-year-old woman whose bride role has remained marooned on one psychologically primitive shore with no bridge available to help her across.

For Georgie, the groom is a less prominent figure than the bride. In all her expressive activity, especially her drawings, the groom is generally smaller than the bride. It would appear that this figure represents the father role. As a role-model, Georgie's father has been paradoxically present and distant. As an academic, he has always spent a lot of time at home and has participated fully in the tasks of raising Georgie. While in Portugal, this was particularly true. Yet, especially in Portugal, he was troubled and professionally stuck, feeling both alienated from the new culture and angry that there was not enough recognition forthcoming from students and colleagues. This was his sabbatical and he was unable to rest. Thus, although he was available to his 8-month-old daughter, he was also self-involved and often emotionally unavailable.

This image of the father, so unlike the prince with the glass slipper, must have caused some ambivalence for Georgie. In taking on the father role, she might well have internalized this ambivalence. It was later, at the age of 2, when she became aware of other kinds of 'grooms', that is, fathers-to-be, who were unambivalent rescuers. Like the image of the bride, the groom might also have served Georgie as a bridge between the imperfect father who was present and absent at the same time, and the perfect lover/husband who would save her from a life of ambivalence.

Through Georgie's first four years, the father has remained smaller in stature than the mother. Many times at 4, Georgie exclaimed: 'Mommy is smart; Daddy is silly.' For Georgie, the smart one is more desirable. Taking on the mother role will give her more wisdom and power. As mother, she will ultimately be able to nurture herself and know what it means to be female.

The silly father, although more distant than the mother, takes on another significance. This kind of father likes to play the fool and Georgie likes to engage with the foolish figure who tells stories and acts childlike and makes up silly songs. The father/fool role is also worthy of taking on as it, too, offers a wisdom, although one more indirect than that of the wise mother.

In the taxonomy of roles, I refer to the function of the father as protecting the family and providing a positive masculine role-model; and that of the husband as providing for wife and maintaining an aura of strength and stability. The role of father and husband that Georgie internalizes during the first four years of her life is much more complex than this. He does provide a sense of safety and stability. But he is also an ambivalent figure. He is masculine, but he also expresses his feminine side; as the mother is one who easily expresses her masculine side.

At 4 years old, it is unclear how Georgie will sort this all out. In her play, it becomes clear that she wishes for a happy, perfect marriage of bride and groom, father and mother, who will be unconditionally loving and accepting of one another. She, too, looks to these figures for an understanding of how to play out her complementary role of child. The gender ambivalence that Georgie internalizes might prove to be confusing in the sense of not knowing what men and women are supposed to do. On the other hand, it might well help her in constructing a non-sexist attitude toward masculine and feminine roles.

Back to the drawing, we find another important figure in the baby. This is the most prominent role of the 8-month-old Georgie, one given at birth. This role has also been socially determined by all the adults who endowed her with the rights, privileges, and, sometimes, scorn attached to their conceptions of how a baby should behave. Thus, the baby is one of the earliest visible roles taken on by a human being. In the first days of life, it is played out automatically, given the infant's biological need for care and nurturance and her psychological need for merging with the mother. As the weeks and months pass, the baby role is highly influenced by parents and other intimate adult figures, and Georgie learned further how to be a baby as she took on those adult points of view. Also, by taking on the generalized role of parents (on the generalized other, see Mead 1934), she learned what a baby is supposed to do in relation to parents.

As Georgie has developed throughout her first four years, the baby role has remained prominent. Generally speaking, the baby is dependent, needy, egocentric, curious, spontaneous, sensual, and playful. As the infant becomes a toddler and child, these qualities tend to diminish as she experiences a sense of decentring (see Piaget 1977), that is, a movement from egocentricity toward sociability. In Georgie's case, many of the baby qualities lingered into her third and fourth years. She was reluctant to give up her dependence upon her mother. She was reluctant to leave her self-contained egocentric world.

There are many explanations for why one needs to hold on to a particular role beyond its apparent developmentally appropriate time-span. For one, people hold on to roles because they provide a way to meet their needs. One plays the baby because of needs to avoid the responsibilities and demands of a later stage of development. Further, picking up on Hamlet's reminder that 'readiness is all', individuals can let go of one role and embrace another only when they are psychologically and physiologically prepared to do so. Some may never feel ready to decentre and take on the responsibilities of growing up. In this extreme, individuals would certainly have difficulties within a conventional society and might seek out relationships or a sub-culture that would support their needs to remain dependent and delay the responsible life.

In Georgie's case, her reluctance to give up the baby role might be based on a fear of losing her mother's unconditional love and attention. The psychologically greatest blow in her young life came with the birth of her brother when she was 2. Suddenly there was another baby to take her place. Her reaction was extreme. She refused any contact with her mother in the hospital and, for several weeks after the birth of her brother, she remained distant and angry. Her only connection to her mother was through a transitional object, a large stuffed dog which her mother gave her in the hospital as a present. She became focused on her mother's breast and would demand a feed herself when her mother was nursing her brother. She would find other ways to regress over the next several years to assure herself that her mother still loved her, even though she had forever lost the role of the baby of the family. All these regressions were duly noted by her parents' who used stories, drawings, and other projective means to help her bridge the gap between baby and child, with the knowledge that both roles are lovable.

The function of the baby role for Georgie was to remain tied to her mother and to delay her fall into a more grown-up, responsible state of being. As an Olà baby in a culture that adored babies, and as an only child with no competitors, she was well reinforced in her role-playing. But upon her return to a more 'baby-neutral' culture and the realization that she was growing up and had been relegated to the role of big sister, the baby role lost its effectiveness. Because of the realities and demands of family and society, Georgie needed to find a way to let go of her baby role or force it into a mould that no longer fitted. Well aware that the latter decision would cause her anxiety, Georgie's parents did all they could to help her through this difficult transition.

By 4 years old, Georgie's drawings of babies had diminished significantly. Much of her prolific output of artwork concerned depictions of the family, most especially of sister and brother. She had, in many ways, diminished the power of the baby role, which is not to say that she had transcended or extinguished it. Roles once taken are not then banished from one's personality, which I have conceived of as a system of roles (see Landy 1993). Rather, they are inflated or deflated as necessary, to serve particular individual needs. Georgie will always have a baby role available within her internal role-system. It will surface at times when she feels most vulnerable, isolated, and unlovable. But as she develops other age-appropriate roles, as well as roles concerning secure feeling states, it will have less control over her. Further, as she grows up, she will discover positive ways to use her baby role, perhaps to counteract the peer pressure to act grown-up before she feels ready, perhaps as a safety valve to help let off hurt feelings that have built up within a relationship or environment that disallows such 'infantile' expression. And should she continue to express herself aesthetically, the baby part might well counteract a burgeoning grown-up tendency to be overly rational and critical.

The final figure in Georgie's drawing is that of the faraway house. As noted above, this represents the new apartment in Portugal, far removed from Georgie's home across the ocean. Although not literally a role, the notion of being removed, separated from home, is a powerful one with many psychological implications. In some ways it connects with the role-type of the lost one, defined in the taxonomy as 'estranged and alienated, lacking a sense of purpose or understanding of one's place in the universe' (Landy 1993).

Most people take on this role either from a powerful role-model who exemplifies these qualities, or from an experience of being removed or separated from home, whether by divorce or war or fire or poverty or, in some cases, a psychologically difficult move from the familiar to the faraway. In some ways the reality is less important than the way the individual internalizes such disruptions. Some will move on from disaster with minimal psychological turmoil, having developed an intact survivor role. Others, with little ability to play the survivor, will experience considerable distress when temporarily moving to a 'faraway' house or when permanently moving from one house to another.

The ability to be a survivor as opposed to a lost one will again depend upon many factors. For many children, change of routine causes much anxiety. But some adjust well to change. One explanation of this, applying to an understanding of why any role seems to be prominent within a person's psyche, is that roles, like temperament, are to a large part genetically determined. The fact that some will survive disasters and others will fall apart when moving to a new town speaks to the way people are individuated genetically. Another explanation is that if one's parents take change and movement in their stride, they provide strong role-models for their children who, if genetically and temperamentally suited, will take on the survivor role and act accordingly.

Georgie, exposed to her parents' difficulties in living and working in a foreign culture, might take on her father's ambivalence, which might surface later on when she is confronted with a similar situation. She, like her father, might have a propensity for playing the lost one. That is not to say that the survivor role will be suppressed. Her parents are also survivors. But like her father, caught between the roles of survivor and lost one, Georgie might also be likely to take on that particular ambivalence.

I have at length extrapolated from a single drawing made by Georgie at 3 years old, referring back to an episode in the month preceding her first birthday. The several roles of gypsy/pariah, bride/mother, groom/father, baby, and lost one/survivor have been explored. Let me now turn to the source of Georgie's fall from grace, her brother, Mackey, and his early acquisition of roles. In my discussion of Mackey, I will also focus upon the relationship of brother and sister as it impacts upon role-acquisition and development.

MACKEY

When Mackey was born Georgie was 2 years old. As noted above, she had a difficult time accepting her diminished status from only child to big sister. Like most older siblings, she feared that she would lose attention and affection from her parents. In some ways, with the birth of her brother, she began to assume the role of orphan, at least temporarily.

There was some real cause for Georgie's concern. Although Mackey experienced a normal and healthy birth, after several weeks it became apparent to his mother that his ability to respond was impaired in some way. He was not smiling like other newborns. His eyes seemed vacant or moved in odd patterns. Further, he quickly developed colic and screamed inconsolably each evening from 6 to midnight. His mother became anxious and his father became distant. Both were exhausted from the evening ordeal of attempting to mollify the frightening screams and hysteria. Nothing seemed to work – neither breast nor pacifier, neither swaddling nor any of several ways of holding suggested by the books. To his parents, Mackey appeared to be in great pain each evening.

Who, then, was Mackey in his first weeks of life? He was a beautiful child with a beast-like disposition. Even during his placid moments, something seemed off – he wasn't connecting. Like Georgie, Mackey was breast-fed from the beginning, but he had a harder time staying on the breast. He often seemed to lose it and became easily frustrated. Yet when he first arrived home from the hospital, only days before the colic would hit, Mackey appeared to his father to be fully content in his own body and contained space of bassinet and basket. His father predicted, in fact, that Mackey would be a mellow child, a 'sunny boy'.

Many of the early roles that one takes on spring from a common source – one's parents or caretakers. As parents view a baby, a baby, in some essential ways, will come to view itself. According to this formula, which, like most formulas, is imperfect, Mackey will take on a paradoxical sense of himself as beauty and beast, lovable and terrible, mellow and hysterical, attached and detached, healthy and sick.

From a future point of view, Mackey at $2\frac{1}{2}$ years old, having long since left the colic behind, appears to play out the more positive role qualities, confirming his father's prophecy of the 'sunny boy'. But the journey from colic to contentment, from the darkness of the moon to the light of the sun, was a very long one indeed.

At 4 months old, after consultations with a number of specialists in the field of ophthalmology, it was determined that Mackey was not seeing anything. Light was passing through his eyes, but for some unknown reason, he had no visual response. His prognosis was uncertain. His parents were suddenly confronted with the reality of having a blind child and the possibility that this condition was uncorrectable.

Mackey, who had just about recovered from his colic and was shedding his hysteria, was again thrust into a disabled role. The doctors were stumped until one retinal specialist made his pronouncement: Mackey had albinism; the prognosis, although guarded, was hopeful. Mackey would see the world, but how much he would take in had yet to be determined.

The images of blind men with white canes, blind blues singers with dark glasses, and old men with seeing-eye dogs selling pencils in the street vanished from the mind's eye of Mackey's parents. Mackey's mother now imagined her son as Johnny and Edgar Winter, albino rock musicians with pure white hair and pink eyes. But Mackey's appearance was not that harsh: with sunglasses, he could 'pass' as a light-skinned boy.

The 'sick' role that had been imposed upon Mackey by the doctors and parents began to shift by 5 months. He had been working twice a week with Joanne, a gifted teacher from the Lighthouse, a state-funded organization that, among other things, sends teachers into the homes of visually impaired children. Within a short time, Mackey was responding to the various visual stimuli presented by Joanne. His parents, instructed by Joanne, implemented the exercises each day, and as Mackey responded more and more another level of bonding was taking place. Over several months, Mackey became quite responsive. His parents began to see him as less disabled and Mackey picked this up.

During these months of visual education, Mackey became attached to a stuffed animal, a tiger, which he later named 'Tigo'. Tigo became his transitional object, which he held and slept with daily through his first $2\frac{1}{2}$ years. A major function of Tigo was clear – to help Mackey move from the physically ill, disabled person who could not take in the world through his eyes, to the healthy, self-contained 'sunny boy', who could take in the multi-faceted imagery and roles and direct his external play accordingly.

With his improving eyesight, Mackey developed motor, cognitive, and verbal skills normally. His capacity to learn and use language actually developed early, as he began to speak shortly after his first birthday. So, too, did he begin to develop a sense of himself as a male differentiated from his mother and sister. Even though he was born with a genetic disability that affected his vision, Mackey was able to move beyond the role of the disabled, having internalized from his parents and teacher the sense that he was worthy and lovable and that he would get better.

Aside from his parents, Mackey's primary role-model was Georgie. He imitated her laughter, gestures, dress, and routines. He even attempted to take on her fears, even though he had not fully internalized them. As an example, Georgie developed a fear of fire sirens which sometimes went off several times a day in the small town where she lived. One day, Mackey, shortly before his second birthday, was playing on his fire truck. The siren went off. Georgie was nowhere to be found.

Mackey stopped his play and looked up as if to say: Should I be scared?

He came toward his father, who asked: 'Are you scared?'

Mackey replied: 'I scared.'

Again his father asked: 'Is Mackey scared?'

'Georgie scared,' he replied.

Indeed, Mackey was thinking about his sister's reaction and attempting to take on her role as frightened one. But because Mackey was indeed undaunted by the noise, he could not fully take on her role this time. Despite this, he was still ever ready to take on the many roles of Georgie in many other ways, to swallow her whole if necessary, even if some of the pieces did not go down too well.

Mackey's wholesale imitative behaviour allowed Georgie to role-reverse, taking on the baby role herself, and hoping for the inherent gratification stemming from being dependent and helpless. Role-reversal, which appears frequently during the early years, is part of normal development. Young siblings, like Georgie and Mackey at 4 and 2, reverse roles in order to either practise new roles or seek gratification from older ones. When the taking on of appropriate roles becomes blocked in later years, role-reversal can be employed as a technique to help individuals recognize another point of view.

At 2, Georgie would revert to baby talk. At 3, she would either pretend to cry or find occasions to justify crying for the purpose of keeping herself tied to the baby role. In her play at $4\frac{1}{2}$ she would cast Mackey in the role of Mommy and demand that he change her diaper, even though she was long since toilet-trained and Mackey, at $2\frac{1}{2}$, was not. This was joyful play as the two would laugh gleefully each time they played out their family roles.

The following anecdote of Georgie at 4 and Mackey at 2 offers another role-reversal, this time as the father takes on the role of baby and the children act out different versions of parents.

It is late in the afternoon and Georgie is in an ornery mood as she is often at this time of day since she gave up her afternoon nap. Her father is exercising and accidentally kicks her with his foot. She is not really hurt but pauses a bit to weight the moment. She cries, in a strained fashion. She goes to her mother and whines: 'Daddy kicked me!' Her mother assures her that it was an accident. Then she turns to her father:

'You're a baby, Daddy! Daddy's a baby!'

Her father takes on the role of baby and responds, childishly: 'I'm not a baby.'

Georgie counters: 'You are! You are a baby!'

Her father whines and says: 'I want a bottle!'

Georgie hits her father several times. Mackey, who has become interested in this interaction, joins in. The father cries some more in an exaggerated fashion and both children are amused. Georgie continues to hit, playing out a punitive version of a parent. When she hits too hard, her father pretends to be hurt. He cries more realistically, asking for comfort – a hug, a kiss, a nice word. Mackey becomes concerned that his father is really hurt. At 2, he has less ability than his sister to separate out play from reality. He comes over and gives his father a kiss and a hug. He demonstrates his ability to role-reverse with his father and to play out the nurturing parent when needed.

Georgie stops hitting her father and moves away, feigning disinterest. For her, the role-play is over. She has been upstaged by her brother who played a more kindly parental role than she did. Unlike Mackey, she knew all the time that this was a game.

Where did each child's version of the parent come from? Could it be that both have internalized the generalized role of parent differently? I think not. The answer may be that Georgie, at an older age, more mindful of the differences between playing and reality, uses the play as a way to express her ornery mood. She projects her mood upon her role of parent and aggressively acts out toward her father. Mackey, caught up in the reality of his father as sad and hurt, plays out the role he would want for himself if he were hurt, that is, the nurturing parent. Each child's version, then, is based upon his/her own needs at a particular developmental stage.

GEORGIE AND MACKEY

If it is true that genetics has a profound effect on the kind of roles we will take on and play out, we should be able to view this state of affairs at an early age. Georgie and Mackey both seemed to be predisposed to certain roles and certain ways of playing them out. Georgie often would take on either hurt or aggressive roles at 3 and 4 years old. Mackey, on the other hand, at 2 would take on more conciliatory roles.

When asked to compare their two children, both parents would agree that Georgie was very sensitive to slight physical discomfort, such as a splinter in her finger, and tended to panic at loud noises. She was generally more difficult and resistant. Mackey, on the other hand, once free of colic and severe visual impairment, seemed less resistant, more light and quick to bounce back from physical pain and disappointment.

It appeared to both parents that these genetically based traits affected the children's choice of role-taking and role-playing. And yet the genetic explanation of when and how roles develop is limited. As we have seen, roles are also strongly based on social factors. Georgie, for example, took on gentle and nurturing roles as Mackey took on aggressive and resistant ones from their role-models. This is more in keeping with conventional social and cultural expectations regarding gender. The following are examples of these more conventional behaviours in role:

> Georgie at 3 is sitting in her mother's lap in the morning. She opens the front of her mother's nightgown and exposes her breast. She examines it attentively and touches it in a very serious way, paying particular attention to the nipple. Her mother says: 'Do you remember when you were a baby and you had your milk from Mommy's breasts?'
>
> Georgie replies: 'When I am a Mommy and you are a baby then I will feed you on my breasts.'

In experimenting with the role of nurturing mother, Georgie imagines a time when she will nurse her own babies. In doing so, she casts her mother in the role of baby, a role that she has only recently left behind.

> Mackey at 2 is with his father at the lake. He climbs on a large rock and straddles it. His father is nearby, watching. A 4-year-old boy approaches Mackey and makes threatening gestures, growling like a tiger. Mackey stands his ground and says, forcefully: 'No!' The boy growls again, even louder. Mackey counters with a more aggressive 'No!!' He then climbs down and sneaks up on his father who is lying on a towel. He growls, trying to frighten his father. He circles around and growls even louder. The father feigns surprise and fear and both father and son laugh heartily. But Mackey goes a bit too far, hitting his father in the face. The father tells Mackey not to hit, but Mackey continues. The father becomes more forceful. Soon Mackey grows tired of his play and moves off.

Mackey in this case is testing out his power at both defending himself against an aggressor and playing the aggressor, seeing how far he can go. In his aggressive play with his father, Mackey enacts the same scene he has just experienced on the rock. The difference is that in the first instance he was cast by the older boy in a victim role. But he refused to take on that role and stood up to the aggressor. Feeling victorious, he did a role-reversal, playing out the aggressor role in a safe context, that is, toward his father. In playing out a frightened role (in a comic, stylized way), the father signals to the son that he is impressed by the son's display of power. This provokes Mackey to act out more aggressively, perhaps catharting his own sense of fear when confronted by the older boy. By standing up to Mackey's aggression, the father causes the aggressive play to stop. Even this mirrors the previous scene where Mackey caused the aggressive tiger behaviour to stop by standing up to the older boy. Mackey has internalized the understanding that aggression can sometimes be stopped by a forceful and aggressive response.

The genesis of aggression is a powerful topic that has been the source of research by philosophers, scientists, and artists for many centuries. In this case, we may speculate that aggressive roles come from two basic sources: genetic, despite the fact that Mackey tends to appear 'sunny' and conciliatory; and social, based upon known and sometimes unknown role-models. According to the work of Jung (Jung 1964) and his many colleagues, aggressive roles, as well as those of sexuality and other identity factors, are archetypal, that is, embedded in the racial experience of all human beings. This point of view is reflected in my own work developing a taxonomy of roles (Landy 1993).

It is hardly startling that Georgie would play out nurturing roles and Mackey would play out aggressive ones. In fact, children from birth to 4 are developing a universe of often contradictory roles from archetypal, genetic, and social sources. In terms of gender identification, Mackey at 1 and 2 had little trouble expressing his anima or feminine side (see Jung 1964) as Georgie at 2 had scant difficulty expressing her animus or masculine side.

At 4, however, Georgie is more connected to the trappings of a feminine identity exemplified in her choice of clothes and toys and identification with such characters as Cinderella and Beauty, and, most important, in her attachment to her mother. The latter point, however, offers a further complexity as to role-development. Georgie's mother is temperamentally quite aggressive and outspoken. Through her identification with these traits of her mother, Georgie, too, plays out her own sense of aggression and power. Some of this is positive, as she learns to assert herself in groups of peers; and some is negative, as she aims her newly learned hurtful language at often unsuspecting targets, such as her brother, parents, and friends.

Certainly Georgie's aggressive role comes from many sources other than her mother. Even though her father's aggression is less visible than her mother's, it tends to explode at times and she internalizes that method of expressing anger as well. As she approached 4 years old, Georgie began to pick up aggressive words and actions from her peers. At that time, she became more aware of aggressive images in the media, such as guns, and aggressive characters, such as tyrants and killers.

Long before her fourth birthday, Georgie had demonstrated a clear attraction to evil characters in stories – witches, hunters, and bullies. In an astonishing statement directed to her father three days before turning 4, she integrated several of these images:

> I don't love you, Dad, I'm gonna get a gun and kill you. I want to poop on your head.

This role of rebellious, murderous daughter serves several functions. It helps Georgie release her negative, angry feelings in a safe way, as she offers up her pronouncement in a matter-of-fact fashion. It helps her continue to test the limits of her own worth as a lovable daughter to her father. In a reversal of the 'Electra complex', it implies an alternative story of a daughter's parricide so that she might have the mother all to herself. And finally, by playing out the killer in a scatological fashion, Georgie tries out her newly learned words and roles safely, knowing that her father will not strike back in a punitive way. She assures this by choosing a style of presentation that is emotionally neutral and non-threatening.

Mackey's style of aggression at 1 and 2 is much different, as was noted in the previous example. He has yet to take in the world of guns and killers. He picks up his sister's reference to 'poop' and will imitate her speech, but his style is without much commitment to the shock value of such imagery. Mackey's aggression at home is confined to fights with his sister, occasional tantrums of screaming and flailing when his needs are not immediately gratified, and imaginary dialogues with rocks and cups which he occasionally sets up to receive his wrath. His words: 'I'm very angry at you!' or 'You're a bad boy!' are taken from his parents, who occasionally express their displeasure toward him in similar phrases. When overwhelmed by anger coming from either his parents or himself, Mackey reaches for Tigo, holds it tightly up in front of his face, and sucks his thumb. He then knows he is safe.

At $4\frac{1}{2}$, Georgie became aware of death and the possible consequences of unchecked aggression. She was not introduced to death stemming from aggression, but from illness. In her four years she had been exposed to two hospitalizations of her father and much anxiety on the part of her mother. And one day, she discovered a photograph of a dog on her mother's dresser. When asked about it, her mother replied: 'This was Cheecha, my dog.'

'What happened to Cheecha?' asked Georgie.

'She died.'

'I'm very sad, Mommy.'

'Why?'

'Because Cheecha died.'

'Cheecha was a wonderful dog,' said her mother. 'We had great times together. But she got very old and died.'

'I'm very sad,' said Georgie.

For some weeks, Georgie transferred her sadness and fear of this terribly complicated death role upon Cheecha. All the while she held on to her own stuffed dog, the present from her mother in the hospital when Mackey was born. The following conversation helped calm her ultimate 4½-year-old fear, that of losing her mother to death. It was provoked when Georgie overheard her mother say that she was feeling very old:

Georgie: Mommy, are you deading soon?
Mother: You mean, are you going to die soon?
Georgie: Yes, like Cheecha.
Mother: No, not until I'm very old. Cheecha was very old and lived a long, long life. I need to see you get bigger and go to school and get married and have your own babies. Only then will I feel ready to rest and die.
Georgie: But you said you're old.
Mother: Sometimes I say I feel old, but that's just an expression. It's like people saying they're so hungry they could eat a horse . . . I'm not really old.
Georgie: For real?
Mother: For real.

The role of death is formidable. In the taxonomy of roles it is listed as a sub-type of demon, a dark inhabitant of the spirit world who is magical and evil, threatening and powerful. Death is also seen as one of the earliest roles personified in ancient dramatic rituals.

It could be that when the role of death appears early in one's life, one lives close to the world of magic and spirits on the far side of the looking glass. Thus at 4, death is more acceptable as a persona than at 24 or 44 or 64, as one comes to reject a magical world view and begins to accept the inevitability of death.

For Georgie, taking on the role of death, personified in a dog, is sad. But there is room for it in her world. Each day, she sets up her stuffed animals, including the transitional dog, and tells them stories. Through these stories, she comes to know her inner world whose magic will diminish as she grows older and accepts more adult, logical explanations for unfathomable events. When her mother explains that she won't die until Georgie becomes an adult and she grows old, Georgie responds: For real? In the asking, she begins to acquire the sense of reality that exists in a realm different from magic. This looking glass is not a window through which one can enter a new world, but a mirror, reflecting back an image of oneself.

Mackey at 2 still lives in the realm of windows. Many of the roles he has taken on still retain a magical quality. He sees the world as animistic. When he is angry, he scolds the rocks. When he is naughty, he calls his father a bad boy. When he is lonely, he throws Tigo out of the crib and cries for his mother to return it at once.

When his father returned home from the hospital, recovering from back surgery, Mackey at 2 came into the bedroom to greet him. He could see that his father was in pain and was told that it was time for his father to take a nap. Before saying goodbye, Mackey lifted the covers and placed Tigo gently next to his father's wound. For that moment, all distinctions between reality and magic were dissolved, all pain was gone. Mackey had taken on the role of healer. And all was right with the world.

CONCLUSION

It could be that roles are pre-existent forms, archetypes in a Jungian sense, dramatic artefacts in an aesthetic sense, that subsist throughout history, culture, and theatrical literature. As such, they are inherited, given as a birthright. By implication, newborns would have the potential universe of roles within their psyches.

It might also be true that roles pre-exist in a culture and society and are, in part, culturally and socially determined. From this perspective, newborns acquire roles as they interact with those in their cultural and social spheres.

So, too, might roles be inherited genetically, both as a means of survival – as, for example, a newborn assumes the somatic role of eater – and as a series of predispositions that will determine the kinds of roles to be taken on and the ways those roles will be played out.

Despite the archetypal, dramatic, social and genetic determining factors, human beings are still creators of their own identities, at least in part. Georgie and Mackey in the many examples above were pictured as active players of their various roles, rather than passive takers of some predetermined substance. Implicit in dramatic playing is the sense of the player as creative (see Winnicott 1971). Even if roles are, to a large degree, predetermined, each individual must still choose those roles that are most appropriate to a given circumstance and most meaningful to that individual. Each role chosen and played must be done so for a purpose, whether to survive, express a feeling, or meet a need. And each act of role-taking and role-playing is creative in the sense that one is building a piece of one's identity. Like theatrical actors, actors in everyday life receive a predetermined script that includes the substance of particular roles. Their artistry comes in humanizing those roles, filling in the personae with the breath of life that is unique to each particular person.

Throughout this chapter we have looked at ways that early roles develop. I have chosen to focus most especially upon the genesis of family roles, as well as those concerning physical ability and disability, fear, aggression, and gender identity. The examples of Georgie and Mackey are typical in the sense that most children from birth to 4 will take on and play out similar roles of parents and siblings, aggressors and victims, males and females. Yet each one will do so in a unique way and not necessarily within the same time-span as Georgie and Mackey.

Some children who are severely emotionally disturbed will not be able to play and thus will not be able to take on or play out a variety of roles. Others, with less severe forms of disturbance or disability, will be able to take on and generate roles, but in a somewhat limited way. Still others, who appear normal by most measures of mental and physical health, will experience trauma through any number of physical, environmental, or psychological circumstances. In such cases, they, too, might experience a diminished capacity to take on and play out roles.

With such children, a treatment through drama therapy based in an attempt to build new roles or restore old ones might well be indicated. Elsewhere, I have outlined a method of diagnosis, treatment, and evaluation of such individuals using a role method (Landy 1993).

Any attempt to understand the ways and means of presenting oneself in role requires a view of young children as they begin to assert their identities through play. This view through the looking glass is one all of us have experienced once upon a time. And this view is one most of us have forgotten. If we try hard, we may begin to recall images. As there are, in Wordsworth's terms, 'intimations of immortality' (see Wordsworth 1807/1965), so there are also intimations of infancy that can be accessed in visions of white rabbits, gypsies, and stuffed animals named Tigo.

If our own memory fails, we can observe the children around us and even those within us who seem to embody the primal dramas of individual identity and family, of power and loss, of sex and death. In their struggles with role lie the seeds of our struggles as adults who live on the other side of the looking glass but sometimes imagine what it would be like to venture forth again through that magical window.

REFERENCES

Green, R. L., ed. (1965) *The Works of Lewis Carroll*. Feltham, Middlesex: Hamlyn.
Hillman, J. (1983) *Healing Fiction*. Barrytown, NY: Station Hill Press.
Jung, C. G. (1964) *Man and his Symbols*. Garden City, NY: Doubleday.
Landy, R. J. (1993). *Persona and Performance: the meaning of role in drama, therapy, and everyday life*. London: Jessica Kingsley.
Mahler, M. (1975) *The Psychological Birth of the Human Infant: symbiosis and individuation*. New York: Basic Books.
Mead, G. H. (1934) *Mind, Self, and Society*. Chicago: University of Chicago Press.
Piaget, J. (1977) *The Origin of Intelligence in the Child*. Harmondsworth, Middlesex: Penguin.
Winnicott, D. W. (1971). *Playing and Reality*. Harmondsworth, Middlesex: Penguin.
Wordsworth, W. (1807/1965) 'Intimations of Immortality'. In C. Baker (ed.) *The Prelude, selected poems and sonnets*. New York: Holt, Rinehart & Winston.

Chapter 2

Fear and tension in children's games[1]

Iona Opie

As regards the fears of childhood and their causes, I want to say that I have never worked clinically. My experience is derived simply from my status as an ex-child, and as an acquaintance of other ex-children; for children – when they *are* children – seldom voice their fears.

The fears of childhood are legion: there is commonly a fear of the dark, and a fear of shadows – especially the shadows in a child's bedroom when a harmless bundle of bedding in the corner looks like a crouching bear.[2] There are fears of dangers of all kinds, especially of car crashes and burglars. Even kindly Father Christmas can become a threat – what right has he to come down the chimney? who is this stranger roaming at large through the house? A worried 4-year-old said in an interview for *Mother and Baby*, December 1971, 'If Father Christmas can creep through my window without my waking up, anyone could . . . tramps or, or TIGERS.'[3] Fear of loss, of death, of sex, of failure – of being in a crowd of strangers, of making a fool of oneself, of being singled out, of being looked at, of *not* being noticed, or popular. Some of these fears are exemplified in children's games.

Large children's parties, I understand, are going out of fashion, and it is more customary for a birthday person to invite a few friends to a film or a circus or a zoo, with a meal afterwards at a McDonald's. This may be due to the recession or the prevalence of working mothers, or it may – partly – be due to the horrible memories people have of the parties of their youth.

Quite apart from the dressing up in unfamiliar clothes and consorting with unfamiliar people, there was the necessity of playing games that seemed designed to embarrass.

Take the game 'How Green You Are', for example. It began, like many other party games, with one person being sent out of the room – not an encouraging start. The others then hid a thimble, the outsider was invited inside again, and must go around looking for the thimble while the others sang 'How green you are!' – softly if the searcher was far away from the hiding place and shrieking loudly if the searcher was staring straight at the thimble. No one likes to be told, in chorus, that he is being stupid; and the disadvantage of being a child is that there is no comfort from historical perspective. How can the child know that this game is probably over two hundred years old, that it was once played by teenagers rather than children, and that it was part of a social scene which enabled young people to mingle and get to know each other in the setting of a formal game. Of course the game had changed – or evolved – over the years. When Dr Paris described it in *Philosophy in Sport*, in 1827, the one coming into the room had to 'perform some action entirely by the power of music'; he must for instance 'go to the mantelpiece, take a rose from a vase, smell it and give it to a certain young lady who he then leads out of the room' – and this entirely by the loudness or softness of the piano-playing.

'Blind Man's Buff' might be seen as another attack on the susceptibilities of a player singled out to be teased and buffeted by a crowd; and were it not that the buffeting is only part of a game and therefore quite impersonal, and that anyone may have to take the role of blind man at any time, and quite by chance, the lonely, blundering blind man might indeed feel victimized. Notice that I say 'singled out to be teased and *buffeted*'. During the thousand or so years of the game's history the buffeting was its *raison d'être*, and it is only recently, in the last century, that the game has become softened. Pictures in the margins of the fourteenth-century manuscript *Romance of Alexander* show men, women and children playing 'Blind Man's Buff', and show that the blind man was blinded by having to wear his hood back to front; and that the rest of the players had tied knots in their hoods – those long pointed hoods – and were scourging him with the knots.

In ancient Greece, according to Pollux, the game was called 'The Brazen Fly'. One boy's eyes were covered with a bandage. He shouted out 'I shall chase the brazen fly.' The others retorted, 'You may chase him, but you won't catch him,' and they hit him with whips made from papyrus husks until one of them was caught.

Part of the discomfort of being the blind man comes from the feeling that you are on your own and that the whole company is against you. It is interesting that when the game was played under the name of 'Jingling', at fairs, chiefly, and public gatherings of all sorts, when a special jingling booth was erected, the positions were completely reversed. All the players were blindfolded except one. He bounced around jingling a bell, teasing the blindfolded players and trying to keep out of their clutches – the prize for so doing was a slice of gingerbread.

Even more worrying were the practical jokes played under the name of games at parties, or as initiations upon newcomers at schools. They are survivals of rougher times, when they were played at wakes and on other convivial occasions when horseplay was accompanied by heavy drinking, or were tricks played by sailors upon new hands at sea. To 7- and 8-year-olds they simply seem malicious. The victim is, for instance, led into a throne room where the King and Queen of Sheba are sitting on a makeshift couch. The royal pair ask questions, and express themselves satisfied with the answers. Indeed they let it be known that they think so well of the newcomer that he or she may, as a special privilege, approach the throne and sit between them. As the victim sits down they get up and, since there has only been a tightly stretched rug between the chairs on which they have been sitting, the victim falls on to the floor with a bump, or into a concealed tub of water.

These games belong to rougher times, as I say, and one might also say times that encouraged a tougher attitude to the mental bumps and bruises of life. They were games that inculcated – though perhaps not consciously – an attitude of 'see if *I* care'.

Certainly wounded feelings cannot be avoided. It is equally certain that some of the wounds received in childhood have an effect that lasts through life. One of the deepest fears is the fear of not being chosen, when two people are picking teams. Nothing can match the feeling of rejection for the solitary figure who remains unchosen, and wordlessly takes the last place. Such failure is entirely personal: it means – or seems to mean – that the person has been rejected as a human being.

However, very few children's games are played in teams. Usually, as in tig, one person plays against all the rest – the chaser is selected impersonally, by fate, or chance, by means of a counting-out rhyme. The whole idea of teams is adult. The idea is to foster a 'team spirit', and games like 'Crusts and Crumbs' and 'French and English' are typically organized by adults. Should I rescind here, and allow that the rather amorphous war games are played by two teams? No, I don't think so. Children playing at war are playing at real life, and the two sides, as in real life, are not exactly matched.

Fear and tension are built into many of the traditional games. It is the kind of artificial, enjoyable fear to be found in stories of ghosts and vampires, in murder stories, horror stories, and some of the so-called fairy stories. The human being's desire to be frightened is almost as primal as the need for love and comfort. Sometimes fear can be experienced vicariously within a circle of love and comfort, as when the family watches the television news together, or the fictitious extravagance of *Dr Who*. Then the mother has to explain – 'Yes, that's in Bosnia. Yes, that man is dead.' But in *Dr Who*? 'No, that man's not really dead. When it's over he will get up and go home.' In children's games, the children are fully aware that the dangers and fears are not real.

Let's go back to the beginning of childhood and think about the oldest game of all, the game of 'Peep bo'. Does the adult think she is frightening the child when she hides behind the sofa and pops up saying 'Bo!'? Of course not: the child is delighted and says 'Again!' Does the child – aged 3 or 4 – think he is frightening the adult when he hides in a shop doorway and suddenly bounces out with a shout?* The surprise is simulated, the event is a shared joke. These games are similar to the play of fox cubs with their mother. The fear and tension are all pretend, and all the tussling and jumping out are presumably a preparation for later life.

The same game in a more sophisticated form has long been played under the name of 'Bogey'. It is best played after dark or in the gloaming, and was traditionally played when walking home from school. The child who is to be 'Bogey' goes on ahead and hides in a doorway, or on top of a wall, or behind a pillarbox. The others, after counting perhaps 'five hundred in tens', follow along with an air of unconcern, but in reality scaring themselves by singing out loud:

> Moonlight, starlight,
> Bogey won't be out tonight.

When, without realizing it, they come to Bogey's hiding place, he jumps out at them and everyone screams. The game was played in Germany at least as early as 1851, and in Flora Thompson's *Lark Rise* she describes the village children, in the 1880s, marching along singing 'I hope we shan't meet any gypsies tonight!' – gypsies being the currently fashionable bogeymen.

Many playground chasing games have the same element of suspense and sudden movement built into them, with or without the pictorial element. These games we called 'suspense-start chasing games'. They accumulate excitement and tension at the very beginning, because no one but the chaser knows when the chasing will begin. In the game 'Poison' (or 'Bottle of Poison'), for instance, the chaser holds out his hands and each player takes hold of a finger and stretches away as far away from him as he can, preparing to run. The chaser says, 'I went to a shop and I bought a bottle of – *vinegar*!' then perhaps, 'I went to a shop and I bought a bottle of *p-p-p-Pepsi*!' and finally, 'I went to a shop and I bought a bottle of – POISON!' The word poison is the signal for everyone to run.

In studying children's games Peter and I were in several sorts of difficulty. Children's games are – in most cases – *not* children's games. They are games that adults used to play – and only children have gone on playing them. Other difficulties were the difficulties perennially associated with folklore. Anything handed on through oral tradition becomes so diffuse and varied that it is almost impossible to categorize it. Also, the interest in folklore is so recent – the word itself came into being only in

---

* *Editor's note.* Gender language: please note that references to he or she or her or his denote the gender of the author, therapist or client. Otherwise non-gender specific terms are used for general reference, or, in cases such as the above, gender pronouns are used to distinguish the therapist/parent from the client/child.

1846 – that early records are few and far between; they occur by the way, very much as asides in general literature.

The games that most fascinate me are those that seem to satisfy a deep desire for vicarious fear carried out in a dramatic form and which, though without any real evidence, we can only suppose were played by adults – and far back in time.

An instinct to dramatize already exists. Girls, especially, have a natural tendency to dramatize quite ordinary games, like tig; they emphasize every moment of danger with high-pitched screams – the very fact of being chased is exhilarating. More pictorial games like 'Fairies and Witches' are naturally accompanied by shrieks and shouts, as the girl who is the Witch takes her captives back to her den, tortures them and puts them in chains. In contrast, the boys' games of war do not involve much self-expression. (They are realistic; the sounds are of machine-gun fire, and, occasionally, groaning from wounded warriors.)

Some of the formalized games involving fear are simple, but contain a supernatural element – as we've seen with the game of 'Bogey'. Others contain no supernatural element, but enjoy the build-up and release of tension – as we've seen with the game of 'Poison' – and in *these* I always suspect a pedagogical influence. Others seem to be dramatizations of old agricultural worries, in which the villains are wolves and other predators. Others seem to approach full-blown theatre, and to ritually encompass the supernatural world in its effect on human life.

Let us consider the old agricultural worries. Everyone knows the game 'What's the Time, Mr Wolf?', which is played by very small children. They promenade along behind 'Mr Wolf', asking their question, and 'Mr Wolf' replies gruffly, 'Eight o'clock' – or any other time – and keeps on walking. They continue, pestering him to tell the time until, suddenly, he says, 'Dinner time!' and turns round and chases them. The one who is caught becomes 'Mr Wolf'. This game, which nowadays has – really – only a kindergarten status, seems to be derived from much more sinister games, in which a thoroughly spooky predator is repeatedly asked the time.

Another well-known game – still known when we were collecting games in the 1960s, but enjoying its heyday in the nineteenth century – portrays the straightforward worries of the shepherd about his sheep, though with a pleasant touch of humour. The shepherd calls to the sheep, 'Sheep, sheep, come home!' The sheep answer, 'We are afraid.' 'What of?' 'The wolf.' 'The wolf has gone to Devonshire, Won't be back for seven year, Sheep, sheep, come home.' Then the sheep run over to the shepherd, and the wolf – who has been lurking at the side – tries to catch one, who either helps him catch at the next performance, or takes his place. Sometimes the words are wonderfully ludicrous. In one version the 'wolf has gone to Lancashire, To buy a penny hankershire'. Sometimes it is not a wolf but a fox, and not sheep but geese. The game is widely known across Europe, and recordings are as old as the interest in folklore – going back to the early nineteenth century.

Now we can approach the acting games, which have longer stories and longer scripts. When you are considering the question of drama, the acting games and singing games must be taken into account. Because they have descended into the possession of children, it has been forgotten that they are a distinct category of drama – they are dramas in which the players themselves alter the action of the play. In a stage play or a ballet the script and the choreography are fixed, decided beforehand, and cannot be varied. In the dramatic games the outcome for individual players is uncertain and sometimes the dialogue can be varied; but in the singing games the players change places through choosing, and any fear and tension is of a social and personal nature. I shall concentrate on the ritualistic dramatic games, with their strange undertones of evil.

'The Old Man in the Well' is an excellent example. When we collected the game from children in Swansea this playlet had a quite domestic and mundane atmosphere. The characters were a Mother, her Children, and an Old Man. The old man goes off and secretes himself in some suitably dark and mysterious place which is designated 'the well'. The children say to the mother, 'Please, Mother, can we have a piece of bread and butter?'

The mother says, 'Let me see your hands.'

They hold them out for inspection.

'Your hands are very dirty,' says Mother. 'Go to the well and wash them. The children go to the well, where they spy the old man crouching down. They rush back to the mother screaming; 'Mother, Mother, there's an old man in the well.'

Mother: Don't be silly, children. There isn't an old man in the well.
Children: But we saw him.
Mother: It's only your father's under-pants. I hung them out to dry.
            Go again.

The children go again, and the same kind of dialogue occurs, until the children persuade the mother to come and see for herself. She sends one of the children to fetch a candle (a twig) and goes to look in the well. As she is about to look, the old man blows the candle out.

Mother, to child nearest her: 'What did you want to blow my candle out for?' She cuffs the child, who sets up a howl. This happens three or four times, until nearly all the children are crying. The mother finally manages to look in the well. The old man jumps up with a horrible shriek and gives chase. Whoever he catches is the next old man.

This all seems quite innocuous until one looks at the older, and continental, recordings. For instance even as late as the 1920s, in Devonshire, the mother had the following conversation with the old man before the chase began:

Mother:	What are you doing here?
Old Man:	Picking up sand.
Mother:	What do you want sand for?
Old Man:	To sharpen my needles.
Mother:	What do you want needles for?
Old Man:	To make a bag.
Mother:	What do you want a bag for?
Old Man:	To keep my knives in.
Mother:	What do you want knives for?
Old Man:	To cut off your heads.
Mother:	Then catch us if you can!

In present-day Austria the situation becomes even clearer, when the mother sends the children to fetch butter from the cellar, and they find a witch. After much play-acting, and pretending the witch is only the butter churn, the mother faces her adversary and says: 'What are you doing here?'

Witch:	Picking up stones.
Mother:	What will you do with the stones?
Witch:	Sharpen my knives.
Mother:	What will you do with the knives?
Witch:	Kill people.
Mother:	Will you kill me and my children?
Witch:	Yes!

In the usual folkloristic way, this game is all mixed up with the game of 'Fox and Chickens' – now much truncated. The children line up behind one another, with the defending mother hen at their head, and march up to the fox saying:

Chickany, chickany, crany crow,
I went to the well to wash my toe,
When I came back a chicken was dead.

Then there is a familiar dialogue – *'What are you doing, old fox?'* and so forth – and the fox springs up and tries to catch the last chicken in the line. There is good reason to think the game was known in this form in Queen Anne's time. The predators can be a fox, a wolf, a hawk, a vulture, or, in a nineteenth-century American version, a witch, for Newell reports that in Georgia the rhyme beginning the game, 'Chickamy, chickamy, crany, crow', included the question 'What o'clock, old witch?' and the children repeated the question until the witch replied 'Twelve o'clock'. After that the threatening dialogue began – 'What are you doing, old witch?', 'I'm making a fire to cook a chicken' and so on (Newell 1883: 155–8).

It is curious, and fascinating, to think how many of these dramatic games are concerned with losing children, of having them stolen or killed.

Sometimes the thieves or killers seem to be after sheep or chickens, as in 'Fox and Chickens' – which we've just been looking at – or the apparently straightforward game of 'Johnny Lingo', in which the sheep stand in a ring and 'Johnny Lingo' prowls around outside. Within the ring is a farmer, who calls out, 'Who's that walking round my stony wall?' and 'Johnny Lingo' replies, 'Only little Johnny Lingo.' 'Don't you steal any of my fat sheep, or I shall make you tingle.' 'I stole one last night, and I'll steal another tonight,' says Johnny Lingo, and he touches one of the children on the back, saying, 'Come on,' and the stolen sheep joins on behind him and they go padding round outside the ring. The game ends with all the children in a line, and the farmer tries to catch them from behind the protecting arms of 'Johnny Lingo', in the same manner as in 'Fox and Chickens'. Again, it is not until one looks at the oldest recordings that the game seems more sinister. In the earliest known, which dates from the 1820s, the thief is 'Bloody Tom':

> Who goes round the house at night,
> None but bloody Tom!
> Who steals all the sheep at night?
> None but this poor one.

An old name for the game was 'Limping Tom', which suggests witchcraft, it being well-known that witches limp.

The cumulative effect these games had on me as they were gathered together from children in the more remote parts of the country was very powerful. The supernatural undertones became more pronounced; and yet I had – and still have – no idea of their origins, history or meaning.

In some of the games the children are undeniably children, and not chickens or sheep; but they are disguised under fancy names. A 12-year-old girl in Cumnock described for us a game called 'Little Black Doggie'.

> 'There are about half-a-dozen players, and two of the players are picked to be what we call "the Man" and "The little black doggie". The "Man" gives each player a romantic name, for example "golden moon", "tiger lily", etc. When everyone has received a flattering name they chant "Little black doggie come a hop, hop, hop, and pick out the golden moon," or whatever name they happen to chant. The "doggie" then hops up in the hope of picking out the right one, which is very difficult to do. And if she does pick the right one she takes the player by the nose or ear and puts her in her den.'

Now the interesting thing is that when a certain James McBain played this in his youth in Arbroath, about 1837, it was in very much the same form, even down to the golden names – such as Golden Rose, and Golden Butter-plate. And he adds that the player who guessed did so in the guise of a 'weird wife hirpling on a broomstick', to whom the children called, 'Witchie, witchie, warlock, come hopping to your dae!' (McBain 1887: 344). It appears that the hopping of the little black doggie, in Cumnock in the 1960s, had remained as an important part of the tradition.

The disguising of the children was sometimes done not by giving them fancy names but by turning them into other things – such as different kinds of birds, or pots of jam. The game of 'Coloured Birds' was widespread and international, and it is difficult to know what example to give from so many. It was still being played when we were running our surveys, and was especially popular in Bristol. One child is the mother, one is a wolf or a fox, and the rest are birds or eggs and choose what colours they will be. Sometimes in Bristol the mother also acts the part of the door, which opens and shuts in keeping with the story. Thus the wolf taps on her head and the door turns round and says, 'Go away.' The wolf taps again and the door says 'Come in.' The wolf is asked, 'What do you want?' 'Have you any coloured birds?' he says. 'What colour?' The wolf names a colour. If there is no bird of that colour he has to go away and try again; but if there is, that child has to run for her life, until she is caught and put into the wolf's den.

In eighteenth-century Germany this game was an established 'game for youth', and the participants were a bird-seller, a bird-buyer, and numerous finches, ravens, starlings and so forth. In France, as is typical in Roman Catholic countries, the setting is religious; the children have turned into animals and it is the Devil who comes to buy: 'Who is there?' 'It is the Devil with his fork.' 'What do you want?' 'An animal.' 'Come in.'

In a game known, nowadays, only in Scotland and the Scottish Isles, the children are turned into pots of jam, or other groceries, and again witchcraft plays a central part in the drama. Here are phrases from children's descriptions of the game as it was played in the 1950s. A child in Stornoway: 'The witch comes and knocks at the door and asks if there is any jams today. The maid says yes, and the witch tries to guess the names of them.' At Westerkirk, the guesser is summoned with the words 'Limpety Lil come over the hill and see what you can find' – the limping witch, again. At Langholm, where the game is called 'Limping Jenny', a 12-year-old says, 'Old Jenny comes into the shop and asks for something. If she asks for lard and somebody is lard she takes that person away with her. . . '

These games, of which there are many, seem to be dramatizations of the ancient struggle between good and evil. The continental versions retain the religious actors: angels, the Devil, and the Lord God Himself. The British versions have retained only the frightening, evil character – the witch. The games might be thought of as having been, possibly, Morality Games. In the morality *plays* the community were spectators. In these morality games the community could all take part.

My mother used to play a game called 'Honey Pots' as a child; it is still being played – or was when we did our surveys. It seems an innocent enough affair of one child pretending to be a honey pot and putting her hands under her knees, and two other children lifting her by the arms and swinging her. If her clasp does not give way she is pronounced to be sound; if it gives way she is rejected and set to one side.

In Italy this game is heavy with allegory. The Madonna comes to purchase the pots, who seem to represent souls. The good ones go to Heaven and the cracked ones to Hell. In France, in the nineteenth century, the actors were God Almighty, the Virgin Mary, the Devil, who came to buy pots of flowers from a flower-seller, and his helper. When the purchases had all been made, the flower-pots acquired by 'le Bon Dieu' and 'la Sainte-Vierge' made horns at those purchased by the Devil.

There is no doubt that the weirdest of these weird games, and probably the basis of all the others, is 'Mother, the Cake is Burning'. Briefly the plot is this. A mother goes to market, leaving her seven children in the care of a maid or eldest daughter. While she is away an evil visitor comes to the door, enters the house on some pretext, and snatches one of the children – 'the youngest child', or 'the most precious child'. Sometimes the evil visitor distracts the child-minder by saying, 'Look, the cake's burning!' The mother returns, beats the maid or eldest daughter for allowing the child to be stolen, and goes off again. While she is away the second time, a second child is stolen. The mother, who seems to be simple-minded, returns and again beats the girl in charge, and again leaves home. This occurs seven times until all the children have been stolen. The mother then seeks out the kidnapper who, it is becoming clear, is a magical person. For a while the kidnapper obstructs the mother's entry into his house, but she becomes indomitable; she will even, in some versions, cut off her feet to gain admittance, and eventually succeeds, only to find that her children are now disguised, or renamed, or turned into pies or other delicacies and about to be eaten. Nevertheless, by skill or luck, she identifies and releases them. Usually the game ends in a chase.

When little girls, dressed in T-shirts and jeans, are seen playing this acting-game at the end of the street, it is difficult to believe that they are not making up the incidents as they go along. Only when comparison is made, scene by scene, with nineteenth-century recordings, does it become apparent they are following an old and international script dictated by folk memory.

In the nineteenth century the game began with the mother admonishing her eldest daughter with a rhyme such as this one:

I'm going into the garden to gather some rue,
And mind old Jack-daw don't get you.
Especially you, my daughter Sue,
Or I'll beat you till you're black and blue.

Today, after counting her children, she merely warns the eldest daughter not to lose them.

The elements of witchcraft have survived: the limping witch, who in Breconshire in the 1950s was called 'Heckedy Peg', a lame old woman who announces, 'I'm Heckedy Peg, I've lost my leg'; the sinister request for a light from the fire – witches were always trying to steal fire from the hearth (in Oxford, for instance, the witch asks for a match; in Alton a fox asks for a box of matches; in Radnorshire the children are called 'Matchsticks').

Whatever the form of the kidnapping and its discovery, and no matter how lengthy, it is repeated for the stealing of each child; and sometimes, even in the present day, the ritual is wonderfully surrealistic, and may go like this:

Mother: Where are my children?
Kidnapper: Gone to school.
Mother: How many miles?'
Kidnapper: Eight. [Or any number.]

The mother and the maid have to take eight steps backwards.

Mother: They are not here.
Kidnapper: They've gone to bed.
Mother: I want to see them.
Kidnapper: Your shoes will dirty the carpet.
Mother: I'll take them off.
Kidnapper: The wool will come off your stockings.
Mother: I'll take off my stockings.
Kidnapper: Your feet are dirty.
Mother: I'll cut them off.
Kidnapper: The blood will go on the carpet.
Mother: I'll fly up!

The game can end in a number of different ways, most of them incongruous – and rather tame, after all that drama. But in Cornwall, in 1887, when the old witch had been caught the children pretended to burn her, 'fanning the imaginary flames with their pinafores'.

As Keith Thomas said:

'We must readily accept the need to explore, however imperfectly, the mental worlds of all subordinate groups, whether women, children or the poor, regardless of whether they were at the time disparaged as 'ignorant' or 'childish'. For it was within the confines of these subordinate groups that all the people of the past spent some of their lives and the majority spent all of them.'

(Thomas 1989:71)

Looking again at these mysterious play-acting games, of which so few traces can be found in earlier centuries, I have tried, through an act of imagination, to understand how – in the days when witchcraft was an accepted fact, and adults and young people played as one community – these games must have had a truly terrifying force and meaning.

NOTES

1 My illustrations in this chapter are based on material from *Children's Games in Street and Playground*, which itself is based on information obtained from more than 10,000 children attending local-authority schools in England, Scotland, and the eastern part of Wales during the 1950s and 1960s.

2 A seventeenth-century writer describes the same fear. 'Children hide their heads within their bed-clothes, though they see nothing, when they have affrighted themselves with the shapes of Devils pourtray'd only in their Phancies.' Nathaniel Ingelo, *Bentivolio and Urania*. 3rd edn (1673), II, 175.

3 The still common custom of leaving out food for Father Christmas on Christmas Eve (a mince pie and a glass of sherry for instance) has resonances of propitiation, and is a reminder that at one time it was customary to leave out food for the spirits of the dead (see e.g. 'Speranza' Wilde's *Ancient Superstitions of Ireland* (1887), I, 225).

REFERENCES

McBain, J. M. (1887) *Arbroath: past and present*. Arbroath.

Newell, W. W. (1883) *Games and Songs of American Children*. New York: Harper & Brothers.

Thomas, K. (1989) *Children in early modern England*. In G. Avery and J. Briggs (eds) *Children and their Books*. Oxford: Clarendon Press.

BIBLIOGRAPHY

Amongst Iona Opie's publications are the following, all with Peter Opie:
The Oxford Dictionary of Nursery Rhymes. Oxford: Clarendon Press (1951).
The Lore and Language of Schoolchildren. Oxford: Clarendon Press (1959).
Children's Games in Street and Playground. Oxford: Clarendon Press (1969).
The Singing Game. Oxford University Press (1985).
A sequence from her playground diaries was published by OUP in 1993, with the title *The People in the Playground*.

Chapter 3

Dramatherapy with children who are trapped in their spontaneous play

Galila Oren

Play should be introduced under proper regulation as medicine.

Aristotle

INTRODUCTION

'It is good to remember always that playing is itself a therapy' (Winnicott 1971: 50). Through play, children develop emotionally and cognitively and maintain their mental health. Some children are unable to use spontaneous play for these self-healing purposes.

In this chapter, I will try to demonstrate how children might use their spontaneous play to protect themselves from emotional development. I will focus on the ways children get trapped in their spontaneous play and lose their ability to play for developmental and self-healing purposes. I will use T. H. Ogden's theory as expressed in his book *The Primitive Edge of Experience* (1989) as a framework. He discusses the ways people get trapped in one mode of organizing their experience. I will show how this manifests itself in children's play and focus on the creative ways used by the dramatherapist to help children rediscover self-healing play. This will enable them to reorganize their experience in a healthier and richer manner. I will demonstrate this work with case illustrations.

OPERATIONAL FRAMEWORK

The case illustrations took place in the Unit for Intensive Therapy for Children, in a state mental health clinic in Rishon-le-Tzion, Israel, where I work.

In this unit, we provide intensive psychotherapy for children who might otherwise be hospitalized. This unit is staffed by two clinical psychologists, a social worker, an art therapist and myself.

For each case we design an individual treatment plan that includes either psychotherapy and/or art or dramatherapy for the child, and separate psychotherapy for the parents.

In view of the complex framework, involving several therapists, an important part of the effort is invested in staff discussions and supervision with a view to understanding the case and the development of the therapeutic processes.

THE IMPORTANCE OF PLAY FOR NORMAL DEVELOPMENT

Many authors have written about the complex processes of playing and drama for normal development. Rather than go into the subject at length, let us say that there is broad agreement that children's play is an important part of cognitive, emotional and social development. (A comprehensive summary of the subject can be found in Jennings 1993: 3–24.)

D. W. Winnicott contributed a great deal to the understanding of the nature of play. He viewed play as an important part of human life: 'It is play that is universal, and that belongs to health. Playing facilitates growth, and therefore health' (Winnicott: 1971: 41). He describes humans as living in both an inner 'subjective world' and an outside 'objective world'. Play belongs to a 'third part of human beings [which is the] intermediate area of experiencing, to which inner reality and exterior life both contribute' (ibid.). In this area the difficult task of keeping inner and outer reality separated and yet interrelated is first developed and later on maintained.

Play develops very early in life. We can observe sensory and motoric play at the age of several weeks. Even before the beginning of language 'make-believe play' develops, starting with imitation, through projective play and, further on, dramatic play.

Through play, children constantly reorganize their experience. They separate inside from outside, integrate objects and develop a sense of self and a view of the world. While playing, children are engaged in a dialogue between the developing inner world and the growing demands of reality. Through this dialogue, children preserve their mental health.

WHAT IS 'MAKE-BELIEVE' PLAY?

Dr Shlomo Ariel defines 'make-believe play' as follows:

> Make-believe play is primarily a complex mental activity, and only secondarily, outward behaviour . . . Simultaneously with the explicit behaviour, (verbal or non-verbal), the player implicitly makes the following 'mental claims':
>
> *Realification*: Some entity, which at the very moment is only in my mind . . . is now in the external reality. (There is a lion here.)
> *Identification*: This material or behavioural entity that I have selected from the external environment is not what it is . . . it has become the

entity in my mind. (This piece of wood is the lion.)
Playfulness: These two claims have not been made seriously. I do not
believe in them.

(Ariel 1992: 37–9)

The 'mental claims' are statements that the player keeps in mind while
playing. According to Ariel, what defines 'make-believe play' is the
simultaneous existence of behaviour with these three seemingly
contradictory 'mental claims'. From now on, I will use the term 'mental
claims' as defined here.

I believe that in the dynamic relationship between these three
contradictory claims lies the secret of the healing power of make-believe
play.

The playing child moves within the whole range between 'owning' and
'alienating' his own symbolism. This motion enables the child to deal with
parts of himself and of reality which would otherwise be overwhelming.

CHILDREN WITH DIFFICULTIES IN PLAYING

Not every child spontaneously develops the ability to play in this creative
and healing manner. Some children stick to motoric and sensory play.
Others are capable of make-believe play, but the relationship between
the three 'mental claims' is static. In this case, play might increase the
anxiety of the inner world, or serve as a defence against dealing with
reality.

I believe that the role of the dramatherapist who works with such
children is to help them develop their spontaneous play. This will enable
them to engage in a dynamic dialogue between their inner life and outside
reality – a dialogue that will help them grow.

Recently, I came across Ogden's ideas, which seemed to offer a
theoretical framework for the development of my observations and
method of intervention.

Ogden further developed parts of Melanie Klein's theory, notably her
opinion that human experience is based on two positions developed during
early childhood:

1 the 'paranoid-schizoid position'; and
2 the 'depressive position'.

The baby develops these positions by introjecting parts of the mother and
of the external world into himself, and by projecting parts of himself on to
objects in the external world.

The 'paranoid-schizoid position' is characterized by a split between bad
and good and by massive projection of self on to the environment. The
'depressive position', developed later, allows for a better integration of

good/bad and a finer differentiation between mother/infant, and me/others. I will elaborate on this subject while describing children stuck in one of these positions.

Ogden explores the idea that human experience is the product of a dialectical interplay of three modes of generating experience:

1 the 'autistic-contiguous mode';
2 the 'paranoid-schizoid mode';
3 the 'depressive mode'.

'Each mode creates, prevents and negates the other' (Ogden 1989: 4).

These three modes are developed in early childhood, starting with the autistic-contiguous position – a sensory-dominated, pre-symbolic area of experience; moving towards the development of the paranoid-schizoid position; and finally reaching the depressive mode, where one achieves a sense of subjectivity, continuity, and the wealth of symbolism.

But these modes also exist synchronically and the movement between them is what gives life its richness. Ogden views psychopathology as the 'collapse of the dialectic in the direction of one or the other of the modes of generating experience' (ibid.).

Children who operate mainly in one mode of organizing experience have either failed to advance from a more primitive position, or they are regressed. Sometimes they achieved the ability to operate in these three modes but have difficulties with the movements between them.

Since children organize their experience through play, remaining stuck in one mode is reflected in the way they play. These children often get trapped in their own spontaneous play, and therefore play loses its healing power.

Through the use of ritual, projective play and drama, the dramatherapist can help the child enrich his spontaneous play and help him move more freely in the area within the three 'mental claims' that define play.

By helping the child organize and develop his spontaneous play, the therapist gives him the tools to reorganize his experience; the dialogue between inner life and reality is released. More often than not, this will enable the child to develop new modes of organizing experience and to move freely between them.

Dramatherapy with children who operate in the autistic-contiguous mode

'The autistic-contiguous' position is understood as a sensory-dominated, pre-symbolic area of experience in which the most primitive form of meaning is generated on the basis of the organization of sensory impressions: 'rhythm, touch and shape, contribute to the earliest psychological organization in this mode' (Ogden 1989: 32).

Ogden and many others view the infant from its very first days as being active in its interaction with others. The essence of this interaction is sensory and physical: 'The body and its relationship with other bodies – through touch and the other senses – forms the basis for the development of identity in all human beings' (Jennings 1993: 25).

Both rhythmicity and experiences of surface contiguity are fundamental to a person's earliest feelings of self and relation with others. The experience of being held, rocked, sung to, covered and fed are of crucial importance for the baby's development of self and its ability to relate to others. The first infant–mother interactions are based on these sensory elements. In this mode of organizing experience, there is no sense of inside–outside, self–other. What is important is the meeting between these shapes, rhythms and textures.

Older children who operate mainly in this mode suffer severe psychopathology. They are not necessarily autistic, but they have great difficulties differentiating inside from outside, possessing only a very vague sense of self and hardly any ability to communicate meaningfully with others.

These children will not spontaneously engage in make-believe play. They will stick to the sensory and physical play which characterizes this mode. Although they might have acquired language, verbal symbolism is meaningless to them. They organize their mental images in shapes, rhythm, texture and motion.

The dramatherapist who works with such children may at first intend to trace the child's tactile, rhythmic and motion patterns. When these patterns are recognized, a ritual will be originated by repeating the pattern. This ritual will usually include swinging, covering with cloth, playing with sand or water, or reproducing rhythm and sounds. *The physical ritual gives shape to sensory experience.* This shape provides a sensory experience of boundaries and containment. Both therapist and child participate in this ritual. Within the safety of this contiguity, the beginning of a sense of me–others can develop.

Usually, after the physical ritual is created and enacted, a symbol will arise from the child's associations. Now the ritual will continue to develop. It will still have a very defined physicality, but it will include a theme, a story or a song.

Originally, in early societies, the ritual was a form of 'make-believe play' since all participants in it shared the three 'mental claims' that define play. In the ritual, heavy emphasis is given to the claim of realification and identification, while the claim of playfulness exists, but is almost forgotten.

Although all the participants in the ritual know each other and know that they are putting on an act with very strict rules, the strong feeling prevails that what is being enacted is almost real. The claim of identification is extremely powerful. There is hardly any differentiation between mask and role, or role and actor. The materials chosen to represent a symbol are treated with great respect, as if they were the soul of the symbol. Actor and audience are all part of the story which has to be told. This provides a very strong feeling of oneness among the participants in the ritual and the boundaries between 'me–others' and 'inside–outside' are diffused.

In normal development, mothers often give their baby a feeling of oneness by responding to its sensory and physical needs. This feeling of oneness is called by Tustin a 'healing-sensory experience' (Tustin 1987). This enables the baby to make bearable the awareness of its separateness. According to Tustin: 'When the mother–infant dyad is unable to function in a way that provides the infant a healing sensory experience, the holes in the fabric of the "emergent self" (Stern 1985) become a source of unbearable awareness of bodily separateness' (Tustin 1987: 43).

Children who experience these 'holes' too often have difficulties progressing out of the autistic-contiguous mode. For them, the feeling of oneness through the enactment of their very own ritual, together with the therapist, provides a 'healing-sensory experience'.

Ritual provides an effective way of re-creating the experience of oneness that lessens the pain of a premature feeling of separation from the mother. It also encourages connections between physical-sensory experiences and themes, a connection that enables movement to more advanced modes.

Case illustration: Uri and ' The ritual of the cocoon'

Uri was 11 years old when I first met him. Since he was born, he was used as a weapon by his parents in their violent struggle against each other. At the time he started treatment, his mother left her husband and took along her children.

Uri seemed completely detached from reality. Although his intelligence level was normal, he did not know how many days were in a week or how long is an hour. Everything fell from his hands. There was a constant smile on his face, even during violent outbursts.

He was referred to our unit because of his severe psychopathology. His father and mother were each assigned to separate psychotherapists. Since the psychologist who tested him recommended treatment on a pre-verbal level, I saw Uri twice a week for individual dramatherapy.

Since I share a room with the occupational therapist, a wide selection of sensory-stimulating elements – swings, large balls, cloth, water and a sand box – is available. Puzzles and cognitive games are displayed on the shelves. A variety of dolls, puppets, miniature toys, costumes, masks and a large supply of art materials are kept in boxes.

During the first meetings, I could hardly follow Uri's play. I had difficulties remembering what he did. He engaged in physical play with most of these elements. I felt exhausted and frantic when he left.

At further meetings, it became clear that almost the whole of his physical activities involved some kind of swinging, covering himself and hiding. We developed a ritual, which we repeated endless times.

Uri would lie on a large swing. I would cover him with a large piece of soft cloak and then swing him. After a few minutes, the cloak would fall; I would say 'Oh! . . . the cloak fell!' and cover him again. This ritual calmed him. After repeating it for almost thirty minutes, he would choose a very easy puzzle, sit near me and play with it, reminding me of a 2-year-old child.

I understood this ritual as an expression of his wish to be held and contained like a baby, and of his fear that, in the course of our interaction, the fabric that holds him, and 'us', together might fall, as it did in his early relationship with his parents.

Such a sensory ritual may contain a complex idea without having recourse to words.

Later on, Uri started a search for more stable containers than a cloak and a swing. He chose a cylinder, hiding inside it and rocking himself. I joined in rocking him and singing a lullaby. Uri said: 'I am a butterfly cocoon!' This was the first time he invented a symbol both connected to and removed from himself.[1]

While rocking Uri, I made up a song about a cocoon who felt safe all covered up; it was not completely protected since wind and rain might endanger it and people might step on it. Then Uri would stretch a hand or a leg out of the cylinder and pull it back in. The song continued synchronically with Uri's movements; it was about the cocoon's ambivalence, and whether it was worthwhile getting out of the cocoon state to become a butterfly, and which state was safer.

In this ritual, there was a strong feeling of oneness between us; we were both storytellers of his myth.

Gradually, Uri initiated the separation between us. One day he declared: 'You are the mother-butterfly and I am the cocoon'. After that, we started to improvise short play interactions between mother and cocoon.

Although we still repeated the cocoon ritual at each session, the balance between ritual and improvisation started to change. Through ritual, Uri experienced a sense of oneness with a caretaker which he had missed at the beginning of his life. In ritual, text, music and movement patterns are clearly defined and repetitive. When he started to improvise, Uri took the risk of surprising me and of being surprised by my reactions. In mutual improvisation, two separate individuals meet and play. Uri started to 'allow and enjoy an overlap of two play areas' (Winnicott 1971: 48). When this occurs, the child begins to experience a feeling of separateness with all its frustrations and joys. From this point on, Uri's ability to play symbolic make-believe play developed rapidly. His play became less physical and more communicative.

From the feedback I received from his mother and his school, it seemed that Uri's relation to reality was starting to change. I believe that the development of his play helped him engage in a new dialogue between his inner and outer life.

Throughout our work together, there was a period of severe regression. This period was related to a 'sudden' worsening of the family's situation. Uri regressed at school, had a psychotic episode at home and completely lost his ability for 'make-believe' play.

While his mother's therapist worked hard to help her reorganize the family's reality and to contain Uri's difficulties with less aggression, I worked intensively with Uri.

New rituals had to be created to hold him through these difficult times. In our sessions, he stopped playing. He walked restlessly around the room, spreading and throwing small toys and parts of puzzles all over the place. My attempts to help him put his feelings into words seemed to do more harm than good. After he had torn the whole room apart, he would throw himself upon a mattress and kick his hands and legs. Remembering his need for covering at the beginning of our work together, I tried to cover him with the cloak but he threw it away violently. I gathered the pieces of puzzle he threw before and covered him with them; he then asked me to cover all of his body so he would not see or hear anything. Gradually, he calmed down.

This interaction was not 'play'. No claim of playfulness existed. It was Uri's only way of showing me his terrible fear of breaking into small pieces and his need to shut himself off completely from outside reality. Once I managed to communicate, in the sensory mode, that I acknowledged his wish to disconnect from reality and that I believed that the pieces of himself could be collected and returned to him, he calmed down. We then repeated the process: he threw little toys in the room and I covered him with them. By doing so, we re-enacted something that had happened in the past, and redefined it as play; this became a ritual that gave physical shape and sensory content to our history.

Two weeks later, when Uri became more organized, we repeated this ritual. Suddenly, Uri told me the story behind it: 'Once upon a time, there was a tiny, tiny baby. Upon leaving the hospital after his birth, he was crushed between two cars that drove like crazy. During the crash, the doctor's medicine was scattered all over. The doctor had to collect the medicine as fast as possible and rush to the hospital to save the baby, because all these little toys were the only medicine that could help the baby.'

Dramatherapy with children who operate mainly in the paranoid-schizoid mode

The paranoid-schizoid mode was conceived by Melanie Klein as the most primitive psychological organization (Klein 1975).

Winnicott (1960, 1971) and Guntrip (1961) talk about more primitive psychological organizations, while Ogden, as we have seen, views the paranoid-schizoid mode as developing out of the autistic-contiguous mode. In it we find the beginning of a differentiation between 'me' and 'not-me'. But there is not yet a full relationship between 'me' and 'real others'. It is rather a relationship between parts of 'myself'and 'other-parts-of-myself-that-are-projected-on-to-others'. 'Self' and 'others' are perceived as 'things' rather than full human beings.

In this mode, the child is capable of feeling love and hate towards himself and others. But loving and hating the same object is intolerable. The fear of causing damage and being damaged by love objects is great. The child therefore organizes his experience by splitting between good and bad, and by trying omnipotently to control the environment.

Children who operate mainly in this mode tend to use free playtime for projective play. It is often difficult to follow their play, since their defensive use of splitting creates a discontinuity of experience. They jump from symbol to symbol, and the thread that holds the symbols together is hidden. Other times, their play is super-organized, with no place for surprises or risk-taking. This rigid organization defends them from connecting with their inner sense of discontinuity.

In this mode, there is very little space between the symbol and the symbolized. 'Thoughts and feelings are not experienced as personal creations but as facts' (Ogden 1989: 21). Children relate to their imaginary creations in a concrete manner that denies the richness of their own symbolism. Concretizing symbols reduces the space between inner and outer life. This eliminates the natural healing power of play.

Whatever character the child chooses to play, the role will be the same. Every character will either be the victim or the aggressor, the villain or the hero. A wolf might have the same voice and body motion as a policeman, a father and a thief, and the poor sheep will behave in the same manner as the baby or the old woman. Although the child jumps from symbol to symbol, they all mostly look and sound similar.

The characters selected by such children are very often mechanized: cars, dinosaurs, machines and especially robots. The child does not emotionally relate to toys; these may easily be interchanged. This might reflect a sense of dehumanization. Humans become 'things' which can control the child from within. People may easily be used and replaced. This mode allows very little space for feelings of loss, missing or guilt.

In this mode, the child's imaginary world is full, with characters, action and intense emotions of fear and hate. Yet it is a dull world. All characters are similar and there is very little variety of emotion. Events just 'happen', with no sense or causality.

The following directions should be considered by dramatherapists while working with such children:

1 help them organize their spontaneous play in a way that will be less chaotic – around a theme, a scene or a story – so they can identify the thread that holds the symbols together and gain some sense of continuity of experience;
2 help them develop their imaginary characters in the following ways:
   (a) encourage differentiation between the various characters by defining each one's uniqueness
   (b) develop in the child a sense of empathy towards higher imaginary creations by associating them with a wide variety of emotion and connecting these emotions to life events
   (c) develop a sense of causality within the make-believe world. Events do not just 'happen'; they also might be motivated and enacted by someone
   (d) encourage the child to develop a variety of relationships among his imaginary creations.

The main aim of such work is to develop the 'make-believe' world so it includes more human figures, with emotions, motivation and reasons for behaviour. This will allow for better integration between 'good' and 'bad' and a more continuous sense of experience.

Enriching the imaginary world in this way will decrease the concrete manner in which the child treats symbols. This will allow the meaning of the symbols to surface.

It is not easy to achieve these goals. Children who need the omnipotent control and who view things and thoughts as facts may easily feel attacked and misunderstood by any intervention in this direction. The dramatherapist has to start by accepting the child's perception without actually agreeing with it; an effective way to achieve this is to join the child in his other make-believe play as an obedient actor. When the therapist accepts the child's will and plays the exact part the child asks for, the child feels accepted. Yet the 'mental claim' of playfulness works to the benefit of the therapist's activities. Both parties know that the therapist may or may not agree with the child's perception as expressed in the play. This is not always easy for the therapist, since the child may ask her to play very cruel and bizarre roles. It is important for the therapist to assume these roles, but to keep the scenario played strictly within the realm of the make-believe play.

Only after the therapist asserts her ability to play together with the child within the 'make-believe area' will the child accept intervention in the direction of change.

Case illustration: Ron – 'The machine that discovered its humanity'

Ron was referred for treatment by his school psychologist and was accepted by the Unit for Intensive Therapy for Children. Although he was 14 years old, his only means of self-expression was through play – therefore the psychologist who tested him recommended dramatherapy which he received once a week.

Ron is the eldest child of a very depressive mother. He has both learning disabilities and emotional difficulties that affected the mother–child dyad from the start. He was one of the most 'bizarre' children I ever met. He talked to himself in strange voices, loved to play with miniature toys, but it was impossible to follow his play. At times, he would give himself behavioural orders in a robotic manner. He was completely isolated socially.

From the very first session, it was clear that Ron felt free only when playing. However, since play isolated him from reality, it was also his prison.

He played with all the miniatures in the room. He divided them into 'bad machine-like figures' and 'good small-(usually) animal figures' which were often harshly abused by the big ones. His play had no sense of continuity. He jumped from one toy to another making strange noises, often forgetting what he had just done. Fragments of songs would just pop up out of his head with no apparent connection to what he was doing at the moment.

Although Ron knew he was playing, his attitude toward his imaginary creations was overly concrete. Therefore it was difficult to discover the symbolism in his play.

Because of the complexity of Ron's difficulties, my work with him included both cognitive and emotional elements. We started our work within the play area, but later also worked on reality-based issues. For the purpose of this chapter, I wish to focus on the ways I helped Ron organize and develop his spontaneous play, to enable him to move from the paranoid-schizoid toward the depressive mode.

I will discuss two main methods of intervention:

1 Organizing frantic play around an image

In one of our first sessions, Ron was more anxious than usual. I had no idea what the reason could be and I could not make sense of his play. He played with a lot of miniatures and small toys and sang fragments of songs and melodies. He asked me to imitate the voices and songs of all these little creatures. I could hardly manage to comply. His imaginary characters became more and more frantic as I failed to do so. I suggested we make a list to help me remember all these characters and songs. Ron was not able to describe his characters, which were all some kind of robot. But he gave each a number and a song or melody. This task had a surprisingly calming effect on both of us and he narrowed down his songs and characters to five:

1 an angry and abusive song;
2 a song expressing fear of abuse;
3 a song about the fear of going crazy;
4 a song with the text 'I'm always happy, I forget my troubles';
5 a frantic, unclear melody which I could not follow.

I suggested we make-believe we have a 'song-machine'. He would press the button with the name of the song and I would try to sing the proper song.

As we played this game, the thread holding all the symbols together suddenly appeared. His singing characters were a way of regulating his emotions. The most frightening theme for him was the fear of becoming crazy. Less frightening was the fear of abuse. Being the abuser had a calming effect on him, and being happy *forgetting* his troubles was the most calming song.

Ron used his 'song-machine' to deal with his fears. I pointed out to him that his machine is like a fairground. By operating this machine, the child scares himself more and more, until he can no longer bear it. He then switches the machine to a calming song, only to re-engage further in a scary one. Ron smiled, and asked me to press button number five. I did so. He started to sing the same melody that I found so confusing at the beginning of the session. It was a beautiful song, with a sense of continuity, a beginning, a middle and an end. It also had a very long, sad part.

This was the first time I saw Ron as a complete human being, a person with a range of emotions that could be experienced and expressed artistically through music. I saw that as the beginning of an ability to relate to the world in the depressive mode.

At the beginning of the session, he treated his imaginary creations and their songs in a concrete manner. There was no distance between the singer and the songs. After we organized the songs around an image, the meaning of the songs started to surface. This enabled Ron to allow distance between the symbol and the symbolized. He was emotionally connected to the melody, but the melody was not him. I believe that in this beginning of artistic expression lies the beginning of an ability to relate to the relationship between inner life and reality in a more mature symbolic manner.

2 Helping Ron gain empathy towards his imaginary characters by encouraging more fully human characteristics and a sense of continuity within the imaginary world

After the creation of the 'music machine' Ron started to develop four parallel little plays which he re-created each session. For each play, he selected a different set of little toys. But the content of these little plays was very similar: in most of them, he used mechanical plastic toys. They were all about frightening and cruel adventures of villains and abused victims. One of these dramas was slightly different. It told the story of 'Good Charade', 'Bad Sherman' and a 'Judge'. Charade was named after a car that was often parked outside the clinic. Charade was a clothmade, very soft beetle puppet. Sherman – who was named after a tank – was a soft-made whale puppet. The Judge was any hard object (stick, wooden cube etc.) that was available.

The play was about some undefined 'crime' that Bad Sherman committed against Good Charade, and the terrible punishments that the Judge inflicted on Sherman. The punishments were extremely cruel. Sherman was often buried, burned alive or mutilated.

Ron gave me the role of Charade while he held the puppet that represented Sherman and the object that represented the Judge. I was expected to repeat Sherman's text as he was slowly dying or suffering.

All my attempts to investigate the nature of Sherman's crime failed. I believed that this play represented Ron's attitude towards parts of himself and towards his therapy. It seemed to me that Ron wished me to help him understand and accept Sherman. I had to help Ron develop Sherman's character in order to allow the meaning of the symbol to surface. It was a difficult task, because Sherman was experienced by Ron as a very negative side of himself and I had to accept his wish to 'kill him', while helping him to develop empathy toward this character.

The following short dramatic improvisation illustrates the way the play went:

Judge/Ron:	He is sentenced to death.
Charade/Galila:	But . . .
Judge/Ron:	Kill him, I said! Put him in jail, and then burn him.
Charade/Galila:	What was his crime?
Judge/Ron:	None of your business . . . (*he turns to me*) Hangman . . . prepare the fire!
Hangman/Galila:	(*Prepares the fire*)
Charade/Galila:	I want to protest . . . I do not understand the verdict!

(*Ron asks me to voice Sherman as he is dying in the fire, while he holds Sherman's puppet in one hand and hits it with the other*)

Sherman/Galila:	'one thousand firemen won't manage to put me off . . .' (*Singing a well-known Hebrew song*)

Judge/Ron:	Shut up! You won't sing for long. Hangman, make the fire stronger!
Hangman/Galila:	(*Makes the fire stronger*)
Sherman/Galila:	(*Sings louder and louder while Ron abuses him, throwing stones at him*)
Judge/Ron:	We finally got rid of him! Hangman, bury him deep so we never hear his voice again!
Hangman/Ron:	(*Buries Sherman deep under the carpet*)
Charade/Galila:	(*Crying*) My friend is dead! I couldn't help it! The Judge never gave me a chance! I know he must have done something to me, but I do not know what! What could have been so bad as to deserve such a punishment?
Judge/Ron:	Go home.
Charade/Galila:	(*Remains seated next to the grave*)
Judge/Ron:	We won't hear him sing again the song of the oppressed!
Charade/Galila:	Was that his crime?
Judge/Ron:	Yes.
Charade/Galila:	No one wants to hear the voice of the oppressed. It is too sad and painful to listen to.
(*We both sat quietly by the grave, and suddenly*)	
Storyteller/Ron:	And then . . . the Messiah came and all the dead came back to life.
Sherman/Ron:	(*in panic . . .*) Where am I? I do not remember anything! Help . . . I am crazy!
Charade/Galila:	Relax, you are not crazy! You went through a lot. You wanted to sing the song of the oppressed but it was not allowed in the society you lived in. So the Judge punished you. You were burned and buried. Then the Messiah came and brought you back to life. No one can remember such frightening things!
Sherman/Ron:	Oh! So I am not crazy? Thank you, thank you for telling me what really happened!

From this point on, the characters of Sherman and Charade and the relationship between them started to develop. Sherman became the symbol for all forbidden feelings – need, love, loneliness, and the pain and guilt of being born impaired. Sherman was oppressed and killed again and again because Ron was overwhelmed by those feelings and lost control of his behaviour. He therefore had to regress to the paranoid-schizoid mode, often forgetting what he had just done and losing his sense of continuity.

Further on, gradually, working first in the realm of the imaginary world and later connecting the 'make-believe' world to reality, Ron expanded his ability to relate to the world also in the depressive mode.

Dramatherapy with children who operate mainly in the 'depressive mode'

The concept of the 'depressive position' was introduced by Melanie Klein (1975) to refer to the most mature form of psychological organization. Ogden's focus is on the 'depressive mode, not as a structure or a developmental phase, but as a process through which perception is attributed meaning in a particular way' (Ogden 1989: 9–11). He talks about the dialectical relationship between this mode and the more primitive modes.

In this mode, a person achieves the ability to relate to himself and others as full human beings. Self and others are conceived with a sense of continuity. The person does not become another person when constantly subject to changes of moods and/or emotions. It is only when 'thoughts and feelings are experienced to a large degree as personal creations . . . that one develops a feeling of responsibility for psychological actions' (Ogden 1989: 12). Therefore, there is space between the symbol and the symbolized and symbols have layers of meaning.

In this mode, a person also cares about others; therefore, feelings of guilt about real or imagined harm that one has caused to others are strong. There is a capacity for feeling loss, for missing, empathy and ambivalence. Life is outside the area of omnipotence. One is often sad about what one never had and, indeed, feelings of grief and loss are experienced towards the unattainable.

Like the others, this mode never exists on its own. 'Every facet of human experience is the outcome of a dialectic constituted by the interplay of the three modes' (Ogden 1989: 4). Children who operate predominantly in this mode do not have access to the other, more primitive modes, of which they are usually terrified.

These children are often very good at school. They express themselves as adults. They are empathic, concerned about others and understand the complexities of life at a very early age. However, they pay a high price for their maturity. They hardly dare desire something for themselves. They do not allow themselves feelings of anger, jealousy and passion. They feel guilty about their thoughts, feelings and the imaginary damage they might have caused. They often feel as if life has passed them by and have morbid thoughts.

These children often stop engaging in make-believe play at a relatively early age. They prefer reading, board and computer games, drawing or writing and sometimes sport. They feel too responsible for their imaginary world to engage in actual make-believe play.

The constant struggle against the appearance of the more primitive modes causes a variety of symptoms, including suicidal thoughts. Being in contact with the more primitive modes is essential to the feeling of being alive.

In working with these children, it is very important to respect their defences. Drama and theatre work enables them to make use of their intellectual curiosity to help them engage in a dynamic dialogue between the three modes.

Myths, legends, plays and stories hold the complexity and richness of symbolism that belong to the depressive mode together with the extreme emotions and magic that belong to the paranoid-schizoid mode. The active process of turning literature into theatre includes sensory and physical work that belongs to the autistic-contiguous mode.

Within the safety of acting a story without being responsible for its symbolism, children are encouraged to search for artistic expression. They move within the range of owning and alienating their emotions and experience themselves as an intellectual, emotional and sensory being.

During the creative process, the child searches for the 'aesthetic distance', which is the point of equilibrium in the artistic form. At this point, the performer 'retains a piece of the overdistant cognitive observer and a piece of the underdistanced affective actor' (Landy 1986: 100).

Through this work, the healing dialogue between inner life and outer reality is released.

Case illustration: Orit –'The Storyteller'

Orit was an 11-year-old girl, talented and intelligent. Her father died during army service. She had one older brother who served in the military and she lived alone with a very controlling mother and adopted the role of 'mother's best friend'. She was referred to a dramatherapy group by her psychologist; while she continued individual psychotherapy with her, she also joined a dramatherapy group in a private practice, which met for two hours at a time every second week.

Orit operated mainly in the depressive mode. She had an amazing ability to use symbolism and was a very empathic little girl. She never wanted or wished for anything for herself. She was socially isolated and felt that life was passing her by. The psychologist who treated her recommended dramatherapy to help her reconnect to her creative self. When starting psychological treatment, she concentrated on trying to please her psychologist.

When Orit joined the dramatherapy group, she was very shy and avoided participating in any acting role. Since she drew very well, she very much enjoyed being the 'set designer' for other children's improvisations. She read a lot, and was familiar with many stories and legends.

For the purpose of this chapter, I would like to focus on two episodes in which dramatic work helped her connect with more primitive modes of organizing experience, and the liberating effect that these modes had for her.

1 The Legend of the Fisherman's Wife

For several weeks, the group had been working on legends. We divided into several smaller groups, each one working on a different legend.

Orit joined a group working on the Legend of the Fisherman's Wife and the Golden Fish. As usual, she was the costume designer. She designed a wonderful costume and mask for the fisherman's wife.

She made a mask out of papier mâché using glue made out of water and flour. She enjoyed the messy, sensual work with these materials. I asked all mask-makers to wear the masks they made, and to show their small group the image they had in mind while creating the mask. Within the framework of the rehearsal, while everyone was working simultaneously, Orit wore the mask and started improvising a humorous monologue for the envious and greedy fisherman's wife.

This character belonged to the paranoid-schizoid mode. She was jealous, greedy and bad and lived in a world in which people were either 'bad and greedy' or 'good and stupid'.

In this role, Orit adopted for the first time a sense of wanting something for herself. At the end of the session, she expressed having had more fun than usual.

2 Snow White's Sleep (a mini-death that gave room to life)

After the fisherman's wife monologue, Orit felt much freer within the group. She started to enjoy acting. She expressed her wishes and ideas more often and loved to play the part of the 'bad guy', a role she never allowed herself in real life. At this point, Orit was trapped in the depressive mode. She viewed life with its complexities, she showed understanding for her mother, her father's death, her therapist, but lacked empathy towards her own anger, need and greed. She felt guilty about these unconscious feelings. Through the use of drama, she could experience them. The character of the fisherman's wife viewed the world through the glass of the paranoid-schizoid mode. When this happened, Orit began to include this mode in the way she viewed her outside world. She created a split between the two treatment modalities. She enjoyed the dramatherapy group and felt cared for and appreciated by me and the group members: it represented the 'good mother', while her psychologist represented the 'bad mother'and was experienced as boring and demanding.

Orit's psychologist worked hard to contain the negative transference while Orit continued to develop her spontaneity with the help of the dramatherapy group.

We were once working with the concept of 'sleep', a metaphor which was brought up by one of the group members. We did a lot of physical work using cloth and pillows. At a certain point, almost all the group members found a place to rest and relax.

Orit was restless. Finally, she sat on a swing and started swinging vigorously. I joined her by swinging her as fast and strongly as possible. I gradually slowed the pace, and she started to relax. I covered her with a cloth, continued to rock her, and sang a lullaby to the 'sleeping' group. When the song ended, I asked each child to write or draw something about their experience.

Orit wrote and read to the group a beautiful story about 'Snow White's sleep'.

> Snow White was afraid to fall asleep, because the moment she tasted the apple, she knew she had been cheated by her stepmother and was afraid to die. As she was struggling not to fall asleep, she heard her real mother's voice singing, and fell into deep sleep. She told her dead mother how hard life was for her. She spoke about her King father being away on important missions, leaving her at the mercy of her cruel stepmother, who turned her into a slave. She was tired of slaving for other people and wanted a life of her own, but she was not sure she would ever obtain it.

Later, her psychologist told me that Orit let her read this story and this opened a new communication line between them. It seems that the physical-sensory work helped Orit get in touch with the autistic-contiguous mode. Together with the psychologist's perseverance, the creative work helped Orit reorganize her perception of childhood, and she gained the ability to move freely between the three modes. She expressed this newly acquired ability through the Snow White story. At this point, she was able to integrate both treatment modalities and to initiate a new search to discover her true self.

CONCLUSION

Ogden's theory emphasizes the importance of the dialectical relationship between the three modes of generating experience.

In this chapter, I have emphasized the importance of play for children's mental health. Through play, children organize their experience and maintain a live dialogue between their developing inner world and reality.

When children are unable to use play in this manner, this important dialogue stagnates and the dialectical relationship between the three modes[2] of generating experience collapses into one single direction.

I believe that the role of the dramatherapist is to help children restore their ability to play in a way that will release this important dialogue.

In order to achieve this goal, the dramatherapist starts a playful dialogue with the child. The communication between the child and the therapist is in the same mode that the child uses to attribute meaning to his experience. If the child operates mainly in the autistic-contiguous mode, the playful dialogue will be physical and sensory. When the child operates mainly in the paranoid-schizoid mode, the dialogue will begin with projective play. And if the child operates mainly in the depressive mode, literature, theatre and drama will be the window to communication. After this dialogue is established, the dramatherapist helps the child enrich his play by encouraging him to discover the live space between symbol and symbolized.

The important dialogue between inner and outer life and the ability for a dialectical relationship between the three modes is often stimulated when children discover the wealth of their own play.

ACKNOWLEDGEMENTS

I should like to thank Marianne Soher for help in writing this chapter.

NOTES

1 Cylinder in Hebrew is '*galil*', and my name is 'Galila'. Cocoon in Hebrew is '*golem*', which also means 'stupid'.
2 This framework follows similar lines to Jenning's EPR (Embodiment, Projection and Role) theory; see Jennings 1993.

REFERENCES

Ariel, S. (1992) *Strategic Family Play Therapy*. London: John Wiley.
Jennings, S. (ed.) (1987) *Dramatherapy Theory and Practice: 1*. London: Routledge.
——— (1990) *Dramatherapy with Families, Groups and Individuals: waiting in the wings*. London: Jessica Kingsley.
——— (1993) *Play Therapy with Children: a practitioner's guide*. Oxford: Blackwell Scientific.
Klein, M. (1975) *Collected Works*, Vols. I–III. London: Hogarth Press and Institute of Psychoanalysis.
—— (1989) *Envy and Gratitude and Other Works*. London: Virago Press.
Landy, R. (1986) *Drama Therapy Concepts and Practices*. Springfield, Ill.: Charles C. Thomas.
Ogden, T. H. (1989) *The Primitive Edge of Experience*. New Jersey: Jason Aronson.
Piaget, J. and Inhelder, B. (1969) *The Psychology of the Child*. Trowbridge: Basic Books.
Segal, H. (1964) *Introduction to the World of Melanie Klein*. New York: Basic Books (English edition 1991, London: Karnac.)

Stern, D. (1977) *The First Relationship: infant and mother*. Cambridge, Mass.:
  Harvard University Press.
———— (1985) *The Interpersonal World of the Infant*. New York: Basic Books.
Tustin, F. (1987) *Autistic Barriers in Neurotic Patients*. London: Karnac.
Winnicott, D. W. (1971) *Playing and Reality*. Harmondsworth, Middlesex:
  Penguin.

Part II

The context of dramatherapy work

Chapter 4

The role a role-play may play
Dramatherapy and the externalization of the problem

Torben Marner

INTRODUCTION

This chapter deals with the relationship between dramatherapy (Jennings 1990) and recent developments in systemic family therapy.

The main trend is towards an approach. The post-systemic family therapists tend to step down from the cybernetic metalevel, to the level where they meet the referred child and the child's family in a personal way.

From yesterday's attempt to understand the dysfunctional interaction of the family, the focus today is on learning what the family finds constructive in the therapeutic dialoque.

Years ago the referred child was the scapegoat. When this label was removed from the child, the parents often became targets. To counteract this, the Milan Systemic Associates (Selvini *et al.* 1980) designed three guidelines for the interviewing therapist: hypothesizing, circularity and neutrality. This resulted in making scapegoats of either all or none of the family members.

Recently the theory and practice of the Australian Michael White and David Epston from New Zealand (Epston 1989, White 1989, Epston and White 1992, 1993) have introduced the technique of 'externalization' to end all labelling and unite the child and her family in a 'freedom fight' against the subjugating problem. By externalizing, objectifying and often personifying the problem as a tyrant, a monster, a troll, etc., they have not only engendered a fighting spirit, but have also transformed the therapist from the supreme expert into a friend against foes, and an ally against all kinds of oppressors.

A whole new language has emerged. Talk about an internal illness has been replaced by a discourse about the real effects of the change; for example, 'I am anorectic' becomes 'Anorexia wants me to. . . ' Externalizing the problem, as well as maintaining a spirit of resistance towards sneaking counterattacks from the problem, demands an encouraging support from the therapist, who needs all his ingenuity, playfulness, persistence and creativity to be an ally in the struggle towards liberation. Thus theory and practice emerge more and more clearly, in an overlap of the ideas and methods of dramatherapy. Every family session becomes 'a play within the play', though most frequently taking the form of an imaginary enactment on a verbal level.

The three case histories in this chapter illustrate the dramatherapeutic elements of imagination, roles, role-reversal and playful magical rituals, which are now part of the family therapy interview all over the world.

The first case history is a family therapy session which took place in 1985, a few years before I came to know about externalization and dramatherapy. What was intuitive then is today a conscious choice of action. Some new theories and practices are integrated more gracefully and naturally than others. This is undoubtedly due to personality and timing, a fit between the therapist, his professional experience and the new perspective inherent in a particular ideology and practice.

1 Case history

When I recall this family session, it seems to have consisted of six sequences:

1 the referral
2 the welcome
3 the story
4 the invitation
5 the role-play
6 the directive.

1 The referral

The general practitioner had referred a 7-year-old girl for anxiety neurosis.

2 The welcome

The parents had telephoned me in the morning and asked for an expeditious session, because they could not 'take it any more'. It was possible for me to meet with them later that afternoon.

The family drove the 70 kilometres to the outpatient clinic and brought with them three children: Lone, 7 years old; Eric, 5 years old; and Anne, 2 years old. Lone appeared to be bright and curious, Eric reserved, bright and calm, and Anne sat observing on the lap of the father. The mother was a clerk (tense, tearful and powerless) and the father a hospital labourer (initially sceptical, reserved and powerless).

3 The story

They told me that five weeks earlier Lone had suddenly started to get fits of anxiety. These fits had become more frequent, now appearing both night and day, and also stronger: she would cling to the neck of either the mother or the father with loud cries of 'I am scared.'

These fits lasted some minutes, during which the parents could not get in contact with her. As the story was being recounted, Lone had an attack of anxiety (preceded by an ultra short side-glance to me, which gave me an insight into the nature of the attack). Crying loudly, Lone threw herself at the neck of her mother, who stiffened and tried in vain to console her daughter. I continued my conversation with the father without interruption.

4 The invitation

When the fit had stopped as suddenly as it had begun, I turned to Lone and asked her with warmth and kindness to show me the fit once again because I had not really seen it. Lone gave me a look of surprise and replied she could not do it. I pressed her, and reached the point where she could tell me what she was used to doing, but she was unable to show it.

5 The role-play

Using the argument that it was important for her that she could have an attack whenever she wanted, I suggested that she should act it out for the sake of training. Lone immediately grasped the idea and the mother volunteered too.

Standing in the middle of the office, Lone explained that she was standing in the drawing room and the mother in another room, 'and then I run to her'. 'Show me,' I asked, and got her to come rushing up to the mother and start climbing on to her. But she could not cry loudly.

'Maybe your father can help you with this,' I suggested, and the father at once volunteered. 'Daddy is in the bathroom and washes his hands, because he has just finished making the car,' Lone explained. 'Yes, and his hands are still a little wet,' I proposed. Lone nodded, ran to the father and started climbing up to his neck, but still without the loud cries.

I now suggested that the mother should play Lone and Lone her mother. Lone sat down on the couch beside me and the mother walked into the 'drawing room' and produced a 'fit' in which, with loud exclamations, she came rushing up to the father, climbed up and hung herself round his neck, continually shouting, until she burst into laughter and climbed down again.

With seriousness, I now asked Lone whether she would judge the acting of her mother to be very good, half good or bad. 'Half good,' Lone replied, 'because she laughed in the end.' 'And what about the acting of Lone?'

'Only half good,' the mother said with a smile, 'because Lone did not look worried enough.'

6 The directive

Shortly after this I suggested the directive: the parents should role-play an anxiety fit, with Lone in the main role, following each spontaneous fit of anxiety.

The parents agreed, and two days later the mother called me and said that there had been a drastic decrease in the frequency of anxiety fits. Both she and her spouse felt supported, because they now knew what to do in this situation in which they formerly had felt so powerless.

To give the parents and Lone even more solid ground under their feet, I wrote them the following letter a few days later:

Dear Mrs and Mr Hansen,

You have let me know that the situation has improved, but as it is important to allow for the possibility of a relapse I suggest that you buy Lone a little toy animal, e.g. a teddy bear, to have if she feels that the anxiety is coming back. Together with the teddy bear she should decide whether she wants to come to another family session at the outpatient department. In that case she should inform you parents that it is something which both she and the teddy bear agree about.

A week after the first session, the mother telephoned again and said that she was sad, because the school had said that she kept Lone away from school.

I replied that I was sure that she would do only what she felt was the best for Lone and suggested that she supported Lone in going to school by giving her permission to leave the school early if she felt bad, and that she got the school's permission to do this. Besides this the mother mentioned that Lone was again sleeping in her own bed and had taken up playing outside with her friends for the first time since the start of the fits.

We agreed upon a follow-up phone call four weeks later. It was Lone who picked up the telephone and with liveliness and brightness described how the fits had disappeared in the daytime, but appeared a few times during the nights. She had been attending school as normal and likewise played with her friends.

The mother took over and confirmed what Lone had been saying. She said that Lone had attended school the last two weeks and 'everything was back to normal'. We agreed upon termination, but I suggested that the family in case of a relapse held a family discussion at home, about the relevance of another family session at the outpatient department.

Thus the 'spell' of anxiety on a 7-year-old girl and her family was broken in a single family session. In the six sequences of the family session, the case history illustrates the power of imagination and the mastering of the problem by techniques I now would call dramatherapeutic techniques of role-playing and role-reversal.

Contrary to dramatherapy, however, it was I, the therapist, who directed the play, which in itself bore no resemblance to 'acting out' in an analytic sense. The child and her parents were not invited to act in some roles chosen by themselves, but consciously to repeat the pattern both as actors and director.

The enactment, however, gave the girl access to a more constructive and creative use of her fantasy and it also let humour and liveliness into the family.

DRAMATHERAPY AND EXTERNALIZATION

White and Epston have expressed their wonder that externalization of the problem was not described in family therapy literature before 1979 (Epston and White 1992). The phenomenon, however, has been an intrinsic part of human life since the dawn of mankind under various names such as exorcism of bad spirits, the splitting of 'I and my madness' as in *Hamlet*, the representations of good and bad aspects in the play therapy of children as well as in dramatherapy.

To illustrate the process of the relationship between externalization in family therapy and dramatherapy, I will give a short description of the development of the notion of externalization.

White became aware of the relative influence of the problem on the family and of the family members' influence on the problem through reading Bateson's analysis of constraints (White 1986), in which he shows that where some actions are possible, others are constrained.

White searched for moments where the child did not allow the problem to have its will and chose the phrase 'unique outcomes' for these moments. This led to the idea of a crossroads, a choice of who should decide, the child or the problem. And once the child decided to resist and fight, White and Epston assisted with playful imagination in the struggle to regain self-control and the change from 'passenger in' to 'agent of' his or her life.

Later, White (Epston and White 1993), influenced by Foucault's analysis of power and the aspect of subjugation and oppression by the problem (Foucault 1973), encouraged children and families to rewrite their problem-dominated stories. At the same time, Epston (1986), influenced by anthropological studies, introduced narrative (Bruner 1986) and rite of passage (van Gennep 1960) as metaphors for the therapeutic process.

The whole idea of externalizing the problem seems to me to be in keeping with basic theories and practices of dramatherapy. It is, however, more a matter of an overlap of ideas than of identical techniques, masked by differences of terminology. As stated above, the family therapist is more active in his direction than many dramatherapists, who usually provide openings and ideas for the client to choose roles, themes and enactments of stories.

Role-play is frequently used in the process of externalization. A brief example will suffice:

> Epston (*To a girl with severe eczema*) : You play the eczema, I will play you . . .
> Epston (*To the eczema, speaking in his role of the girl*): If we were to compromise, what would you wish I did for you?
>
> (Epston 1993)

2 Case history

The parents brought their child Thomas, a stuttering 11-year-old boy who was haunted by obsessional rituals and school-phobia. Both parents had bcen married before. The mother had a teenage son, who lived with his father, and the father had a teenage daughter who lived with her mother and her new spouse.

Thomas's father had had the painful experience in his first marriage of losing his first son by sudden infant death at the age of 4 months. Thomas was therefore a precious baby for him, leading to a certain overprotection which was openly spoken about in the first of seven therapy sessions.

In the first session the notion 'Troll' was introduced. It was suggested that *it* made Thomas do the rituals and sabotaged his going to school. The rituals consisted in obsessionally walking up and down the staircases in the house.

The notion Troll was adopted by Thomas and by the parents. Thomas described how the power of the Troll was expanding and that it was now putting pressure on him to demand that both parents should be at home close to him the whole day.

I mentioned that I experienced the three of them as a close, loving family which for the time being was burdened by an extra family member, the Troll, which would be too much for any little family.

A metaphor of a 'campaign with many battlefields' was developed and I suggested that Thomas and his allies, the parents, should fight in one place at a time. Together they chose going to school, and the mother and Thomas decided to contact a schoolmate as an extra ally.

In the second session it was still the Troll who was mostly in charge. The father expressed irritation over its power and wonder that the Troll evidently had no power when Thomas was visiting the grandparents. The Troll had made Thomas try to prevent his father from participating in a five-day business workshop. The father said Thomas had given him a bad conscience by saying that if he went away he would work on the side of the Troll. The mother remarked that neither the Troll nor Thomas could give her a bad conscience.

The family was invited to pretend it was quite an ordinary family until the next family therapy session. In the third session they all smilingly talked about this task as a mutually accepted defeat. Hereafter the father mentioned that the last days had been very positive and Thomas explained that the rituals had decreased and he now slept the whole night in his own bed. He had started to go alone to school in the morning.

At the end of the conversation, the father asked for advice about whether he should call the parents of the schoolmates to invite the schoolmates to their home. The family therapy took place a year before I read Epston's inspiring article 'Temper tantrum parties: saving face, losing face, or going off your face!' (Epston and White 1992). In it Epston suggests inviting schoolmates to a party to watch the child's fits. To avoid this, the child normally fights her problem and thereby regains freedom and self-control. I chose to underline the importance of Thomas's expanding his domain of actions by playing with his friends outside the home.

Some weeks later the parents in the fourth session were able to describe how the rituals had decreased to almost nothing, and how the Troll, whom the parents talked about almost as a family member, had lost a lot of its restraining influence. What was left was that Thomas, now and then, when asked to take his plate from the table, would exclaim that he was unable to do it – and thereby show that he could have the Troll as *his* ally! Thomas laughed when I gave this interpretation.

The school situation was now normalized.

Some weeks later the family came for the fifth session and Thomas was looking happy and had grown in many ways. Everything was functioning outside the home, but the Troll somehow still had Thomas in its grip, forcing him now and then to repeat sequences of action in the opposite way. Thomas explained that he was quite tired of this. Contrary to the parents' testimony, he didn't think that the parents could see when it was him and not the Troll who was in charge. This led to a 'prediction task' in which family members kept a secret diary, marking a plus if they thought Thomas was to be in charge the following day and a minus if they thought that it would be the Troll – to see who was best at predicting.

As Thomas was talking very much about his rituals, it was agreed that the parents would find ten minutes daily, during which Thomas could have a talking time and the parents were to listen without comments.

Finally it was agreed that Thomas and the father should make a graphic expression of the relation between the power of Thomas and that of the Troll.

Three weeks later they came for the sixth session. Thomas brought an

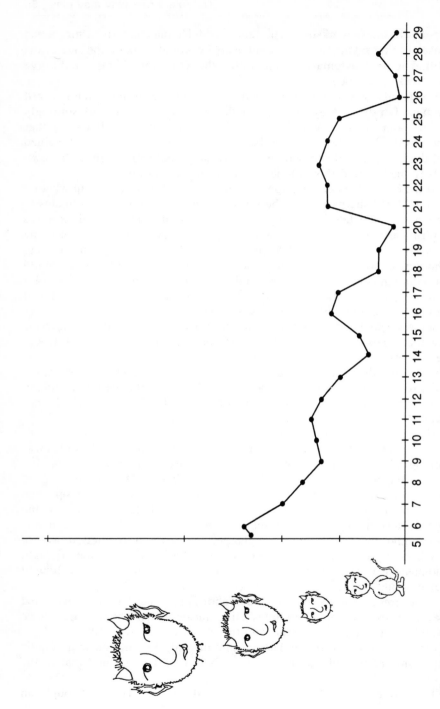

Figure 4.1 Graph plotting the power of the Troll between the fifth and sixth sessions

impressive graph (Figure 4.1) and everybody brought their predictions. These were used to point out that there were days where Thomas was completely in charge.

When the parents talked about how the Troll succeeded one day in making Thomas obstruct their wish to jog in the forest, I supported their not giving in and their developing a clear and firm attitude. For example, they could now and then do something for themselves, such as going out to dinner together. The parents didn't think that Thomas should be left alone, but Thomas solved the problem by declaring that he could visit his aunt while they were out.

In the seventh and last session Thomas announced happily that now there were only the last two hairs of the tail of the Troll left, and the parents confirmed that Thomas was in good spirits, was helpful in the home and liked to argue with his father.

The final test of strength was for Thomas to join the summer camp of the school, from where his father last year was forced to fetch him after one and a half days. I recommended 'dress-rehearsals', and that Thomas should take a small photo of the parents.

Four months later I received a postcard from Thomas, who wrote with childish misspellings:

Dear Toben.

I am on the island Arø, and have seen the bottleship museum.
The Troll has gone and I have no nostalia, but a little loning home.

Greetings Thomas.

In this case, the 11-year-old Thomas was helped by the externalization of the problem through the therapist's indication of a Troll which might have forced him to do his ritualistic walkings up and down the stairs.

Again we see both similarities and differences to the dramatherapeutic way of treatment. The use of magical thinking which is implicit in externalization represents an evident overlap.

The suggestion of the personification, a Troll, was, however, made by the therapist and was not a choice of the child. Both Thomas and his parents took part in playing that the Troll was an extra member of the family for a time.

The idea of making a graph showing the power of the Troll was introduced by the therapist but carried out by Thomas and his ally, the father, following their own design.

In the externalizing conversation, a new language is developed with an emphasis on equality. The referred child becomes a consultant or a veteran once the problem is reduced or gone. When this has happened in one or very few sessions the child is interviewed about how this new competence or freedom was achieved. Subsequently, permission is obtained to use these co-created documents to help other children caught in the grip of the same problem.

To accelerate the regaining of the child's power, notes are taken during the interview and used as a basis for consolidating and encouraging letters.

My third case history will serve as an illustration.

3 Case history

A 6-year-old girl was haunted by nightmares, and as I had to leave the town in which she lives I made an intervention in the form of a letter:

Dear Gudrun,

You are so young that you do not yet understand Danish, so I will let your mother read my letter aloud to you.

It was fun to meet you and to do mimes with you. You are a nice and clever girl who manages many things, but your mother has mentioned to me that you once in a while allow nightmares to outwit you during the night.

Luckily it is a fact that nightmares are a little stupid, and therefore it is possible for children to learn how to cheat them!

Nightmares are so foolish that they believe it is only exciting and interesting dreams which they bring at night and so stupid are they that they believe they have the right to rule over you.

But I will tell you what you can do when they come to rule over you and give you dreams which *you* don't like, but which *they* think are really funny and exciting.

You can either call on your mother and father or go to their bedroom like you used to . . . but even wiser would it be to get hold of a little box with a keyhole! You see, nightmares are not only stupid, but also very curious – so if you say to them, when they come to rule over you, 'Behold my box!' they become *so* curious that they slip through the keyhole and are *so* stupid that they can't find their way out again! And then you and your mother and father once in a while can drive out into the countryside and set them free there!

In this way you will be the one who rules. And when you have become a good nightmare-catcher you can maybe help some friends of yours that have also let themselves be outwitted by these foolish nightmares who love to rule over children.

Good luck with your catching of nightmares!

Your friend
Torben

The letter had an immediate and lasting effect which was confirmed by the mother in a letter eight months later. She also wrote that she had heard

Gudrun counsel a playmate who was also in the grip of nightmares: 'but it must be the grown-ups who take the box to the countryside'.

Epston has stated: 'Don't talk about the problem – talk against it' (Epston 1992), and this creates a drama in which neither child nor parents are blamed for the problem. The parents as well as the therapist are now able to side with the child as allies in an imaginary fight to reduce the influence of the problem. Based on stories of unique outcomes the child is offered the choice of an alternative to the problem-dominated story. By focusing on the preferred story the child and her family are assisted in re-authoring their lives into a thriving-family story.

White has made an analysis of this deconstruction and reconstruction of practices and has shown how it leads to a change of language, of actions and of lived experiences (Epston and White 1992, 1993, White 1989). This new language embodies a new attitude to children-and/or-families-with-a-problem. The actions that spring from this attitude include from time to time techniques also used in dramatherapy such as role-play, role-reversal, storytelling, letter-writing, etc. in a playful and concerned dialogue with the child, young person and adults (Epston 1993).

White and Epston both emphasize that the method of externalization should not be applied in cases with different kinds of abuse towards children. They have, however, described positive results with men who acknowledge violence towards their spouses (Epston and White 1992).

Failure of the techniques has been reported in cases where, for various reasons, it has not been possible to engage the parents in either the idea or the therapeutic consequences of the externalization of the problem.

CONCLUSION

The purpose of this chapter has been to explore similarities between dramatherapy and the methods of externalizing the symptoms. It is argued that, looking through the disguise of terminology, there is an overlap in therapeutic techniques (role-play, role-reversal, storytelling, drawings and documents), but they are identical neither in theory nor in the role of the therapist.

A knowledge of dramatherapy and of the works of White and Epston will undoubtly be enriching for therapists who work with children and their families.

REFERENCES

Bruner, J. (1986) *Actual Minds, Possible Worlds*. Cambridge, Mass.: Harvard University Press.
Epston, D. (1989): *Collected Papers*. Dulwich Centre Publications, South Australia.
——— (1992) Personal communication.

——— (1993) Personal communication.
Epston, D. and White, M. (1992) *Experiences, Contradiction, Narrative and Imaginations*. Dulwich Centre Publications, South Australia.
——— (1993) *Narrative Means to Therapeutic Ends*. New York: Norton.
Foucault, M. (1973) *The Birth of the Clinic: an archaeology of medial perception*. London: Tavistock.
Jennings, S. (1990) *Dramatherapy with Families, Groups and Individuals*. London: Jessica Kingsley.
Selvini, M. P., Boscolo, L., Cecchin, G. and Prata, G. (1980) Hypothesizing, circularity, neutrality: three guidelines for the conductor of the session. *Family Process*, 19 (1): 3–12.
Van Gennep, A. (1960) *Rites of Passage*. Chicago: University of Chicago Press.
White, M. (1986) Negative explanation, restraint and double description: a template for family therapy. *Family Process*, 25 (2): 169–84.
——— (1989) *Collected Papers*. Dulwich Centre Publications, South Australia.

Chapter 5

How individual is individual therapy?

The use of contextual therapy principles in the treatment of children and adolescents in dramatherapy

Jan-Berend van der Wijk

INTRODUCTION

This chapter looks at the theories of Ivan Boszormenyi-Nagy in the application of dramatherapy to work with children and adolescents in a clinical psychiatric setting. It illustrates how Nagy's ideas can provide the dramatherapist with a framework to maximize the effects of the individual dramatherapies.

THE CONTEXTUAL THERAPY PRINCIPLES OF IVAN BOSZORMENYI-NAGY

Dr. Ivan Boszormenyi-Nagy was born in Hungary in 1920. He has lived in the USA since 1950. Nagy is a prominent family therapist, with an approach that is unique in the field. In his contextual theory, insights from psychology, psychoanalysis and general systems theory have been integrated within an ethical view on relationships. By ethical he does not mean a dimension signalling a moral value like good or bad. In the eyes of Nagy ethics is about concepts like loyalty, justice, trust, giving and receiving. The context of several generations is an important issue in the treatment of families.

Key concepts

For a very long time the child is totally dependent on its parents. This need for the parents to live and survive leads one to speak of an existential dependence. Because of this existential fact, children owe their parents loyalty. On the other hand, parents are obliged to their children in the same way. They are responsible for the fact that a child is born and therefore they bear responsibility for their children's lives. Parents and children are fundamentally tied together in a bond that can never be broken. They owe each other loyalty. Loyalty is a fact. It is always there.

Nagy makes a difference between vertical and horizontal loyalty.

Vertical loyalties are the loyalties between parents and children, parents and grandparents. Horizontal loyalties are the bonds between brothers, sisters, friends, and husbands and wives. As children get older, they make more relations outside the family. The quality of already existing loyalties has great influence on the way the child developes these new relations. Generally people find a balance between horizontal and vertical loyalties.

Nagy mentions a number of problems that can arise from these feelings of loyalty. He speaks of invisible loyalties, of being over-loyal to one's parents and of split-loyalty conflicts.

When a person denies or neglects the vertical loyalties, Nagy speaks of an invisible loyalty. The feelings of loyalty may then become a hidden power which causes damage to new generations. For example, the person who has to rebel against an authoritarian religious education expresses their protest by joining a rigid political movement in which they experience the same lack of freedom as in the religious church they belonged to in childhood. In this way they remain loyal to their parents without being aware of it. Their children will probably get the same kind of education as they had.

Another loyalty conflict is the situation in which one is too loyal. Nagy speaks of being over-loyal. This is the kind of loyalty in which children don't leave their parents because they feel they are needed: they don't develop new relations in order to be available for their parents.

A very dangerous form of loyalty conflicts is the split-loyalty conflict. This is a situation in which both parents try to win the loyalty of the child for themselves at the cost of the other parent. The child is not allowed to speak about the other parent or to be in contact with him or her. The child, however, wants to be loyal to both parents. He or she will be torn apart and in the end will lose confidence in both the father and the mother.

Children receive legacies from their parents, certain tasks they have to fulfil in their lives. Trying to live up to the expectations of one's parents is a way of showing loyalty to them. Adopted children from third world countries, needing psychiatric help, often have difficulty integrating the legacies from their biological parents and the legacies from their foster parents. (This will be explained in more detail in the case example of Sander, below, pp. 82–4.) It is also possible that children are given a legacy of failing. (This will be illustrated in the case example of Annie, p. 79.)

Another concept is 'the ethical balance between give and take' (Onderwaater 1988: 46 – author's translation). This is, as it were, a bookkeeping balance between, on the one hand the obligations one has towards another person, and on the other the benefits one has acquired from this person. When one benefits more, the other is more obliged. In a relationship it is always important that balance is restored. This is a dynamic process because the balance is always changing.

In a parent–child relationship there are always moments of imbalance. In the beginning the child is very dependent. According to Nagy, children may redeem their debts by doing something with the legacies they have recieved. In this way they earn the right to be taken care of and to be loved by their parents.

A characteristic of disfunctional families is the long-lasting disturbance of the ethical balance between give and take. Children are giving lengthy support to their families without acknowledgement, or parents are giving too much to their children without a reciprocal arrangement. In the first case the child feels exploited and in the second case the child may develop feelings of worthlessness. In both cases the child develops a right of destructive entitlement, as Nagy calls it. The child is entitled to be destructive, because the sources of trust are exhausted.

Although it is likely that the child would blame its parents for the emotional damage suffered, in most cases they won't do so. Instead, other people are to blame for their suffering. Their partners or children have to supply their unfulfilled needs. The adult tries to get from these relationships what they have missed in the relationship with their parents. In this way they spare the parents and stay loyal to them.

The last concept of Nagy's theories concerns the attitude of the therapist. It is called the multidirectional partiality. For a family therapist it is very important to develop an attitude in which he is able to take the side of all the different members of the family, including the members that are not present in the therapy. For the client it is very important to feel that the therapist doesn't want to place her in a disloyal position to her parents. In the family-therapy training this is one of the most difficult barriers to overcome for students, because everyone grows up with norms, values and prejudices.

This is a brief summary of the theories of Nagy and is in no way intended to be complete. Only those concepts that seem important to give an elementary understanding of his theory, and therefore of its possible applications to dramatherapy, are mentioned.

DRAMATHERAPY

Dramatherapy is a rather young profession in Holland. One of its origins can be found in the creative therapy course in Amersfoort. In the 1950s students studying to become groupworkers were taught to use creative activities in their work with children. The special and often therapeutic value of these activities was soon discovered. Lecturers on the course tried to develop methods of using drama, art and music in therapy. This was the basis for a new theory, called the Creative Process Theory. It is important to mention this theory because I use methods derived from it.

Creative Process Theory is based upon psychoanalytical views combined with a theory about the effects of creative materials and situations upon clients. The therapist tries to discover what sort of creative materials and situations appeal to the client, what emotions are expressed in the handling of these materials and what emotions are rejected or repressed. The therapist should offer a great variety of situations and materials in which clients can experiment with their manifest and rejected emotions in order to integrate them into the personality and learn to accept and understand their different aspects.

As the original Creative Process Theory is mainly based on individual therapy, it offers many opportunities for therapists in child and adolescent psychiatry, where most therapy is given on a one-to-one basis. There are, however, disadvantages. In general, therapies based on this theory are long-term and clients must have the capacity to integrate rejected parts of themselves into their personality. In the population of a relatively large psychiatric hospital (about eighty patients aged 5–18), such as the Ruyterstee, many patients do not fit into these categories. Helping clients to enlarge their problem-solving abilities by means of role-play, imitating specific social situations, becomes more important, while strengthening intact ego-functions may be one of the goals in treatment instead of stimulating, for instance, regression in order to work through problematic life events. (This is often one of the effects of working with the Creative Process Theory.) It is the responsibility of the dramatherapist to assess which methods he will work with. No dramatherapy method should be used at random. The dramatherapist must have the skill to interpret the results of his own observations, as well as those of observations of other disciplines.

Besides therapy on a one-to-one basis, dramatherapists also work with small groups of three or four young children and larger groups of adolescents (four to eight adolescents aged 15 and older). The case examples in this chapter, however, are examples of individual therapy with children and adolescents who were allowed to stay for one or more years in the clinic. Very often a combination of directive and non-directive approaches is used. With children like Sander, for instance, a purely non-directive approach wouldn't have worked because of the lack of a healthy basis to his personality due to long periods of neglect and abuse in his early childhood. Directive corrections of his behaviour and of the themes he wanted to enact were often necessary for therapy not to stagnate.

In the case of Martin, on the other hand, the therapist could be more non-directive. It was more appropriate to let Martin decide the direction and the tempo of the therapy. Martin had not been neglected in an emotional way in his early childhood. His capacities to develop himself into a balanced person were more intact than in the case of Sander. This brings us to the description of various case histories.

The case histories

Children receive legacies from their parents . . . It is also possible that children are given a legacy of failure.

Annie

Annie, a girl of 13 years old, was admitted to the clinic while she had a school-phobia and anorectic symptoms. It was her first year in secondary school. This new stage of Annie's development seemed to be a very threatening one for her mother, a neurotic person who kept her anxieties and fears under control by means of compulsive actions. She had never really loosened the ties with her own parents, who lived in the same village and were very dominant in the family. Annie, like her mother, was not allowed to untie herself from her family. The girl developed the same symptoms as her mother.

Nagy shows some pitfalls of individual therapy. He claims that, as a result of strong attachment of the child to her parents, the therapist is often regarded as a rival, especially in the case of a positive transference. He states that the feelings of guilt increase with the development of a positive working relationship with the therapist. The child feels disloyal. When the symptoms are no longer apparent, it is possible that she feels this improvement as a psychological betrayal of her parents. In order to protect herself from feelings of guilt or to protect her parents, she has to adopt her symptoms again. (Onderwaater 1988: 65–6). Another way of being loyal is to share everything one does in therapy with one's parents. Take Lia, for example.

Lia

Lia is an 18-year-old girl with severe *anorexia nervosa* problems. On a rational level, she wants to become an independent adult; on an emotional level, she wants to stay a little girl. Annie is afraid of losing her parents one day. She is also afraid of quarrels, doesn't know how to react when she is confronted with one. Quarrels and how to deal with them is one of the problems she wants to work on in therapy. During one of the sessions the therapist asked her to think of a situation in which she had been angry or had been confronted by a quarrel. She couldn't think of one. He then asked her to think of situations of a few years back, when she was 14. At first she couldn't remember one either. However, after talking about her life at the age of 14, she suddenly smiled and remembered a few quarrels. She wanted to play the situation where her father forced her to study the piano after dinner for one hour. She wanted to play with friends in the street.

The first time she played it, she obeyed and did what her father asked her to do. The second time she said the things that she had really wanted to say and went to her friends. She played the second situation with great involvement. Afterwards she told the therapist that she always felt guilty after quarrels like these. In the next session she told him that she had talked with her parents about what she had played in dramatherapy. Together they had laughed about it.

In this way she seems to find a temporary (in the end non-effective) solution for both her problems. By telling her parents in detail about the therapy, she tries to ignore the fact that the therapy is meant for her, so that she can develop her own individuality, and by ridiculing the situations she had played she tries to minimalize the quarrels that took place in the past (and of course also her negative feelings in the present).

Maarten

Maarten, a boy of 9 years old, was admitted in the clinic after a crisis situation at home. The problems started after the birth of his younger brother when Maarten was three. Maarten was very jealous of his younger brother. He became incontinent again. This ended in a severe encopresis problem. Maarten grew more and more stubborn. Especially around meals there were power conflicts. Of course the soiled pants of Maarten were also a source of trouble. The parents felt more and more incompetent.

Most of these problems were treated very well in the group of which Maarten was part. In the contacts with the social worker, the parents learned how they could react to Maarten's stubborn behaviour. They learned to understand the meaning of his moods and the things he really needed and was asking for. In the therapy Maarten worked through a lot of his jealous feelings as well as his fear of not being accepted by his parents. In all kinds of role-playing he was allowed to enact his resistance to growing up, and, afterwards, to investigate the possible advantages of being older than his brother.

In one of the sessions Maarten invented the story of the little boy who had been naughty and for that reason had been sent to a magic orphanage. Afterwards the parents felt sorry and wanted to have him back but then the little boy, who was called Jack, refused to return. He had made himself invisible and wanted to come back only under certain conditions.

The therapist and Maarten played this story. Maarten took the role of Jack, the therapist had to play the role of father. Suddenly Maarten introduced a little baby which he also called Jack. 'Baby Jack' is represented by a doll. During the session the therapist mentions the differences between 'Jack' and 'baby Jack', the differences between a boy of 9 years old and a baby of six months old. In the role of father the therapist also expresses his love for both children. As '9-years-old Jack' still refuses to talk with his parents, the therapist asks the baby for help. In the role of father he asks 'baby Jack' to help him understand '9-year-old Jack'. Maarten answers with a baby voice and tells the therapist that '9-years-old Jack' wants to come back only if his parents will listen better to what he has to tell them. In return he promises to be less stubborn.

The next scene is the scene where the father comes to the orphanage to take his son back home. The therapist wonders which role Maarten will take, '9-years-old Jack' or 'baby Jack'. Maarten chooses the role of '9-years-old Jack'. However, as soon as Jack is confronted with his father, he 'shrinks' to the size of 'baby Jack'. In the role of father, the therapist doesn't accept this. He tells Jack that he wanted to do a lot of nice things with him, things that only 9-year-old boys can do with their fathers, such as swimming, playing football, etc. Jack takes a 'magic draught' and returns to his original size. The session finishes with a wild game of football.

During the two years of treatment Maarten gained more openness towards his parents and playmates. It was obvious that he was enjoying life again.

However, what everybody secretly hoped for didn't happen. Maarten didn't give up his encopresis. Despite all the trouble gone through, he didn't give up this aspect of his problems. The last remnants of this problem didn't disappear until rather a long time after his discharge.

The staff had hesitated a long time about choosing the right moment for discharge. Afterwards they were glad that they had not waited until the time Maarten would be clean again. It could be seen as an act of loyalty for Maarten to save the exact moment of overcoming his encopresis problem for his parents.

The case example of Maarten shows how it is possible for children to work through intrapsychic problems in dramatherapy without losing their feelings of loyalty towards their parents. By means of symbolic play the child is able to externalize inner conflicts.

One of Nagy's basic rules is that every therapist should be aware of the danger of placing a child in a position of disloyalty to their parents. This may easily happen in the case of admission to a clinic. From the point of view of loyalty this is a very complex situation. Very often for parents an admission means that they have failed in their role of father and mother. For the child, giving up problematic behaviour may mean a confirmation of their parents' assumption. Consent and preferably involvement of the parents in the therapy are both important.

Sander

This example is about Sander and his therapy. In terms of contextual therapy, Sander is a special case. He was adopted when he was 5 years old. During the first years of his life he lived in Korea as an orphan. Sander lived in different kinds of orphanages as well as on the street. He had identified himself with the leaders of the gangs he belonged to. It is very likely that he fantasized about his biological parents as well. His main care was to stay alive, to adapt himself to different situations, to look after himself, as no one else did. His foster parents were very intelligent, educated people. They belonged to a rather strict Christian church community. They expected their children to be honest and open and they tried to be warm, caring parents for their children. Sander was their third child and their only son. They had lost a child some years before Sander was adopted.

It is clear that it was very difficult for Sander to live up to the expectations of his foster parents. They projected the ideals they had had for their lost son on to him. The issue of legacies is a very complicated matter in the case of Sander. According to Nagy one can show loyalty to one's parents by doing something with the legacies one has recieved. For Sander this is very confusing because he feels loyal to different backgrounds. The relationship between Sander and his parents had never been really good and they had asked for professional help several times, but without the results they had hoped for. At the time they brought Sander to the clinic the situation had deteriorated so far that they were not able to feel anything positive for him any more. They complained about his lack of emotions, about the fact that he lied constantly, that he stole things from shops and that he showed no real emotional attachment.

In his observation period in the clinic Sander was observed in drama-therapy and this resulted in a positive indication for this form of creative therapy.

In the first period of the therapy Sander enacted a role-play in which he was a boy who found an entrance to an underworld, a kind of jungle where he felt really at home, in contrast to the world above where he had to live. He always went there secretly without telling his parents. In this secret world his position was similar to that of a king. He dressed himself up in all kinds of fancy clothes. He was happy there, enjoyed being with his own people. The therapist had to play the role of his companion, a friend from the world above who had to follow Sander into the jungle world. In the role of companion the therapist played that he wanted to go back to his parents, to the world above, where he belonged. Sander told him to forget about his past. He had to get used to the rules of the jungle. At the same time Sander made it impossible for his friend to feel at home in the jungle-world. He maltreated him as a slave and punished him without reason.

This role-play offered a lot of important therapy material. In a nutshell, Sander presented one of the problems of adopted children from third world countries: the gap that exists between their native country and the present country they live in, the gap between past and present. He also showed some of his impressions of adoption and probably repeated events or fantasies he had in connection with his memories of living in Korea.

After they had played, the therapist and Sander talked about the memories Sander had of Korea and about the fact of being adopted by parents in a completey different country.

Some time after this period, another theme appeared in his play. Sander wanted to enact family situations. In these situations he wanted to play a son of 16 or 17 years old who was very rebellious and who was fighting for his independence. He acted as if he were the one who could determine everything he wanted to do. He blackmailed his parents and didn't care for the punishments they came up with. The therapist had to play the father who tried to gain control over his son and who was very suspicious of everything his son did or intended to do. Sander threatened his parents that he would leave home and find an apartment for himself. When the father didn't object, Sander reproached him with being a bad father, as parents don't allow their children to live on their own at the age of 16. Sander's wish for independence is still very ambiguous.

In these situations the father and the mother were to quarrel all day long. Beside the role of a 16-year-old boy, Sander played the role of mother. The quarrels of father and mother mainly concerned the education of the son.

All these fantasy situations were in a way very much the same as Sander's own reality. His father did indeed try to control every aspect of his life. Of course Sander had given them reasons enough in the past for reacting in this manner. Sander's conduct however had improved during his treatment in the clinic. He still stole and lied occasionally, but not as frequently. The father reacted towards Sander as if he hadn't changed. For Sander this was a very frustrating situation. He felt misunderstood and he was angry about this. The quarrels between the parents that had to be enacted in his dramas were also images of real quarrels between the parents. They had marital problems which they denied. During the period of treatment they didn't want to discuss their relationship and how this could possibly influence the whole situation around Sander. The overwhelming anxiety they had for Sander's problems diverted the attention away from their own.

As the therapist tried to talk with Sander about his family and the position he had at home, in the same way they had talked about the jungle and his fantasies in the first part of the therapy, he felt an enormous resistance. Sander didn't want to talk about his father and mother other than in a positive way. In the different situations he played, it was clear what his negative feelings were. Sander was able to express what he really felt about the situation at home without giving up the loyalty he felt for his parents.

In this case, working by means of symbolic play functioned very well. With most young children this technique of acting out their fantasies is effective. When working with adolescents, however, just acting is often not enough. Integrating the therapy experiences into their personality can be achieved by making use of their developing abilities of reflection and introspection. It is very important to verbalize, in a methodical way, what has happened in the therapy session. This doesn't mean that every unconscious feeling or thought should be made conscious. The therapist has to assess whether the client is ready to regard what he has expressed in an unconscious way and whether this is stimulating to the therapeutic process. The case of Selma may illustrate some of these thoughts.

Selma

Suicide or a suicide attempt means, in a contextual way of looking, going to extremes to find a solution. As soon as there is any sign or motive of suicide danger or one suspects a client of having suicidal feelings, it is necessary to investigate the presence of a split loyalty conflict.

(Heusden and Eerenbeemt 1988: 44 – my translation)

Selma is a girl of 15. Her situation at home is very chaotic and confusing. Her parents live alternately apart and together. Selma started therapy six months ago. After a suicide attempt she was admitted in the clinic.

Selma's depression expressed itself partly in long periods of listlessness, withdrawal from social contacts, and partly in over-active behaviour, a kind of maniacal state of mind. She was fascinated by music of the 1960s and dreamt of being a great songwriter and singer. Very often she wanted to enact her fantasies in therapy. Afterwards the therapist tried to test her sense of reality by asking how she saw her future. Her reality was inextricably tied up with her fantasy. She saw herself within a few months playing in a successful band. She was sure that she would have a professional career as a musician.

During these therapy sessions the therapist often wondered what Selma's fantasies really meant. A lot of adolescents do have their idols and dreams of being famous and rich. It helps them to deal with the reality. This was surely true for Selma but it didn't answer the question: why *these* fantasies? The answer was given by Selma a few weeks later.

After she had enacted in detail how she would give an interview in a pop-magazine, she told the therapist that both her parents were very fond of hippie music. Besides 'the flight from reality' function, her fantasies had another, hidden, meaning. They could be seen as an attempt on her part to stay loyal to both parents, perhaps even an attempt to bring them together again. This is of course a desire that lots of children have in Selma's situation. From a superficial point of view, Selma seemed not to have this desire.

Not very long after this session she told the therapist that she became very angry with her parents. The fact that her mother sometimes lived with them until she had too many quarrels with her husband, then left them again, made the situation at home very complicated and tense. She wanted to chase her mother away to help her father. He was always so indecisive. He was afraid his wife would commit suicide if he finally made an end to their relationship. Selma talked about her intentions in therapy. She gave a description of what she wanted to say to her mother to chase her away. The therapist advised her not to do so. He made clear to her that normally parents have to make their own decisions in such matters.

Carrying out her plans wouldn't do Selma any good because she would not be acting as a child but as an adult, as a mother who tries to stop two quarrelling children. Moreover, she would ignore her very deep desire to bring together her parents again. Choosing one parent would cause an enormous feeling of guilt towards the other. During this session the therapist encouraged Selma to express her feelings about the situation at home. During role-playing she tried out different ways of telling her parents what bothered and worried her.

Selma's unconscious attempts to bring her parents together again were not verbalized by the therapist. She would have denied it. The splitting process, which her parents had manoeuvred her into, had already gone too far. Instead the therapist confronted her with a general norm: children don't interfere with quarrels of their parents. This was something she could more easily accept. It was an attempt to get her out of her parent-focused position and it worked.

Selma's case is an example of split loyalty. Both parents tried to gain Selma for themselves. Selma felt she was forced to choose one of her parents. This is very unnatural for a child. A child always wants to be loyal to both parents.

A lot of children in need of psychiatric care struggle with the problem that they never get the appreciation for what they had done for their parents. These children live for years in a situation where they have to be supportive towards their parents without getting something in return. In Nagy's terms, the ethical balance between give and take is disturbed. One of the consequences is that children lose faith in their parents. In this way a child gains destructive entitlement.

> The first thing a therapist should aim at is the anger and the pain that is caused by this injustice. These feelings should be accepted and expressed first. Only then, when a person has the feeling that he is fully understood and that his feelings are accepted and acknowledged, is there a chance that he is able to see what harm he is doing to others.
>
> (Heusden and Eerenbeemt 1988: 61)

Martin

Martin, a 15-year-old boy, had dramatherapy for almost one and a half years. In Martin's family there were a lot of diseases. Martin's mother had had a lot of gynaecological problems and a few operations, his father had lost his job which had turned him into a depressive with many psycho-somatic complaints, his sister was a diabetic and needed a lot of care for that reason. Martin seemed to be the only healthy person in the family. His parents asked a lot of support from him. Their illnesses and handicaps were discussed in detail with Martin so he was constantly worried about his family. Because of the constant atmosphere of crisis, the parents were not able to give Martin the education he needed. Martin was treated as an adult, not as a boy of 15. This resulted in a situation where Martin tested limits in an increasingly aggressive way until his parents asked for help.

The first half-year of the therapy, Martin played out a lot of aggressive fantasies. Again and again he played murderers who were revenging themselves on innocent people. Beneath these very aggressive fantasies, there was always the cry for acknowledgement of the fact that he had been taken advantage of. Giving room to these feelings was the first thing I wanted to aim at in the therapy. Sometimes I wondered if it was a good decision to let Martin play out his aggressive fantasies. I was afraid that in this way the therapy would be too isolated from the rest of the treatment and I wondered what the effect would be in the end. I must admit that these doubts were partly influenced by all kinds of feelings that emerged as a result of processes of transference and countertransference.

Dramatherapy with a client like Martin, at the stage he was then, means a heavy task for the dramatherapist. The dramatherapist in individual therapy is very often the opposite number in the play, and in this role he will be confronted directly with the often contradictory emotions of his client. In the case of Martin, for instance, he had a great hunger to fight and struggle with the therapist and on the other hand he showed very clearly how he enjoyed playing with him. Partly this is an adolescent way of dealing with adults: fighting for independence and at the same time needing a supportive adult. In Martin's case, however, the point was the very egocentric way of thinking and feeling and his extremely aggressive fantasies. For the therapist this meant a considerable investment in terms of energy without the prospect of reciprocity in the near future.

After six months, the intensity of Martin's emotions decreased, and the subject of his fantasies became less aggressive. One of the roles he wanted to enact, for instance, was that of an office clerk who saved a whole office from bankruptcy. When someone else tried to get the credit for this, Martin let everybody know that he was the one who should be honoured. He was very proud. This role was less aggressive than that of the murderer. Gradually Martin was able to reflect on himself and his family. In the beginning period of the therapy there was never time for talking. Every attempt on my part to talk with him was regarded as an assault, as a curtailment of his desire for playing. Later on, however, he liked to tell of his feelings towards his parents, of the periods of fear for their lives and his loneliness. Anger about what he had missed, especially in the relationship with his father, seemed to have disappeared. He had worked out these feelings in the many hours of dramatherapy.

CONCLUSIONS

This chapter opens with the question: how individual is individual therapy? In the course of this chapter it may have become clear that an individual client never comes alone to therapy. The family always comes too, one way or another. Especially when one works with children and adolescents it is very important to be familiar with concepts of transgenerational mechanisms as well as loyalty ties, because these clients are often, not only in an emotional way but also in an actual way, dependent on their parents. These mechanisms will influence therapeutic processes.

One might conclude that family therapy is the most appropriate way of treating children and their families. Reading the literature on contextual therapy, one might come to the same conclusion, because Nagy pays hardly any attention to individual therapy for the child who has been suffering from long-term exposure to traumatic circumstances, whether mental or psychological. He especially focuses on the relationship of parents and grandparents and expects that, by improving this relationship, the relationship between child and parents will improve automatically.

However, with regard to children already in clinical psychiatric care, Nagy seems too idealistic and sometimes even naive. In the first place, not every family is able to attend family therapy. Their resistance towards therapy might be too strong or therapy might not be indicated where the family system is not robust enough to deal with the stress that accompanies therapy. In this case it is an unrealistic option to wait for the family's willingness to attend therapy and not to offer help to the child or adolescent who needs it.

Furthermore, research tells us that it is mostly not enough when a child is treated only by means of family therapy (Verschueren 1986). Children who have lived a long time in dysfunctional family circumstances are mostly damaged in a way that makes it impossible for them to integrate the results achieved in family therapy. This often forms a stagnating factor. On the other hand, when a child is the only one who is treated and the result is positive, these results won't last long when the family system remains the same. Therefore it is always necessary to offer a form of additional support for the parents. These two forms of treatment, family therapy and individual therapy for the child, are interdependent.

Nagy emphasizes the pitfalls of individual therapy. According to him the therapist may easily take sides with the child. This is wrong as it stimulates the feeling of disloyalty, especially in the case of a positive transference. The therapist should be aware of the loyalty of the child and of his own countertransference feelings. He should try for the attitude of multi-directional partiality which Nagy describes as optimal for the family therapist.

One of the important advantages of dramatherapy is that it offers a good many appropriate methods by which the therapist can avoid some of the risks Nagy describes. In dramatherapy the client has the possibility to work through all kinds of conflicting emotions by means of symbolic play. It allows him or her to externalize intrapsychic conflicts without being disloyal to their parents. When children have to talk about things that went wrong in relation with father or mother, this often causes more feelings of guilt than acting out these situations would, in a fantasy-play, when they can tell themselves, 'I just acted as if I was a child who was angry with my mother,' or, 'I just invented the story that my parents quarrelled all day long and that I wanted to run away.'

It is very important that the dramatherapeutic methods are chosen with care and not applied randomly. The use of fantasy is very important in dramatherapy with children and adolescents. The pleasure that accompanies the acting out of fantasies is often one of the most important motivations for them to come. These fantasies give much information about the client. The dramatherapist is trained to understand the symbolic language of his client. When regarded from a contextual point of view these fantasies often clarify hidden messages of loyalty. This often improves the understanding of the client. For instance it may explain why clients can't give up certain symptoms of their problems (see the case of Maarten, pp. 80–1).

Nagy's ideas are very important. By applying his ideas to the dramatherapy I offered, I was able to work more effectively. As a dramatherapy trainer I decided that the students in my programme should have several lessons based on his theories during their course. In this respect, it is important that they should find answers to questions such as:

● In what way am I loyal to my family? What does my loyalty look like?
● What legacies did I get from my parents?
● In what situations have I been disloyal to my family and how did that feel?
● What do I think of the attitude of multidirected partiality and what might be the pitfalls for me?

Studying one's own experiences is very often a useful way of learning and understanding. I hope that the case examples in this chapter have shown the importance and the usefulness of contextual therapy in dramatherapy.

REFERENCES

Boszormenyi-Nagy, I. and Spark, G. M. (1973) *Invisible Loyalties*. Hagerstown: Harper & Row.

Heusden, A. van and Eerenbeemt, E. M. van den (1988) *Ivan Boszormenyi-Nagy and his Vision of Individual and Family Therapy*. Balance in Motion. New York: Brunner/Mazel.

Onderwaater, A. (1988) *De Onverbrekelijke Band Tussen Ouders en Kinderen* [The bond between parents and children that cannot be broken]. Amsterdam Lisse: Swets en Zeitlinger.

Schaap, R. (1992) The ideas of Ivan Boszormenyi-Nagy and their implications for arts therapies. Paper given at the International Conference for Arts Therapies Education, Sittard, October 1992.

Verschueren, R. (1986) Kindgerichte therapieën binnen een gezinsgerichte residentiële werking, enkele bedenkingen [Child-focused therapies within a residential setting where the emphasis is on working with the family as a whole: some thoughts]. *Tijdschrift voor Orthopedagogiek, Kinderpsychiatrie en Klinische Kinderpsychologie*, 11: 181–9.

Chapter 6

Dramatherapy for survival
Some thoughts on transitions and choices for children and adolescents

Sue Jennings

INTRODUCTION

This chapter explores some of my own thoughts on what I see as the essential nature of dramatic development in children and adolescents. I include some of my personal experience in relation to discovering 'the actor' as well as 'the wanderer' in myself, as well as observations of the Temiar life cycle during a period of living in the Malaysian rain forest.

My belief is that dramatic development is part of all human development that brings together the biological, psychological and artistic into an integrated whole. People who miss out on this aspect of their development are likely to have problems of body image, perceptual distortion, reality-ground and role confusion.

My contention is that an increased amount of drama and ritual should be reintroduced into education and society in order to have a 'preventive' effect, and that dramatherapy should be used increasingly with 'difficult' children and adolescents and in forensic settings in order to promote a 'curative' effect.

I no longer talk about the desirability or utility of theatre, drama, dramatherapy. I maintain that they are essential components of our life experience and contribute substantially to our maturation and the taking on of adult responsibilities.

Without the capacity for making use of our 'dramatic imagination', or the opportunity to 'dramatically play' our thoughts and emotions, or the encouragement to expand the 'repertoire of roles' which makes up our emergent 'character', we will be unable to participate fully as an individual as well as a member of a group in the business of life.

This may sound like a major claim, but I have observed the gradual erosion of artistic dramatic experience; the denigration of play as important; the cut-back of drama and theatre in education; and the assumption that somehow drama and theatre are the soft options, that they do not have value in economic terms in the new purchaser–provider economy.

I maintain that drama and theatre, starting from birth and continuing until death, are crucial to our survival in all spheres of living; that they are therefore economically sound because they will actually help to prevent crime, relationship breakdown, illness and despair. Not only would we see vigour and potency in the population, there would be less dependency on welfare and aid as people develop more initiative and autonomy. The root of our culture is at the foundation of human society, which came about through dramatic expression and dramatic ritual. Drama is part of the foundation of human society as well as the structure which can effectively manage change. It is the means through which we understand both our individual as well as our corporate identity.

Through looking at their roots, both historically and in other cultures, we can see how drama and theatre have struggled alongside medicine/science and religion/belief systems *to enable human beings to express what is unexpressable and to understand what is otherwise inexplicable.*

I conceptualize these relationships in triangular form in order to move away from a unilinear perspective and into an integrated view of 'body–mind–spirit' or 'art–science–belief' or 'theatre–medicine–religion' (Figures 6.1–6.3).

THEATRE, MEDICINE AND RELIGION

Dramatherapy, or 'theatre of healing', has always emerged from the relationships between theatre, medicine and religion (or in more general terms, art, science and belief system). It is important to remember:

1 the development of theatre, medicine and religion does not move in straight lines but comes about through conflict and division;
2 the growth of these major institutions is organic both in their own right and in relation to each other;
3 movement or growth in any or all of these comes from individual and collective struggle;
4 since there has always been a relationship between these three institutions, the struggle is often for the dominance of one of them;
5 since medicine and belief state 'how things are' and theatre states things 'as if', we can see the interdependency of these three forms and their need for each other.

If we look at healing rituals or at ancient Greek theatre or at our own medieval theatre, we can see the continuing struggle between 'actor, doctor and priest' and the rules, roles and forms within which they practise.

Dionysian ritual theatre used chorus, dance, masquerades, revels; performers dressed up with masks to portray gods and 'animal-men', as we can see from illustrations on vases of the time.

The classical theatre emerged in highly structured form and content, with increasing numbers of actors and complex scenery. Popular and classical

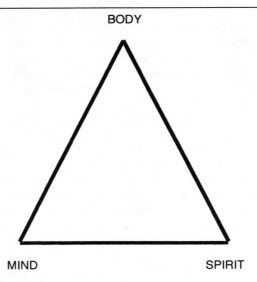

Figure 6.1 Integration of the person

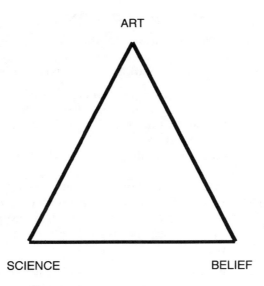

Figure 6.2 Integration of society

theatre both used hillside amphitheatres and both were thought to have a therapeutic effect. Both made use of masks (Figure 6.4).

The theatre of Epidavros in Greece was also a temple of healing, where priests worked with people's dreams. Healing stayed very much under the

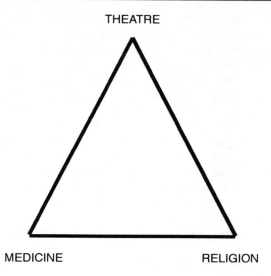

THEATRE

MEDICINE   RELIGION

Figure 6.3 Integration of person in relation to the world

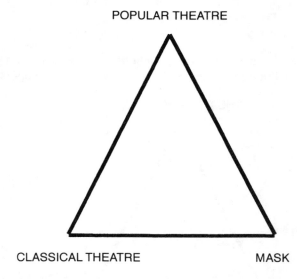

POPULAR THEATRE

CLASSICAL THEATRE   MASK

Figure 6.4 Integration of preventive and curative theatre through the mask

control of priests and ritual specialists until the fourth or fifth century AD, despite the attempts of Hippocrates to separate medicine from the temples. However, Aristophanes mocked temple medicine in his play *Plutus*.

Whereas Dionysian rituals could be said to be 'preventive' in that they celebrated wine, youth, energy, fertility and action, the temple healing could be termed 'curative' since it was under the guidance of Asclepius, the god of healing, together with his two daughters, Hygeia, 'goddess of health', and Panacea, 'she who heals everything'.

Nevertheless, within the above we can see both the struggle between the different forms and the attempt of medicine/science to separate from belief and art, and also the art mocking the religious medicine.

Note that, in the Dionysian revels, youth is celebrated.

Nearer to home, we know that entertainers and storytellers, or 'jongleurs', were always being banned by the Church because they were thought too excessive. Church and populace struggled and new dramatic forms emerged; there was also a popular medicine and a priestly medicine.

In 975 AD, St Ethelwold, Bishop of Winchester, wrote down in his *Concordia regularis* for the Benedictine Houses in England, instructions for the 're-enactment' of the following lines from the Easter Mass:

Whom seek ye in the sepulchre?
  Jesus of Nazareth
He is not here; he is risen as predicted
when it was prophesied that he would rise from the dead.
  Alleluia! The Lord is risen!
Come and see the place.

The two aims of this enactment were celebration and explanation (Figure 6.5) – i.e. both celebrate the risen Christ as well as educate people through

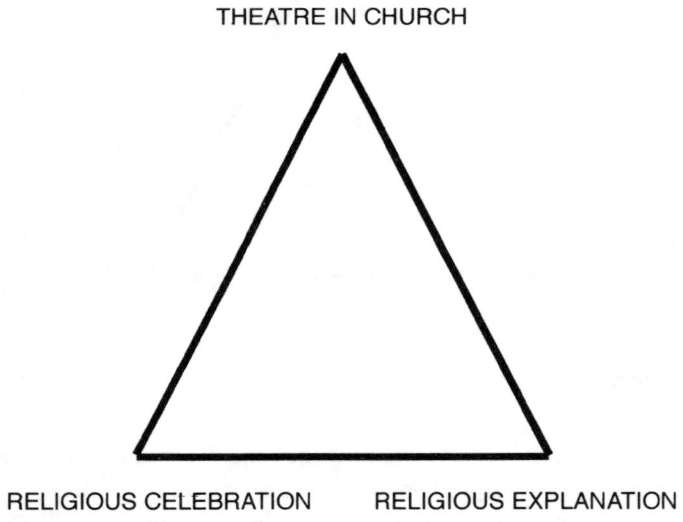

THEATRE IN CHURCH

RELIGIOUS CELEBRATION   RELIGIOUS EXPLANATION

Figure 6.5 Integration of historical facts with the dramatic 'as if' principle

the drama about what happened. Although these instructions are for the re-enactment of an historical event, the Latin words *quasi* ('as if') and *quamodo* ('in the manner of') are used. The dramatic mode of 'as if' is used to illustrate the narrative story within the religious framework.

For example:

A chair is made ready in a suitable place *as if* it were Jerusalem;

The three Marys are making their way *as if* they are sad.

Drama expanded within the churches and to other festivals as well, although inevitably there were conflicts about excess, especially when performers resorted to improvisation instead of text.

In 1098 and 1209 respectively the Cistercian and Dominican orders of travelling priests were founded. They travelled the countryside using storytelling, mimes and dramas to communicate religious truths as well as healing. Many of the convents took in the sick, and orders of nuns became the forerunners of nurses: we can note the similarity of costume.

Theatre as entertainment and theatre as healing were intertwined with the practice of religion whether the priests were travelling or settled. And of course many young people and even children were apprenticed to these religious orders.

Early medical tracts were based on the *herbaria* of the religious orders, and one which appeared in the year 1000 and was later illustrated, in the late thirteenth century, was known as *Theatrum sanitatis*. A medieval herbal known as 'Healing Theatre' again makes the connection between the language of theatre and the language of medicine, much as an 'operating theatre' does in the present day. These brief examples illustrate how medicine, theatre and religion were intertwined, and struggled for supremacy (Figure 6.6).

In modern times we have seen a separation of science, art and belief, and the hospital, the theatre and the Church are three independent institutions, with medicine and science given the strongest position in the hierarchy. White coats have replaced black robes and many hospitals do not have a chaplaincy. Theatres are seen as places of entertainment rather than having any essential function in our lifestyle, and 'high-tech' medicine relies less and less on dramatic ritual. Instead we watch programmes about hospitals and are drawn into the hospital drama whether as a documentary or a soap-opera.

The twentieth century has seen the fast development of medical practice, often outstripping the development of the accompanying law and ethics. The century has also seen the very rapid rise of drama and theatre-in-education; children's theatre; and of course dramatherapy. This expansion took place while popular rural theatre decreased and was replaced in the towns and cities by 'fringe' theatre. However, the educational surge was

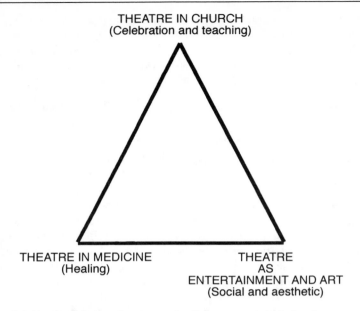

Figure 6.6 How medicine, theatre and religion were intertwined

short-lived and there is currently a major cutback in drama teachers and drama programmes in schools as well as of educational theatre companies. Drama and theatre are classed within the expendable sector; they do not appear in the core curriculum, and are not essential subjects in schools. The progress that was rapidly made from the 1940s to the 1970s has been superseded by technology, not only in science but also in education and entertainment. Video games and video films are popular entertainment, and exposure to them starts at a very young age.

My concern with this shift in emphasis is not that I think video technology is bad as such, but that it rules out the human interaction that takes place in dramatic play, drama and theatre.

The next section examines the early dramatic play of young children and my belief that it is an essential part of human maturation.

DRAMATIC DEVELOPMENT

Babies are born with a dramatic heritage which gradually develops into both art and culture. Babies are born with a predisposition to artistic communication that in the early months can be observed in rhythmic movement, sound patterns, mark-making and imitation (Jennings 1993b). How this develops is dependent on the milieu into which the child is born, especially in relation to how much handling and stimulus is provided during the first twelve months or so. During the first year, a baby responds through its own body in relation to the body of another. There are physical sensations of many sorts, and exploration of the senses, temperature, relaxation and tension.

Dramatherapists call this stage 'embodiment', and it is a crucial time for the beginning of body-self awareness. As the child progresses to exploration of the immediate world outside itself, there is a noticeable shift from the earlier embodiment play to 'projective play'. Objects and toys outside the child take on significance as well as having special attachments (Winnicott's theory of the transitional object is elaborated in Winnicott 1971); the child starts to express things through the imagination. The special toy may be a symbol of mother, security, sameness, as well as being 'Teddy': Teddy can also be cross and can be naughty and shouted at and confided in. Through projective play the child expresses and discovers imaginatively, fears and hopes, stories and puppets, plays – old favourites for secure repetition and new scenarios for adventure and change. If we observe projective play, it gradually takes on more and more dramatic qualities and the child begins to experiment with roles through dramatic role-play. The passage through these three stages of embodiment, projection and role contribute to the emergence of character (Figure 6.7).

Throughout this time the child's imagination is expanding, as well as

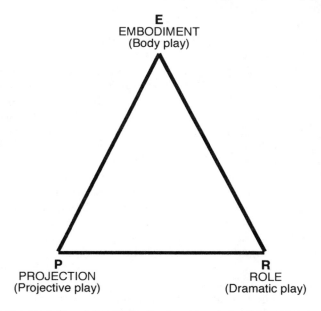

E
EMBODIMENT
(Body play)

P
PROJECTION
(Projective play)

R
ROLE
(Dramatic play)

Figure 6.7 Relationship of the dramatic development of the child through Embodiment, Projection and Role (EPR), leading to character formation

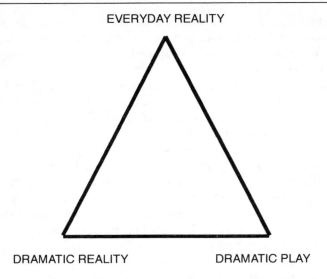

EVERYDAY REALITY

DRAMATIC REALITY   DRAMATIC PLAY

Figure 6.8 Relationship of the two realities through dramatic playing and games

the capacity to form concepts and make use of symbols. The dramatic imagination is crucial for survival, as without it we would not be able to imagine how things might be or how they could be, or indeed we would not be able to hypothesize.

During these early years, a child is beginning to experiment and differentiate between 'everyday reality' and the 'reality of dramatic play'. There is often misunderstanding on this matter as people equate dramatic reality with fantasy, and suggest that too much fantasy can be dangerous. However, 'dramatic play' is the testing time for reality: a playful space where life can be experimented with and choices explored (Figure 6.8).

The capacity to differentiate between everyday reality and dramatic reality appropriately is a sign of maturation and therefore a key concept in child and adolescent development

When the media was shocked at the death of the toddler James Bulger in 1993 and the crowds were baying for blood at the trial of two 10- and 11-year-olds, much time was spent in asking about the whys and the hows and in debating the evil nature of children and whether or not adult videos could be blamed. During the trial I was very struck by one of the boys who said that the child would not lie down so he kept on hitting him. If we can stand outside the shock of this incident and the disbelief that children can kill, it is possible to consider the incident in relation to the development of the dramatic imagination as described above. In conventional children's play, hitting and dying are commonplace actions: 'Bang-bang, you're dead' is considered harmless enough *in play*. It is through play that children experiment with limits of hurt and destruction and learn how to play at fighting, rather than fighting for real.

When a child says that someone would not lie down so he kept on hitting him, it demonstrates a lack of capacity to differentiate between the two realities – everyday reality and dramatic reality. The only way to learn this differentiation is through dramatic play, where children are actively engaged in dramatic scenes with others.

Therefore, I contend that videos and video games are not destructive in themselves, but only when they replace active playing which involves the participants. We have only to look at the structure of children's games and play (see Chapter 2, above, for Iona Opie's discussion of the fear in children's games) to see what social and cultural learning takes place through dramatic involvement in these structures. For example, 'Grand-mother's Footsteps' teaches self-control, co-ordination, excitement, as well as the overcoming of fear. Such games also teach a ritual structure, a set of rules – as with sports – regarding how things are done. These rules can be repeated even if there is variation in the content; they give security and a framework with which the self and the world can be experienced. The game or the dramatic play is like the world in miniature, just as the theatre is also an encapsulation of the larger world. Both symbolize in reduced, apprehendable form, the larger world that is infinite and too overwhelming to take in all at once. Both the dramatic play and the theatre necessitate an active engagement and participation in a human and artistic process, rather than a passive absorption of received images such as formulate films and videos.

On this basis I would argue that the active encouragement and provision of dramatic play, social rituals and dramatic and theatre experience are essential for the maturing child.

THE ADVENTURE OF ADOLESCENCE

As the child matures and grows through childhood with opportunities for the development of the active imagination, the next staging post is the transition between childhood and adulthood. We need to remember that not all societies acknowledge a period of adolescence. You are either a child or an adult, as is the case with the Temiar tribe that I discuss below. However, Western society has an extended period of 'in-between' when there are often problems of identity and selfhood; where young people are expected to make choices about their future in terms of relationships and occupations but are often not allowed to act on these choices. We as adults are often unsure as to what should be expected of adolescents and vary in our responses from treating them as children, and then expecting them to behave as adults. However, drama itself can be part of the maturation

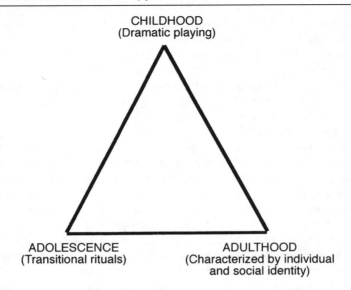

CHILDHOOD
(Dramatic playing)

ADOLESCENCE
(Transitional rituals)

ADULTHOOD
(Characterized by individual
and social identity)

Figure 6.9 The relationship between development stages in the maturational process

process for testing possible choices before they need to be used as a melting pot of thoughts and ideas through which one's actual reality can be formulated. We find, though, that adolescence is often the time when drama (if it is on the curriculum) is replaced by increased academic learning or technical practice (Figure 6.9).

The social necessity of the drama and the emergent artistic and crafting process of drama and theatre make for healthy development into adulthood.

During the in-between years, we need to consider what experiences can be useful and satisfying. Young people themselves need to be able to contribute to this process rather than having purely prescriptive education and recreation. One experience that is rarely addressed is the urge of many young people to wander or to journey.

Traditionally, most human groups were either 'settled cultivators' or 'hunter-gatherers' in their way of life. Major influences of economic change and technology have obviously changed many of these lifestyles; however, there is still a predisposition for many people to choose a settled lifestyle or a wandering way of life. We could discuss in very general terms the contrast between scientists in laboratories and social scientists who live with tribes; uniformed police and uniformed soldiers; bankers or accountants and diplomats or travelling salespeople, where we can see the threads of settling and wandering. However, as well as a preferred way of life, my belief is that there is also a personality influence involved: some people are 'settled cultivators' or 'hunter-gatherers' by temperament. This unfortunately does not always fit in with Western societies' expectations of an adult, settled, way of life. People who are nomadic or who are of 'no fixed abode' or who are gypsies or itinerant travellers cause suspicion, prejudice and often discrimination. We like to know where people are and expect them to aspire to house ownership or at least a reasonably permanent abode.

Whereas I would suggest that all people have a leaning towards one lifestyle or the other, I am sure that a large number of adolescents and young people go through a 'hunter-gatherer' stage. The experiments of the mind in academic learning or experiments of the imagination in artistic expression are not satisfying enough, and young people need to push their own spatial horizons and often physical limits in a protracted time of 'wander-lust'. Many of them return to home base and then decide to settle and choose to raise a family. Some stay settled, whilst others return to wandering once child-rearing is over. Others find a way of accommodating the need to continue wandering, and either leave a family behind, or carry it with them.

Adolescent and young people need to make these journeys in the real world, across water or foreign terrain: they need to be able to move at will – a need that is not sympathetically understood. 'Travel therapy' for adolescents is dismissed by press and politicians as an expensive soft option rather than being appreciated for the very real benefits it affords. The journey assists in our battles for a place in the world, often in an alien environment, and frequently combatting the forces of nature. It responds to the 'wander-lust' need in young people and its unavailability may indeed have been the reason for problems in the first place.

However, drama and dramatherapy should assist young people to prepare for the wandering. Preparation needs to be made and journeys rehearsed within the drama before the actual journey can take place. This means that a ritualization of the journey can be established – the starting point for the map discovered – before the embarkation.

I would suggest that many young people have not had the opportunity to integrate these two aspects of themselves or to put into practice any choice of staying or going. Certainly young people 'at risk' have always responded with vigour to themes based on The Odyssey or Journey to the Bottom of the Sea or expeditions that they have created through improvisation.

One way in which we can look at this strategy is shown in Figure 6.10.

A PERSONAL EXPERIENCE – STRUGGLES OF A 'SETTLED HUNTER'

I suppose that I can view my own childhood with a certain amount of disbelief when I remember just how many houses we moved to during the war years (I can recall at least eight by my seventh birthday), combined with a heightened energy to 'settle down at last' in a farming community in

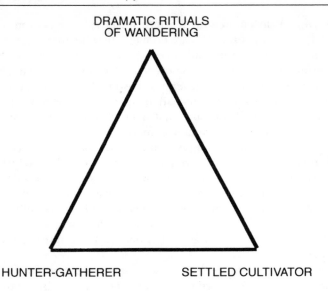

DRAMATIC RITUALS
OF WANDERING

HUNTER-GATHERER   SETTLED CULTIVATOR

Figure 6.10 The relationship of 'staying or going' or 'settling and wandering'

a small village. The farm years were glorious times of 'journey play', when
frequent expeditions were acted through, on my own or with other children,
through fields and large orchards with ponds and streams. Dens were built
in trees and barns, as staging posts; while maps were drawn, and bows and
arrows hidden for defence.

Entering my teens was an enormous shock as I made the lonely transition
by bus from a two-roomed village school run like a cosy family to a bleak,
uniformed all-girls' grammar school. The first morning, I sat in silence in a
fourth-year group, and nobody noticed that I was in the wrong classroom!
The journeys to and from school became more adventurous in my imagination as we drove through miles of copse and countryside. My hero was a
tramp who lived in an old water-tank in a small wood that could be seen
from the bus. I would mark his progress through the seasons as he came and
went, eventually to disappear in winter and return once the snow had gone.
He was the Tom Sawyer of my dreams that one day I could be, whether I
ran away with the gypsies or stowed away on a ship.

Most of my energy was spent in planning a theatrical career, convincing
myself that I did not understand maths, science or technology, and reading
plays and poetry by torchlight. My early theatre work was weekly touring:
revue, musicals, Shakespeare to schools. We often played fourteen shows a
week – twice-nightly, plus two matinées – and then travelled to the new
place on Sunday. We were 'on the road', or rail as it usually was. However,
all these smaller journeys seemed to be preparing for the big journey which
I knew would happen one day.

It must be remembered that I am describing emergent life in the 1950s, when there were still strict ideas about what girls were supposed to do. The main directive was to grow up to be wives and mothers, whereas I made three major moves within the first five years of marriage and then formed a 'therapeutic theatre group' which toured European hospitals and schools. However, the map became clearer when I returned to study a course of social anthropology and, for my final essay, travelled to Malaysia for three months' observation. Expeditions in and around the rain forest, meetings with hunter-gatherers when they touched base, and travels with the army when they went on patrol, steadily fuelled the 'big journey' plans.

I eventually managed to travel back to Malaysia with my children, to live with an aboriginal tribe in the central rain forest. We reached them by river boat and Land Rover, in the middle of a monsoon. My plan was to study the drama and rituals of the Temiar people, and to compare their pregnancy and birth practices and child-rearing with my own social and cultural norms.

As the seasons came and went in our bamboo stilt house, and the tribe understood that we wouldn't rush away after a few weeks, we gradually became accepted into the lifestyle and were encouraged to understand their way of life.

The Temiars first and foremost are genuinely child-centred. Children are not hit or threatened and are allowed to choose from an early age. They understand what Temiar behaviour is expected from them in relation to belief and practice. Fear is inculcated towards thunder and tigers, and consequently parents can be very loving and indulgent. Children walk very early, and breast-feeding continues until about 4 years of age. There are rules concerning food (who can eat certain things and where and when); space (which spaces are dangerous and which are protected); illness (which actions cause illness); and birth and death (who can move in and out of the village). Children are aware of these 'rules for living' from birth and, since they are constantly with adult members of the community, have a continuous role-model of adult behaviour.

Dramatic seances with music, singing, dance and drama form the basis of both their entertainment as well as their preventive and curative rituals. The whole village attends, unless a person is too ill to move: babies are carried in a sling; children join in the singing and dancing; shamans spontaneously give the children 'healing' to keep them strong. Babies and children stay until first light, like everyone else, and sleep peacefully amidst all the noise. There is little in Temiar culture from which children are excluded and parents see this as a way of children learning how to be grown up and take on responsibilities. Yet nobody makes anybody do anything, as the Temiars feel it is wrong to force your will on another.

The Temiars, to my surprise, thought I had a good system going. Since my children settled down to do lessons most mornings, the parents asked me to make their children go to school! The bargain with mine was that, if they did lessons for an hour each morning, then the rest of the day they could join in with their friends. The Temiar parents see a vested interest in their children going down-river to a little school where they would be given food and clothes, and maybe their lot could be improved by their children having some basic education. However, when we were there, the children had a different plan. They went off to school and then diverted to a logging camp in the forest where the loggers cooked them food and allowed them to play!

The Temiar life cycle is divided into three broad categories: childhood, fertile years, old age. So there is not the age-stage we have of adolescence. Either you are a child and in many ways a carefree, playful person, or you are fertile and start to plan your domestic routine. After the child-bearing years, you are considered old and therefore to be respected. In each age-stage, people's names change: therefore, names denote identity. Both myself and the children were given Temiar names and expected in broad terms to keep the Temiar code. They participated with their peer group in Temiar activities which ranged from versions of playground games to domestic and fishing routines. The Temiars, although settled and cultivating for periods of time in villages, also move on, either as individuals or families or the village as a whole. They are a riverine people and will take time to visit other villages up and down the river network, as well as hunting and gathering wild fruit and vegetables. Thus they integrate cultivation with hunting and gathering.

As a personal journey for me, despite the discomfort of combating monsoons and leeches, illness and hunger, I knew this journey was right. We fumed at delays and became frustrated at lack of progress, but even so, we had found a way of wandering, even though we had eventually to return to our own culture. After we returned to the UK, it was time to reflect on the many processes that had been activated during this time away.

What is interesting is that the most criticized aspect of this journey was the fact that I took the children with me – that somehow they should have been left behind or should have gone to boarding school! One bout of very severe criticism came from a group of 16-year-old girls who thought I had been very selfish in depriving my children of a settled home. They would not accept that the children were given both the choice to go and also the choice to stay.

Although this journey continues to be a most formative time for me and my children, it also gives me insights into the debate concerning 'settling and wandering', as well as new perspectives on age-stages and adolescence. Why is it that some people feel more comfortable in a nomadic lifestyle whereas for others it is the epitomy of insecurity? Why is being a home-owner given as the symbol of security as well as status in our own culture? Why does the idea of travellers and gypsies cause such anxiety amongst settlers?

Figure 6.11 Integration of the dramatic processes of theatre art

CLOSING THOUGHTS

In this chapter I have looked at two major themes in relation to the survival of children and adolescents. The first is the primacy of the dramatic development of children and its influence on the maturation of human beings. I emphasize that we need to be able to distinguish between every-day reality and dramatic reality in order to function appropriately as responsible adults.

The second theme is that of recognizing the need to wander in people, and especially during the period of adolescence. I suggest that although this journey theme can be explored in drama and dramatherapy, there is a primeval need to actualize the wandering experience in the real world before young people settle down into chosen lifestyles. The opportunity to wander enables people to have a greater flexibility in living as well as fostering greater survival skills.

The overall philosophy of this chapter is how theatre art, medicine and religion are interdependent and need to be integrated in both the individual as well as the collective.

As such, we need to acknowledge the importance of:

drama as development
drama as ritual
drama as therapy

which can be integrated into an acceptance of drama as theatre art at all stages of life, but especially during childhood and adolescence (Figure 6.11).

REFERENCES

Jennings, S. (1993a) *Playtherapy with Children: a practitioner's guide*. Oxford: Blackwell Scientific.
——(1993b) Settled-cultivators or hunter-gatherers? A view of Shakespeare's *The Merchant of Venice*. Keynote presented at the Dramatherapy and Shakespeare Symposium, Stratford-upon-Avon.
——(1994) *Theatre Ritual and Transformation: the Temiar experience*. London: Routledge (in press).
Winnicott, D. W. (1971) *Playing and Reality*. Harmondsworth, Middlesex: Penguin.

Part III

Dramatherapy with adolescents

Chapter 7

Pinocchio – a handicapped brother
Working with healthy siblings through dramatherapy

Pamela Mond

INTRODUCTION

This chapter is about group dramatherapy with healthy siblings who have brothers or sisters with handicaps. The aims of the work are:

1 to create a support group;
2 to improve self-image;
3 to explore the roles of healthy siblings in family and social spheres;
4 secondary aim: to increase the community's awareness of handicap with projects prepared by healthy siblings.

We will look at three such groups, each of which met together for ten sessions. Within the supportive environment of the healthy dramatherapy group with the focus on the building of trust, self-confidence and creativity, we hope to help the group own and examine some of their themes and conflicts. The 'creative expressive' model of dramatherapy practice (Jennings 1987, 1990, 1993) was used, whereby the imaginative aspects of the individuals are stimulated and built up. In order to activate the change, without creating additional anxieties, we used the following areas of dramatherapy methodology: the use of the therapeutic metaphor via the story of Pinocchio, movement, relaxation, guided fantasies, art, puppetry, games, creative writing, psychodrama techniques and improvisations.

Comparisons made of individual and family drawings before and after group meetings showed an increase in self-image, positive changes in family dynamics and with regard to their relationship with their handicapped sibling.

The healthy sibling is, in fact, 'at risk' and accordingly deserves our professional attention in assisting him with his 'handicap'. These are not easy issues for the siblings to talk about (see Table 7.1), neither with parents, nor with friends, and often they feel isolated and lonely, thinking that they are the only ones with feelings such as these. Because of its unique distancing techniques, dramatherapy can contribute in a positive way to overcoming some of these difficulties. We therefore advocate the introduction of ongoing sibling support groups similar to those suggested in this chapter.

SETTING THE SCENE

Eighteen healthy children aged between 10 and 14 years, each of whom had a handicapped sibling, took part in the project. They were divided into three homogeneous groups:

1st Group   six girls aged 10–12;
2nd Group   five members, two boys and three girls, aged 10–13;
3rd Group   seven members, three boys and four girls, aged 11–14.

1st Group

Apart from one, all the members' handicapped siblings were very young, either in kindergarten or in first grade. Three had Down's syndrome and the other three were quite severely developmentally delayed and suffered from hydrocephalus, Cornelia de Langue syndrome and the third with a degenerative, genetic kidney disorder. The group was very involved with 'denial' – denying that any problems existed in the family because of their handicapped sibling. Taking this factor into consideration, the core of our work centred on the recognition of feelings. Another theme which was central to this group was the outward physical appearance of their sibling in comparison to one another's siblings and to siblings without handicaps.

2nd Group

The siblings were very close in age to their handicapped brothers or sisters. The latter were all studying within the regular school system, two were physically handicapped, one with cerebral palsy and the other who had become paralysed from her waist down in an accident and confined to wheelchairs; one, with development delays most marked by her absence of speech, was in a 'special education' classroom. This group dealt with the subject of the integration of their handicapped siblings into society. Another topic which the group approached was their need to work with their parents around the problems arising from the responsibility placed on them with regard to the amount of care they had to give to the handicapped member.

3rd Group

These older children had handicapped siblings who were suffering mainly from developmental problems including autism, severe mental retardation, personality disorders and the like. The main theme worked on by this group was (1) the need to keep 'secrets' and (2) social stigma. The majority of the handicapped siblings were older than their healthy brothers and sisters.

The groups ran for ten consecutive weeks on afternoons for one and a half hours per session. (Free transportation was provided by the town council and the therapist was employed by the Ministry of Education.)

The location was the large conference room at the Child Development Centre which also doubled as the therapists' work room and was furnished with all materials to suit the needs of the group. (A staff volunteer was also present and videotaped each session for learning purposes.)

It was decided that a workable number in each group would be between three to eight children, also that only one sibling per family would be accepted into the same group. All siblings referred were interviewed and in order to choose clients for each group we were guided by:

1 analysis of the dramatherapy work done by children during their home visits;
2 the siblings themselves and their ages;
3 the accounts and descriptions given by the parents as to their children's coping resources.

There was no definition as to any specific areas of handicap in the sibling.

Also referred to was Dr Yossi Zeider's doctorale work on siblings (Zeider 1985) which suggests that certain siblings are likely to have more difficulty in adapting to their handicapped brothers and sisters, for example:

1 if the healthy sibling was younger;
2 siblings from large families;
3 if the healthy and handicapped siblings were of the same sex;
4 in general, girls were at a higher risk because of their inclination to try to take care of their handicapped sibling.

Those children (hereafter known as 'sibs') who have handicapped siblings – and in most cases it does not matter what form the handicap takes – are often regarded as a 'Healthy Population'. But in fact they carry a very heavy burden. Of course, we cannot actually see their problems (as we may do with a person who has a physical handicap), and so in most cases their difficulties are not fully addressed or understood, neither by the children nor by those around them, yet their problem touches much of their daily life, 'family' and 'social' roles. By way of introduction to my dramatherapy groups for healthy sibs, let me tell a short story.

One afternoon on my way back from work, I found myself on the seat next to a chatty lady in an Israeli-style communal taxi (to ride in one of these is a real dramatherapy exercise!) and was soon encouraged to tell her my life story. I mentioned my work with the sibs groups. 'Well,' she exclaimed, 'that is certainly a population that needs help.' She went on, 'In the block where I live, there is a family with a child that is handicapped and three other healthy children, but in a way they all behave as if they had disabilities – differently from other children. They hold themselves back, keep a low profile.' I was very impressed by this lady's understanding; it had taken me five years of working at the Child Development Centre to reach the same conclusions. She was referring to what the literature (Hanochi 1986, Zeider 1985) describes as 'distorted' or 'low' self-image and the consequent difficulties with expression and ability to cope with social problems. Working on the improvement of these two areas became the main aims within our support groups.

It is the child with handicaps whose problems dominate the stage and the other child-actors in the 'family drama' are needed to fulfil supplementary roles, for example (1) the need to live up to parents' expectations for him to compensate for the handicap of the special child, or (2) over-responsibility in assisting parents to look after the sibling with the handicap (Table 7.1).

I was not the only one to 'miss' the sibs' cues. When I was interviewing families to find potential group members, 90 per cent of the parents would have preferred me to run a group for the children with handicaps as 'the healthy ones don't have any problems'. The sibs themselves, during pre-group work, would ask disbelievingly, 'Doesn't my brother have to come to the meetings with me?' When I stressed that the meetings were for them alone, the relief was enormous. Their sense of responsibility was so strong

Table 7.1 Common issues of sibs

1 Distorted self-image.
2 Problems created by ambivalence of feelings towards the handicapped sibling: love, pity, responsibility versus guilt, anger and anxiety.
3 Fears regarding genetic inheritance.
4 Growing up in an environment of anxiety, lack of confidence and stress within the family circle.
5 Emotional and behavioural neglect due to attention most often being centred on the handicapped sibling.
6 The need to live up to parents' expectations to compensate the handicap of the special child.
7 Over-responsibility in assisting parents to look after the handicapped sibling.
8 Danger of regression in overall development.
9 Social problems – the need to cope with problem areas of:
   a social stigma;
   b inviting friends home
   c the difficulty surrounding 'explanation' of the problem;
   d the need to learn to cope with strange reactions in the street when out with the handicapped sibling.

Source: Hanochi 1986: 2 – my translation

that, at the end of the first session, I was asked, 'Well, we had a lot of fun, but when will we learn how to take better care of our handicapped brothers and sisters?'

Sara Wheeler, an adult sib who discovered only this year that being the sib of a child with disabilities had caused resentment and emotional turmoil which she had carried into adulthood with her, wrote for the *Independent* (1993): 'I felt angry that nobody ever explained anything to me, or acknowledged that as 'the other child' I had special needs too.' These are the 'needs' – often carefully guarded, denied and kept as 'secrets' which make sibs feel lonely and isolated - that we attempt to address with the help of dramatherapy. Sara's hope, that sibs who are children today do not have to drag that confused and needy inner child into adulthood, is also our hope and the reason for advocating sibs groups to our colleagues in child development, psychological services, in education and the social services. The community still needs to receive information on the subject of handicap to understand the personal emotional and social suffering it brings with it to all family members (Bax 1990).

Considering the sensitivity surrounding the issues of those children who have disabilities and their families, I decided to use the telephone as a way of introducing myself to the parents of prospective group members. In some cases I was asked by them to speak to the children and tell them about the support group being formed. Wherever interest was expressed, a date for a home visit was set up. This period, between talking over the telephone and the time-lapse before I visited the home, was the start of the therapeutic process. It allowed time for the sibs to think about the issue of having a sibling with a disability and often encouraged discussion of the subject between the sibs and their parents.

A clear example of this occurred with Sally, aged 12, whose mother was waiting for me on the street outside their home as I arrived for the interview. She wanted me to know that Sally had been very upset, shortly after talking to me on the phone. She had sobbed to her mother, 'Why did Pamela say he had a disability?' to which the mother replied, 'Because he has. . . ' thus bringing about a long and first-time-ever conversation for them around this issue.

At this point, I should like to emphasize the importance which I attatch to the time spent on individual work during the home interviews. Because of the difficulties with these clients around the area of expression of their feelings and their concern about social acceptance surrounding the subject of handicap (as we shall see later more clearly), I doubt whether many of the sibs would have made it at all to the first group meeting had I not spent this time with them. Later on, in the very first group session, when the sibs 'shared' regarding 'why they had come', about 80 per cent said that, 'After I'd spoken with you, I thought. . . ' and it was clear that some real trust had already begun to develop between us during that home visit.

HOME INTERVIEW

The home interview was divided into a number of areas:

1 family interview
2 bibliotherapy
3 story-making
4 small object projection
5 figure and family drawings
6 questions, answers and feedback

and took between forty minutes and an hour and a half, depending on the needs and dynamics of the client and their family. I would like to spend some time looking at some of the bibliotherapy from which we found out the sibs' individual specific key issues and then at the six-piece story-making (Lahad 1992) and Basic Ph. (See Table 7.3) configurations which helped us decide further the group issues likely to need working on within our sessions.

Bibliotherapy

The bibliotherapy now to be described had an immediate effect on the clients. I brought with me two copies of a book written by 'siblings for siblings' called: *Straight from the Siblings: another look at the rainbow* (Murray and Jampolsky 1982). We found the pages I had chosen and then looked together at drawings or articles, with me role-playing what was written (whilst looking at the sibling). Sometimes I would improvise a little, make changes in the text to suit my client's needs, e.g. the age and sex of the writer and/or the sibling.

The areas I chose for work from the book were those about:

1 coming to a sibling group
2 the establishment of trust in such a group
3 letting go of feelings
4 fear
5 loneliness
6 jealousy
7 guilt.

Below are some examples of ways in which the material can be presented.

The first article examined was by a girl called Sue, aged 11, who wrote that when her mother first mentioned the idea of going to the centre, she hadn't wanted to go and would only do so if there were another 11-year-old girl with a 7-year-old brother there. She thought that there was nobody else going through what she was going through. After a while, she realized that there were other people like her so she agreed to attend a sibs group. 'After a couple of meetings it got easier to talk. I found that I could tell things to the group which I couldn't talk about with my parents. I found out that we could trust one another. Sometimes, I felt lucky that I wasn't having some of the problems that the other people were having. Now we can talk easily to each other. We joke around and talk about previous experiences. I am really glad that I have a place to come to when my brother has problems.'

John, aged 9, wrote that he was pretty scared at first because he didn't know what was wrong with his sister. 'When your sister has something and you don't know what it is . . . only the name . . . that's pretty scary because you don't know what's going to happen to her in the future . . . When I felt sad I would go to a friend's house or to school and try to forget about Dalia's sickness and my sadness. If I played football I would forget all about it except when I would kick the ball and then I would think I was kicking the good health back into her body.'

The next piece chosen was a picture drawn of a girl inside a tree house. She was thinking: 'Did I cause it?' and she was 'feeling guilty'.

Next, two children were drawn lying in separate beds. One had drawings and many toys and was saying aloud, 'Whee! What fun!' - he was the sibling with the disability. The other, a healthy sib, appeared angry and mumbled to himself, 'Oh, shut up, can't you!'

Eve, aged 12, expressed that jealousy is envy! Most of us are envious when someone else gets all the attention. 'Sometimes it's hard for us to know why our brother or sister gets more attention than we do. Many times we think we are getting ripped off when we are actually the lucky ones.'

Tara, aged 16, told how she felt she had to hold her feelings in when she was around her parents. 'I let my feelings out only when I am with my close friends.'

Bill, aged 12, brought up the subject of his sister's seizures which had been getting much worse. 'I am really frightened. I stay in my room and let my parents take care of her, as there is nothing I can do to help. It is kind of scary to talk to my friends about her, but I would rather have them ask me than stare.'

In many cases the sibs sat in a kind of trance – wide-eyed, open-mouthed, quite stunned at hearing, often for the first time ever, some of their private feelings dramatized aloud. The 'creative' media aroused their interest and, without creating additional anxieties, allowed them to identify at their own level. The younger sibs, who verbalize more easily, would even begin to talk about similar instances and give examples from their own lives. After looking at the 'other' sibs' contributions, I asked my potential sibs to prepare an article, drawing or entry for a similar 'sib magazine' and then to share it with me if they wished. In the sibs' work which follows, not only are we able to hear and see their difficulties expressed, but in a number of instances we are clearly shown how this media helps them to go one step further and begin working on the process of behavioural change.

Sandy aged 11

This sib chose to draw. There were two figures on his paper. One was a fat, muscular woman with one hand on her hip, her face drawn without eyes. Behind her stood an 'eyeless' smaller figure of a boy with his arms folded in front of his body over his stomach. After drawing, Sandy said in an explosive, angry tone, 'This is me. That is her. I'm small. She's big. She controls everything. I have to do everything she tells me.' He then changed his tone and added, 'But I forgive her.' After this torrent of words, the boy sighed heavily and returned to his drawing and drew a balloon from the boy's mouth and wrote in it the word 'me'. (NB On a visit to our town's sheltered workshop one morning, I saw his sister, who bore little resemblance to the 'fat muscular' figure portrayed in his drawing. She was in fact short and thin.)

Mike aged 12

'I'm very happy with my brother. I play with him, help him with many things. I give him food and drink. I dress him, care for him; I do like him, but sometimes it annoys me that my parents play with him a lot and they never did so with me. They buy him a lot of things but don't do the same for me. However, they don't hate me, I need to understand this. Sometimes my brother breaks things and makes my parents angry, that's when I know they don't hate me. Anyway, I'll take care of him and play with him – he's my brother after all, isn't he!'

Sara aged 12 (Fig. 7.1)

This sib drew a picture of her sister with a smile on her face in a reclined position on a sofa-bed opposite the television. There was a row of cushions on the floor next to the bed with a child sitting on one, her face towards the television. A balloon from the girl on the bed said: 'Bring me some juice, bring my medicine.' The sib told me after she had finished drawing, 'She takes up the whole sofa, exactly opposite the television, the best place, and the rest of us have to sit on the floor. At first it was okay bringing her everything, but now I'm fed up with it. I don't want to, but I'm afraid not to. I do it but without the will from inside. She did it for us when we were young, when she was well; now she's ill, it's her turn to be looked after.' When she'd finished speaking she returned to her picture and wrote on it in a balloon near the child on the floor, 'No, I don't want to.'

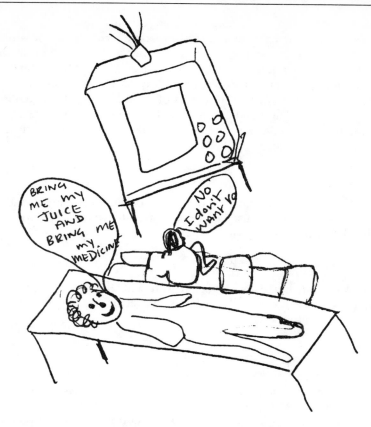

Figure 7.1 Drawing by a 12-year-old girl showing her sister (lying on a sofa-bed) and herself

Lily aged 14

'I prefer to speak up and tell my friends about my older sister, even though it's difficult. I don't want them to think that because she learns in a special school that she's abnormal, etc. I don't want them to pity her, just to understand what's wrong with her and why she learns there. Sometimes I'm asked if I'm the oldest, but I'm ashamed to answer and don't know what to say. So I reply, 'There's one older and one younger than me', and when they ask me if she learns here in our school, I don't actually tell them where she learns, but say that she goes to a different school.'

Heidi aged 13

'Usually my friends and I speak about my sister and why she doesn't speak, and how I cope with her. They never ask me though how I 'feel' about having a sister with a handicap. I love her very much and worry about her, and try to make contact with her. But sometimes when I go out with her, I feel that everyone is looking at me and at her and I feel very uncomfortable. They sometimes laugh and point saying, 'Look at her', sometimes I get very angry and feel protective towards my sister, I tell them it's not nice to laugh and ask them to stop. But most of the time I simply keep quiet and give my sister my hand and carry on walking with her in spite of all the faces she makes and the way she behaves, like a retard, and in spite of all those looks and laughs.'

Melvin aged 14

'As soon as my friends arrive, my older brother gets angry and starts shouting at me – it's because he doesn't have any friends. He won't admit this, but I feel that this is why.'

Ada aged 10

'I feel okay with my sister, I get on well with her. I help her a lot, for example, with homework. My sister is fine at home. She finds speaking difficult, but we manage.'

Fay aged 11

'I couldn't accept it at first – seeing a wheelchair in the house. I don't think I have to be jealous, only thankful that I'm healthy. There are times when I think of the future and how she'll cope. I'm sure something will be worked out. I have to help her a lot, so she will feel normal and not different from anyone else.'

Suzy aged 11

'I don't think my brother gets extra attention. I take it very hard that I have a brother with a handicap; e.g. when my friends call me to play after school, usually just at that same moment my brother calls me to help him with his homework – this makes me angry. Or if I want to go into town with my friends and at the same time my parents decide to go out as well so I have to stay behind with him. I'm not to blame for having a brother who is handicapped – no one's to blame. God wanted it that way and I have no choice but to accept it.'

Jim aged 10

He drew three stick figures and told me what each was, saying: (1) his sibling was crying; (2) his mum told him, 'Go and look after her'; (3) he answered, 'Oof, it's always me who has to look after her.'

Saul aged 13

Drew a picture of children playing football, and in the 'goal' area sat a child in a wheelchair who was saying: 'Why can't I be like you?'

Tamar aged 10

Drew a picture of herself and two other sibs looking at the baby who has Down's syndrome and a heart problem. Mum calls out hysterically, 'Don't touch her!' (Figure 7.2)

Ruth aged 11

(There are two handicapped siblings in this house.) She drew a boy and a girl. The brother was stuttering, inside his balloon was written '*ggzzss*' and she answered him, 'Shut up already, you're annoying me.' (Unfortunately, Ruth never again expressed such 'open' aggression.)

Paula aged 14

'On one hand I'm happy to have a brother like him because he helps to wash dishes, empty the rubbish, etc. but on the other hand, I'd rather not

Figure 7.2 Drawing by a 10-year-old girl showing herself and two sibs in relation to their handicapped baby sister

have such a brother because sometimes he embarrasses me when my friends see him, they talk about him.'

Sally aged 12

Chose to draw two pictures, one opposite the other. In the one was a boy lying on a bed in the hospital and in the other a girl behind a door in tears. After drawing this she said, 'Here's my brother in hospital, and I'm at home alone, with my thoughts about him and crying.' I asked, 'How did you feel when you were drawing this?' She sighed, then replied, 'It was as if I was telling it to someone; it came out from a place deep inside.'

Story-making

The six-piece storytelling technique used by me with each client was based on work by Dr Mouli Lahad in 1991 (Lahad 1992). Briefly, it consists of the child making up a six-piece story in words or in pictures in response to six questions asked by the therapist:

1   Who is the hero/heroine of the story? (Or more simply – who/what is the story about?)
2   What is his/her 'mission' or 'task' in the story?
3   Who or what (if at all) can help him/her achieve this?
4   What is the obstacle preventing him/her from achieving this task?
5   How (if at all) does he/she cope with this obstacle?
6   What happens next/at the end of the story?

These stories can then be looked at to suggest the clients' 'coping skills', 'themes', 'conflicts' and current emotional state. They also offer us a clue to the 'language' of the child, so helping us create an easier rapport.

Here are three examples of stories made in the groups:

Sara, aged 12, from whom we heard previously, comes from a large family; her eldest sister 'suddenly' became 'ill'. She stopped going to school, dropped out of everything, stayed home and, during the previous year, underwent a battery of tests, the outcome of which indicated no clear physical reason for her 'sickness' to date. A personality disorder was suggested but she refused to go for therapy. (Two years later, I learned that the sister had gone to live with an aunt out of town and has resumed her studies.) Here is Sara's story:

Sara's Story

1   *Hero:* A young boy, not old, who got injured by a car or something. He wasn't born like it, now he's handicapped.
2   *Task:* To walk. He wants to get well and walk again.

3 *Who can help?* A specialist doctor.

4 *Obstacle:* Money – there's not enough money. The parents do not have strength to work any harder.

5 *How to overcome?* Nothing at this stage.

6 *The ending*: In a totally unexpected way, the father receives an inheritance from an uncle; enough money. The specialist performs the operation which is successful. The boy can walk.

The next two stories are written by girls asking for help, both wanting to 'go for it' in spite of the difficulties - and both, in fact, did make it to a group (not the same one), but sadly only Doris saw it through to the end (ten sessions) whilst Lily left halfway through, though I continued to post her invitations to meetings and other group members phoned to keep her informed. The first story is 14-year-old Lily's, who, we heard previously, has so much difficulty socially and whose feelings of 'shame' are very strong. Then comes Doris, aged 12, the eldest in a large family, who left the room during the interview after hearing the bibliotherapy examples, supposedly to go to the lavatory. Five minutes later, her mother came in and told me of Doris's difficulty in facing up to her feelings. She managed to return, however, and said she wanted to continue – we left the 'magazine' work and went on to story-making.

Lily's Story

1 *Heroine:* My best friend.

2 *Task:* To encourage her; to be together with her when needed.

3 *Who can help?* In my opinion, only my best friend can help, because I am not ready to tell everyone.

4 *Obstacle:* The heart – in order to help and be ready for this, you need understanding, love, a good heart – to have these qualities, you need to know how to behave.

5 *How to overcome?* The heroine overcomes her instincts and comes towards the other person with a lot of love, understanding and consideration.

6 *The ending*: The heroine comes and admits she wanted help but something unknown stopped her and she put up boundaries.

Doris's Story

1 *Heroine:* A small, innocent girl.

2 *Task:* To learn about things that interest her. To research and talk about them with someone.

3 *Who can help?* Her parents or anyone who works in these areas which interest her.

Table 7.2 Description of fifteen six-piece stories

Sib no.	Hero	Minus or unusual scores in Basic Ph.	Conflicts	Themes	Additional remarks*
1	Princess	Ph– S–	Good v bad	Escape Magic Loyalty	Rescue story Heroine saved herself
2	An 'invisible' boy	S– No A No Ph	Strong v weak	Attention stolen from him Rescue	Rescue story This sib attended erratically & left with no word
3	Lion tamer	A– no A no I	Id v superego	Aggression Fear	
4	Red Riding Hood		Id v superego (Puberty age approp. conflict)	Threat of being devoured (by her sibling?)	
5	A boy called Shi aged 15	no I	Adolescent conflict	Girl needs help	Rescue story
6	Rambo	S– No A	Good v bad	Too many people Strength Inventions	Rescue story
7	Will Parker (boy)	S– no A (0·5)	Control v loss control	Suppression of feelings Running away	Rescue story
8	Chief of police	S– No I Very high 'C' score	Good v bad	When is a friend not a friend?	Rescue story
9	Young boy in a wheelchair	B– Ph– No A Low S&I (0·5)	Give up v faith	Money Miracles	Rescue story

10	Young innocent girl	A- S- No I No Ph	No one understands me, lack of comm. (age approp. conflicts)	Searching for and finding help	Rescue story
11	My best friend	A- 2S- Low I&Ph (0·5)	Holding in v letting go	Fear to share Fear of society	Was sending a message re. her fear of a group
12	Herself	S- I- No C	Good v bad	Fighting against odds and winning (miracle)	Rescue story
13	Saddam Hussein	B- A- S- No I Very high 'C' score	Good v bad	Identification with aggressor	
14	A cat and its mother	B- S- No I	Independence threatened	Need for reassurance Help from mother	
15	Himself	No I No A No Ph.	Parental problem	Escape persuasion	Rescue story

* Existential idea of Rescue
Rescue = My sibling from his problem
Therapist = the cure

4 *Obstacle:* Misunderstanding – can't find her 'place' – no one listens to what she is saying.

5 *How to overcome?* Tries to speak to someone, to ask someone to talk to her. Someone who knows about these things that interest her – a lot of understanding from this other person.

6 *The ending:* She finds the suitable people and they help her to cope with the problems and obstacles she encounters.

We analysed fifteen stories according to Basic Ph. (a model for understanding an individual's capacity for coping and resilience under stress. A detailed account of the model is given in Lahad 1992). Tables 7.2 and 7.3 give some of the results, comparisons and configurations.

We see that the 'average' scores are quite revealing (Table 7.3). They suggest that we will find an above-average use of 'C' (Cognition) and a minimal use of 'I' (Imagination). Although the sibs' scores in 'S' (Social) skills are good on average, however, a large number of sibs have 'conflicts' or 'no scores' in this area, which is also significant. It may be plausible to consider that families with handicapped children often use social and cognitive Belief Systems (BS, BC) as a means to control their emotions (A). Scheff (1986: 99–100) calls an individual whose primary mode of experiencing is a cognitive one 'overdistanced'. The extreme of overdistance is a state of repression – the overdistanced individual has blocked her ability to experience painful emotion. The past is remembered but the person detaches from present feelings associated with past experiences. We often heard statements in our groups like: 'His illness doesn't affect the rest of the family,' and, 'I'm not at all embarrassed by her; I just don't like to talk about it when people ask me,' or, 'My sister looks okay. She just can't speak, read or write,' and 'God wanted it this way,' and, 'We shouldn't pay attention to the things he says but we should give him all the attention because he needs it.'

Small Objects/Spectograms

In the interviews, the subjects I worked on via the small objects were family dynamics and/or social position in school.

Table 7.3 Comparison of scores of fifteen sibs according to Basic Ph.

	B	A	S	I	C	Ph.
Total	30	27	39.5	9	66	34.5
Average score	2	1.8	2.6	0.6	4.4	2.3
Nos. of minuses (−)	−3	−4	−11	−1	none	−1
Nos of no scores	1	5	none	7	1	3

NB 2.3 is average overall score

*B = Belief and attitudes; A = Affect; S = Social; I = Imagination; C = Cognitive; Ph. = Physical

I presented the sib with a colourful box which I told him contained the 'actors' for a play. However, they were not people but animals, animals which could represent the characters in a play about the family/school. We spoke about how often when the curtain went up in the theatre, for the first time, we might see the characters on the stage in a friezed position. This gave the audience time to look at and ponder about the theme of what they were about to see. The sib could choose any scene from the play, he could place the animals in front of him, on the floor or table, to represent the details of the story which he could then share with me. At the end I also asked him which role he would choose to play. Some of the scenes have been reconstructed below in diagram form to show examples of their work.

The following is a scene created by Jim, aged 10, the eldest brother in a family of six children.

Spectogram 1

Jim chose all 'wild' animals in dark colours for the 'family scene' and placed six of them in a row (a) whilst another two were put in front (b).

	✕	✕	✕	✕	✕	✕
a	Monster	Dinosaur	Lion	Tiger	Wolf	Leopard

b   Two Black Gorillas – the same size

✕   ✕

He then said, 'The boy and the father are the gorillas.'

Spectogram 2

For the school scene at 'play-time', he arranged any animal which came out of the box, without looking, into a circle.

Then he carefully looked at the assortment, chose a white stallion and put it into the middle (c).

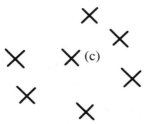

'This is the eldest brother,' he explained seriously.

DEVELOPMENT OF WORK PROGRAMME

Embodiment and Projection (Jennings 1990)

Before the home interviews took place, it seemed clear that I would be able to plan in advance to explore some of the main sibling conflicts, e.g. jealousy, guilt, fear, etc. However, on meeting and working with the children, most clearly of all arose their great need for assistance first and foremost in the area of recognition of such feelings, which were in the main carefully suppressed or denied.

The bringing together of such children and creating an environment for them to share with one another material which they had been unable to bring up in any other forum had to be my main objective and group aim.

I decided that the first sessions would definitely have to centre on the building of trust and self-confidence, hoping then that work on control and release of emotions would be made easier. If, by the end of the group sessions, we would be able to 'accept' some of our less comfortable feelings, the group would have achieved one of its major aims.

We know that 'Ph.' (Physical) work using movement and all physically active media can lead one, albeit 'unconsciously', quite directly to the area of emotions. Elaine Segal (Segal 1974) describes how, when a specific motor sequence is suggested to the client, it changes their inner situation, e.g. a client who was helped to work with tensing muscles and making fists, said, 'That reminds me of an angry person,' and then went on to recapture particularly angry personal life situations. An over-simplification but an example tracing the stages of work one gets into from a mere clenched fist!

Let me add also an example of how a piece of movement work which we did in the group around the subject of an 'erupting volcano' allowed one girl to realize, 'That is just how I feel inside,' and then for another to add, 'Watch out for me when I explode!'

Therefore, I would consider that as a beginning the 'Ph.' areas of dramatherapy, e.g. movement, clay and puppetry, should work well for these clients. 'Overdistancing' techniques such as the use of masks are also a helpful medium for beginning groups. Masks worked well with our clients in their second session (Table 7.4) as a way to reach intra-psychic material and for use in dialogues with other group members, so helping, too, to experiment with interpersonal exchanges.

Working with 'line/colour/shape' drawings, which clearly bypass the mind and its intellectualizations and go directly to the source of feelings, also allowed the clients a unique opportunity vividly to capture 'feelings' on paper and to visualize their emotions.

During such experiential initial sessions and through the sharing of experiences, the 'group' begins to come together; by recognizing their 'shared experiences' the clients feel freer to trust one another.

Table 7.4 Development of work with sibs

Subject	Ways of working	Sessions
Sibling groups Me and my family Me and my friends Basic Ph.	Bibliotherapy Small object projection Spectograms Figure & family drawings Six-piece story-making	Home interviews
Getting acquainted Group work on cohesion	Movement, Mime Indiv./Pair/Small group games Creative art work using maga- zines leading to individual and group stories	1
Expression of feelings	Music, movement & mime dialogues Line, shape & colour drawings Masks	2
Personal and inter- personal relationships	Clay work Pinocc. metaphor begins Improvisations (1,2,3)	3
Denying or facing reality	Creative writing Improvisation – (4) Voice & body sculpting	4
Social stigma	Improvisations (5,6,7) Creative diary writing	5
Feeling ashamed Sharing feelings	Line, shape & colours Art work Puppet improvisations	6
Expressing feelings Experiencing handicap	Set induction – guided fantasy Collage work, posters	7
Me and society Wishes for the future	Creative art work Making of gifts for group members	8
Telling of secrets My family, my sib & myself	Family sculpts Secret writing Improvisations (8,9)	9
Closure	Exhibition of works done in sessions, art work, writing improvisations (10)	10
	Family and figure drawings	In separate room after conclusion of 10th session

We can then begin to move on from our work in the embodiment and projective stages of group work to enter the next stage of role.

WORKING WITH 'ROLE PLAY'

Therapeutic metaphors

Stories have been used for hundreds of years to help motivate people to discover their own solutions to their problems. According to David A. Lee (1991: 242), when you tell a 'story' which bears a resemblance to your listener's problems or relevant issues, the unconscious mind 'tunes in' and 'locks on' to it – gaining one's attention and arousing interest. The images, emotions and perceptions which are evoked by the therapeutic metaphor create experiences and perspectives that form the foundations for change, at both the conscious and the unconscious levels. Metaphors are effective, says Lee, because they (1) bypass the listener's resistance and self-limiting beliefs; (2) access unconscious resources; (3) stimulate right-brain functioning, which is closely linked to emotion. So, when people hear such stories, they connect up with those of their own life experiences that are similar. This allows the therapist indirectly and respectfully to stimulate someone to think about and address particular issues. Therapeutic metaphors allow their listeners vicariously to experience themselves as responding in new and different ways. Also, because it is 'just a story', the person is able to hear it without feeling the need to defend learned limitations, or deny a new point of view. A person can 'try out' new perspectives and solutions without having to 'save face' by defending current ones. The listener has a sense of freedom, and can create his own meanings, giving personal relevance and value. There is a great variety of types of metaphors, e.g. true stories, fables, analogies, jokes, art, music, etc.

Pinocchio as a healing metaphor

In our sibling groups, in order to help the children to select and construct scenes which would offer useful material for exploration and which would approach and address their inner conflicts, we translated the 'explicit reality' into 'dramatic reality' (Gersie 1987). I chose to adapt the story of Pinocchio (the Walt Disney version) as the starting point for our improvisations.

Gheppetto and his 'only son, Jiminy Cricket', enjoyed many years living peacefully together when along came a new addition to the family – a long-awaited brother for Jiminy called Pinocchio. As with all sibling arrivals, a whole new set of changing dynamics was created in the family!

The magical, mythical nature of this fairytale matched up well with the child's view of the world. Our aim in presenting the metaphor is to create what Rossi (quoted in Mills and Crawley 1986: 65) termed 'a shared phenomenological reality'. The story is chosen so that the child will feel a sense of identification with the characters and events portrayed. The children, say Mills and Crawley, need to create a bridge of personal connection between themselves and the events of the story if they are to bring 'parts' of the story back into their 'real' life (Mills and Crawley 1986). In the effective therapeutic metaphor, this is facilitated by representing the child's problem accurately enough that they no longer feel alone, yet indirectly enough that they do not feel embarrassed, ashamed or resistant. In the story of Pinocchio, we were offered varied opportunities for our clients to explore the many resemblances in characters and situations to the story in which they often found themselves.

The 'wooden' appearance of Pinocchio and the fact that he is a 'doll' offer immediate possibilities of comparison to a child with a handicap. Perhaps also the well-known fact of the 'miracle' which happens to Pinocchio at the end of the story – i.e. he changes into a 'real live boy' – was the 'allowing' of our clients' secret wishes. (See the large number of 'Rescue theme' stories in Table 7.2.) The character of Jiminy Cricket represents the 'healthy sibling' and allowed many explorations of such a role, both at home with parents (Gheppetto) and outside in the street or with school-friends. The character of Brutus, as the 'best friend', was used to explore the importance of 'sharing' one's feelings. The character of the Blue Fairy allowed for 'difficult moments and memories' to resurface and be addressed.

The following are examples of how these characters were used in the group to explore the issues of:

1 personal and family relationships;
2 denial of uncomfortable feelings and difficult thoughts;
3 society and how it relates to children with handicaps and their families;
4 parents – can they be told the truth, or who should protect whom from whom?

All sessions were videotaped, and a presentation film has been made of one group's sessions.

Improvisations

We began our improvisations after I had carefully told 'our' version of the story's beginning, making it clear that from now on 'we' were in charge of making up and changing the story in any way we wished. We could try out new ideas and then add or edit from them after we had acted out the scenes or rehearsed them using puppets, movement or any other media we chose.

The first scene was set:

Improvisation One

(group meeting no. 3 would be a suitable session to begin this work)

Characters: Gheppetto and Pinocchio   Jiminy is just going off to play (as he does every afternoon) with his best friend Brutus. Before he leaves, Gheppetto suddenly calls him back and tells him to 'take Pinocchio' with him or invite Brutus to the house to play so that Pinocchio can join in too.

This scene, as with the other suggested improvisations, can be acted out a number of times to explore the different responses by the characters. For example, in one variation Jiminy was portrayed by a sib as being totally compliant to Gheppetto, but another sib played him as the rebellious son. As the children become more adventurous within their work and as the group progresses, they will begin to play a number of different roles for themselves, subconsciously trying out new patterns of behaviour, without feeling afraid. A clear example in one of my groups was Sally, who, we remember, had never dared to admit that her brother had a handicap, not even at home with her parents. The male children in her family were susceptible to liver disease which stunted their growth dramatically and eventually led to their dying at a young age. Sally had already lost one brother when she was younger and very likely was still grieving for him whilst at the same time living from day to day and looking with fear at her younger, 8-year-old brother who was suffering from liver problems too. In her bibliotherapy work, carried out during the interview, she had given us clues about her crying behind closed doors. As expected, Sally had been a very slow starter. In the first sessions, she chose to participate from the sidelines, watching carefully, but keeping her 'sharing' to a minimum. This continued until we began improvising the Pinocchio story, when she suddenly began to 'volunteer' eagerly for parts in the different scenes. She started to 'try out' as many characters as possible. At the start of session 5 she called out, 'Hey, I want that part today, because I feel like I have been playing it all week and I know it well now!' (It was the role of Jiminy, talking to his classmates about his brother, Improvisation Seven).

Improvisation Two

Characters: Jiminy and Brutus   Jiminy goes off to meet Brutus to tell him about Pinocchio (does he? doesn't he? how? etc.)

Improvisation Three

Characters: Jiminy, Brutus and Pinocchio   Jiminy and Brutus are together, Pinocchio arrives.

Creative writing and drama (session no. 4)

The next series of improvisations explores the theme of 'Denial'. Here we dramatize material which 'comes up' during the 'sharing' of the following

Picture One

Jiminy knows he should be very happy to have Pinocchio for a new brother because................... *(write down reason)*

Picture Two

The truth is, I have a lot of problems because of Pinocchio. Things like...

Picture three

Whenever anyone asked him what was wrong or if anything was bothering him, he just couldn't admit the truth and he would 'deny' any problems, saying things like...

Figure 7.3 Pictures used for creative writing activity in relation to issues arising from the Pinocchio story

creative writing activity. Three pictures of Jiminy Cricket are handed out to each group member, one where he looks happy, the second where he looks troubled and the third where he is avoiding looking at us, even hiding (Figure 7.3; illustrations from Snoonit 1984). Each picture has an introductory thought written below it, which needs to be completed by the client (who writes on the back).

Picture One allows expression in the sibs' usual modes of behaviour (i.e. Social and Cognitive Belief Systems) and our group members offered suggestions like:

● Because I look after Pinocchio, I feel mature and responsible; at least he will always be 'faithful' to me
● When my friends or Gheppetto are busy and don't have time for me, Pinocchio will be there for me
● If Jiminy doesn't react 'happily' to getting a new brother, people will look at him as if he is unusual
● It may sound hard to believe, but you can be proud of a brother even though he is made of wood – in spite of everything, Pinocchio is very cute!

It was as important for us to work with those last two points as it was to explore those pretended 'happy' reactions.

Picture Two allowed much previously undisclosed material to emerge and be shared – writing in the first person singular but as another character was our protecting distancing technique. The responses listed were:

● I have to look after him all the time, share with him
● He invades my privacy, interferes with me and my friends
● He makes me feel jealous and ashamed
● He hurts me, gets the best of everything, shows me no respect and I'm fed up with him.

After the writing of Picture Two was finished, we could call out whenever we wished the things we had written, and what began slowly turned into a ritualistic chant with sibs feeling free of inhibitions and able to shout out and bemoan their fate together because, as one sib put it, 'We're all in the same boat here.' Sara, whose sister had 'suddenly' become ill during her late teens, really opened up here. Apart from myself and the group, very few others in the community even knew of the difficulty which the family had been desperately trying to cope with over the last eighteen months. It was this 'secret' which was adding to Sara's problems, stifling her usual chatty and relatively open style of personality. She shared with us here, 'It's so important to know that there is someone else on your side of the coin.'

After the group, she explained to me why she had been able to tell her 'secrets' for the first time ever in the group. 'It was really meaningful and important for me to hear the puppets and the others in the group speak out, so it was only fair that I did so too.'

Picture Three allowed us, after feelings had been ventilated whilst working through Picture Two, to laugh at ourselves a little and playfully 'over-act' the roles it suggested and which we know so very well from our everyday lives – the things we say or do when we are asked awkward questions or when we just don't want to speak to the person in front of us. Here are some of the sibs' ideas:

- I change the subject, e.g. 'Want to play football next week?'
- 'I don't know what you mean.'
- 'I have a headache and don't feel well.'
- I just try to disappear, pretend I'm not there, or say 'excuse me, I have to go now, maybe we'll talk tomorrow'.

Those who did not directly avoid answering said things like:

- 'It's a family matter'; 'I can't tell you'; 'It's a secret.'

One girl wrote:

- When friends ask me, I say, 'He's a good brother,' but when he arrives I tell him, 'Oof, why did you have to come?'

Another wanted to tell Gheppetto:

- 'What a rotten father you are, for bringing me such a nuisance as a brother!'

And a number of Jiminys were secretly saying:

- 'It's just my bad luck but maybe he'll get well and be like everyone else's brother.'

Improvisation Four

Some groups who had advanced well had members who were willing here to work and try to change the ending. We did this using pair work, the pairs acting out some of the scenes between Jiminy and another person in the street using the above texts. Then the same pair or other pairs could act out 'alternative endings' with different ways for Jiminy to react. (Slower groups just acted out the first scenes and we worked on the theme of changing behaviour patterns in later work.)

Dramatization leading to diary-writing (session no. 5)

Improvisation Five

Here we start exploring the theme of 'Society, my sibling and I'.

Characters: Pinocchio, Jiminy and his classmates   Jiminy wants to show off his new brother to his friends at school. Jiminy's friends are all 'crickets' like himself. Jiminy is popular at school and has many friends there. Pinocchio is, of course, a puppet and not a cricket. However, Jiminy doesn't think of Pinocchio in any other way than as a 'brother'. Let's see what happens when Jiminy comes into the classroom (where his friends are gathered); Pinocchio is with him.

Improvisation Six

Characters: Pinocchio and Jiminy's classmates   The next day Jiminy has to go to the doctor before school. Pinocchio goes alone to school today. Let's see how the children receive him now without his brother.

Improvisation Seven

Characters: as above plus Jiminy   Jiminy arrives late and sees some of his friends (who don't notice him at first) making fun of Pinocchio in the playground.

Following this series of improvisations (Five, Six and Seven) comes some *creative writing* which is then *shared*.

Choose to be either:

a One of the children in the class
b Jiminy
c Pinocchio

and write one of the following:

'Dear Diary, I have a secret to tell'
'Dear Diary, I feel bad about something'.

The diary-writing varied, depending on how the groups' improvisations developed. For example, in one of the 'younger' groups where 'all came out well in the end' after the intervention of a teacher and the classmates' consciences had been pricked, one diary entry said:

> Dear Diary, I want to tell you about something good which happened to me. Today, my brother Jiminy took me with him to school and I had a very successful time there. At first, the children laughed and made fun of me, but later when they saw that I had no friends and that I was by myself and lonely, they came over and made friends which made me feel really good. After all the nasty things they'd been saying about me and

laughing at me, suddenly everyone wanted to make friends with me – I was so happy that they'd changed their minds about me, otherwise maybe I'd never have had any friends at all!

In another group, whose Pinocchio 'stayed on the outside' of the group of schoolmates, one sibs' diary entry said:

Today was a 'bad' day for me at school. It was great getting ready to go, I was excited. On arrival, however, my brother Jiminy and I got an unexpected welcome! My brother's friends (by the way, my brother until now was very popular with his classmates) were rude to me and Jiminy, who had been so proud of having a brother, just blushed and didn't know what to say. Until now, I had thought that I was cute, but in class everyone was whispering about me. 'Look at the funny doll' - maybe I won't go back again tomorrow. I feel bad about Jiminy's new social status, and yes, I feel sad for myself too! Before I ever went to school, I was happy staying at home and being with Gheppetto who gave me a lot of help. Now what shall I do? Go back to school or not? Perhaps I should talk about it with Gheppetto and Jiminy? (Signed: 'A sad Pinocchio')

Another entry from the same group written from a different perspective:

Dear Diary, Something unpleasant happened today, and now I'm feeling sorry about what I did. Today, when Pinocchio came into the class, I spoke to him in a rude manner and I asked him all sorts of questions which actually weren't any of my business. When I saw how it hurt him, I began to realize that I'd done something wrong, but it was too late. I want to say that I'm sorry, but how? (Written by a friend of Pinocchio)

In one of the older groups that same issue of 'needing someone else's advice' came up at the end too. (We later used this theme for work with puppets.)

Dear Diary, Shalom, how are you? It's two weeks since we last spoke! I want to tell you about a 'new pupil' in our class called Pinocchio. He's a doll made of wood and he's sweet, he's the brother of Jiminy also in my class. However, I don't feel very comfortable with this new brother, he is cute but the truth is that it's not possible to include him in our 'group' of friends because we're all 'crickets' and he's a 'doll'. He's not suitable – he's different from us. Some of the classmates speak rudely about him because they don't feel comfortable with him. However, there are other kids who do feel okay towards him. He comes to class every day and I don't know how to behave towards him, to accept him or not – maybe you can advise me, dear diary. From your loving friend, Gingey.

Art work (session no. 6)

Following the diary-writing, we experimented with 'line/colour/shape' art work; the subject offered was: 'Show how Jiminy felt after his day at school.' This work was put aside for later and not shared at this point.

Puppets

Puppets were our next media, and the group members were asked to choose two puppets each, one to be Jiminy and one to be Brutus (the best friend). They then prepared a short scene in which Jiminy tells Brutus how he is feeling after what happened in school. Interesting to note here was the sibs' choice of puppets. In most cases the 'best friend' puppet was a strong or large styled figure, e.g lion, happy face, whereas 'Jiminy' was nearly always a small, weaker, even ugly or broken doll. Their voices took on similar proportions of strength or weakness and the sibs' bodies, arms and faces would alternate too between confident, open, high movements and lower, more withdrawn, weaker movements, showing low self-image. In all the puppet plays Brutus managed to help Jiminy to speak up and tell what was bothering him and to offer him support, sympathizing and often making suggestions of how Jiminy could change things.

Comparison of 'before' and 'after' art work

A second line/colour/shape picture is then made by each client to represent and show how Jiminy felt *after* he had spoken to Brutus. On completion, we took both 'before' and 'after' pictures and compared them. The two illustrations serve as clear examples as to the difference between being alone with your problem and how you can feel if you share it. Figure 7.4 shows some work in this area.

Set induction and guided fantasy (session no. 7)

The continued work on Pinocchio is now experienced via set induction and guided fantasy. A new character, 'The Blue Fairy', is introduced. Set induction and relaxation is achieved via colours floating and flowing through the body. A blue sparkle in the distance begins to come closer. It is the Blue Fairy, who says, 'I have come to help you.' From within, large light bubbles, which she produces with her magic wand and scenes from Jiminy's past arise. Bubble no. 1 shows Pinocchio in the school playground, fooling around and acting stupidly, children are laughing at him. The Blue Fairy says to Jiminy, 'I saw how ashamed you were of Pinocchio's silly behaviour.'

She magics Bubble No. 2 – 'Do you remember yourself here, Jiminy?

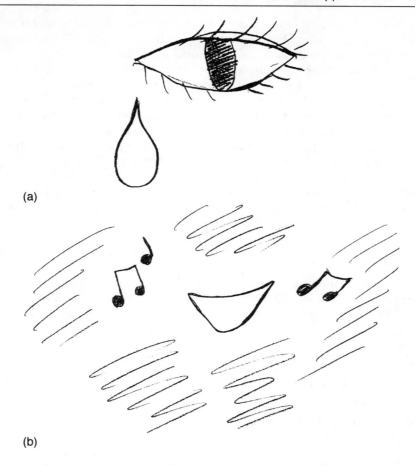

(a)

(b)

Figure 7.4 a and b 'Before' and 'after' work on the Pinocchio story: line/colour/
shape pictures

You were wishing that he'd never been born and that you had had a
'cricket' as a brother.'

In Bubble No. 3 she points out Jiminy, who is looking very depressed,
feeling afraid of what the future will bring for Pinocchio when Jiminy or
Gheppetto won't be there to look after him. Also on Jiminy's mind, the
Fairy reminds him, was his fear that one day he himself might have a child
like Pinocchio.

Collage work

After the telling of this story to the group, who have their eyes closed, each
client is asked to make a collage of one of the scenes which the Blue Fairy

brought – or of a new scene (bubble) depicting Jiminy having a hard time. The collages were then shared. Next, a group list was prepared combining all the problems Jiminy had, and a title was designated.

A very interesting phenomenon took place with the writing of the posters. Pinocchio's and Jiminy's names were often used during the group's joint work. However, during the discussion on what points to use in the posters to summarize the difficulties that Jiminy had, the children were clearly relating to their own problems on individual and group levels. They were choosing, albeit subconsciously, to leave the 'dramatic reality' and come back into their 'everyday reality' (Jennings 1987, 1990, 1993). From this point of progress in the sibs' work process, it would be feasible to hope that a place was being reached from where behavioural change could begin. Secrets and difficult feelings were beginning to be expressed and shared.

Poster presentations

To go further into new areas the set induction was then continued: 'The Blue Fairy decided to *give Jiminy some wishes to help him have a better life.*' The siblings were then asked as a group to write down all the things which could help Jiminy. Here are two examples of posters which the siblings made:

Poster 1: What can help in the future?

- Self-confidence
- The ability to influence others
- Explanations to friends
- A 'Magic Potion' which will cure him and, therefore, help me too: if he gets well and becomes normal, all my problems will be solved
- Accept everything happily
- Not to feel ashamed
- To learn more about his problem(s)
- To seek advice
- To share with someone who will understand
- Not to get into a panic

Poster 2: Thoughts for the Future

- I'll talk to Pinocchio and tell him to change his ways and to stop coming along with me everywhere I go
- When it reaches the limit, I won't keep it inside, I'll tell Father
- I'll ask someone to speak to my brother
- What will I do if all this doesn't work?

- Whom shall I call upon – Mother or Father?
- If that doesn't work, I'll go to a friend and talk to her about things, maybe that will help

Magic wishes and gifts (session no. 8)

Continuing to work from those ideas conjured up by the Blue Fairy, it was the themes of miracles and cures and ways for Jiminy to cope in society that were most frequently referred to. The siblings were asked to choose one of those wishes for themselves. They mostly chose, in one form or another, 'for my sibling to be healthy', because then their lives in turn would be better.

As we were nearing the end of the ten sessions (meeting no. 8) and separation work was already being introduced, the group here made 'gifts' for each other (each for the person on their right) from scrap materials – each present had to relate to the friends' 'wish' for the future. We had cure-all medicines, books containing 'all you ever needed to know', charms which increased self-confidence, and words of encouragement and strength which popped out of locked boxes, etc.

Puppets

Finally, to end this part of the work around 'society', a summary of it all was made, using puppet play media in which Jiminy told Brutus all about the Blue Fairy's visit.

Secret writing (session no. 9)

The final area of work which the group looked at using the Pinocchio metaphor was 'My family, my sibling and myself'. Here we used some 'secret writing', a piece of work which I stressed, beforehand, would not be 'shared' in the group. The idea I suggested was that Jiminy wanted to share his problems, caused by having a handicapped brother, with Gheppetto. But he just couldn't summon up the courage to tell him. Instead he decided to write down all the things he'd never been able to tell him. 'Now,' the group was told, 'you, too, have the opportunity to write down (without sharing afterwards) all the things you have never been able to tell your parents.'

It was interesting that many siblings asked if they could share what they had written. 'We're so used to sharing now,' was one comment. I did ask the question, however, 'How did you feel after you'd written your list?' One client compared it to the puppet work done previously, when Jiminy 'shared' with Brutus and felt such relief! (The children may want to make a group 'poster' listing problems caused by handicapped siblings which 'can't be told to parents'.) Most of the older girls (12+) felt the need to be extremely protective of their parents' feelings and so hide from them any difficulties they themselves were having. Younger children, in contrast, decided to talk to their parents. The next improvisations were designed to address this very need.

Group improvisations

Improvisation Eight – The Nose Job

Characters: Gheppetto, Jiminy and the Blue Fairy, and all the rest of the siblings to participate from the side   Gheppetto felt 'something was wrong' and so he called Jiminy in for a chat. The Blue Fairy was watching. Each time Jiminy didn't answer one of Gheppetto's questions truthfully/to the point/evaded answering, etc., *she made his nose grow longer!* When he told the truth, *it got shorter!* Those group members not 'acting' in the scene as Gheppetto, Jiminy or the Blue Fairy, call out 'nose grow' whenever they spot that Jiminy has not answered honestly. Similarly, they call out 'nose shrink' when they hear him answer truthfully.

Improvisation Nine

Characters: Jiminy and Brutus (only needs to be acted if work on this issue still needs exploration)   Jiminy tells Brutus all that he couldn't tell Gheppetto.

Suzy, aged 11, from whom we heard earlier, whose only brother John, aged 12, is physically handicapped with cerebral palsy and in a wheelchair, had many problems as a result. Those which bothered her the most were to do with school and her friends. John had been mainstreamed and, for various reasons to help him, was kept down a year and put into his sister's class! On school trips she had to slow down and help him; at home she had to assist with his homework. All this was interfering with her social life. Until now she had been biting her lips and pinching herself whenever she was unable to cope with her anger over the situation. 'He just *has* to tell his parents,' she called out, watching the last improvisation between Gheppetto and Jiminy, and when her turn came to play Jiminy that wooden nose grew not one inch! By the way, I am very happy to tell you that now, two years later, Suzy goes to a boarding school out of town! John, her brother, can manage quite well without her help, he no longer uses a wheelchair and is learning to walk well on a special frame. I work with him in a special cerebral palsy after-school group and he is now one of the star swimmers and horseback riders!

Medal-presentation ceremony (session no. 10)

An imaginative way to see if the sibs' self-image had improved was made in the final Pinocchio scene.

Improvisation Ten

The children were given a picture of Jiminy wearing a large medal around his neck – Olympic-style. I then asked them to decide which medal – gold, silver or bronze – he had received and why he had been awarded it. (They wrote their answers on the back of the picture.) During the 'medal-presentation ceremony' which we then acted out, it was really entertaining to see how much the sibs enjoyed applauding and bowing, but most of all it was gratifying to see that every sib awarded Jiminy a gold medal for his brave and outstanding behaviour in spite of all his problems.

These were the basic 'Pinocchio' ideas I worked out to explore the siblings' conflicts. Dramatherapy and 'flexibility' are, of course, synonymous and so some pieces were used, others not, or changes were made when the need arose. As one would expect, the children themselves had many ideas of their own and often came up with completely different material to that which I envisaged! For example, in Session no. 8, in one of the older groups (12+), *all* the members decided to make only 'miraculous' gifts and they were thrilled to receive 'magic spoons', 'miracle potions' which cure all problems, 'amazing' hammers which knock on extra amounts to one's self-esteem and other 'wishful-thinking' accessories. This, of course, was all right with me: dramatherapy is all about using material which is relevant and meaningful for the clients.

RESULTS

Figure and family drawings

Both during the home interviews and in a separate room after the final session was completed, each group member was asked to draw: (1) a figure; and (2) a family picture.

Comparisons were made of the drawings by an art therapist and a developmental psychologist, in order to note changes in the children's self-image, expression of feelings and changes in attitude. Notice was taken specifically of the following details:
In the 'individual' drawing:

1 size of the figure
2 body shape
3 any emphasis made on the body
4 placement of the figure

In the 'family' drawing:

1 additions or omissions of family members
2 placement of individual figures
3 the style in which individuals are drawn

Some 'before' and 'after' drawings were examined and compared with the following results. (Note that some of the drawings are not illustrated.)

The 'individual' figures

'Before' (Fig. 7.5a)

1 Sexless figure
2 Stick-figure without a well-defined body image
3 Negative facial expression

'After' (Fig. 7.5b)

1 Clear female figure
2 Good body image
3 Positive facial expression

'Before' (Fig. 7.5c)

1 Girl figure
2 Side profile of face and body
3 Drawn very small

'After' (Fig. 7.5d)

1 Girl's face only
2 Full view
3 Whole-page drawing

The 'family' drawings

This sib is the eldest daughter in the family. She had an older brother with Down's syndrome.

'Before' (Fig. 7.6a)
All eleven family members are drawn as stick figures and there is no way to identify any individual.

'After' (Fig. 7.6b)

1 The eleven faces have been clearly and carefully detailed and named
2 'Mother's' eyes are closed
3 The eldest brother's hat fits straight on to his forehead, he has no 'head' area drawn in

(a)   (b)

Figure 7.5a and b 'Before' and 'after' figure drawing

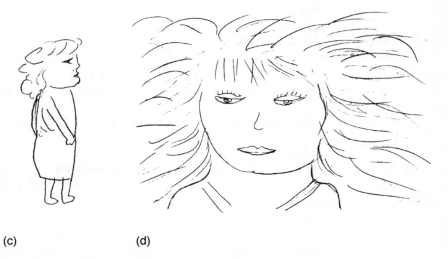

(c)   (d)

Figure 7.5c and d 'Before' and 'after' figure drawing

(a)

(b)

Figure 7.6a and b 'Before' and 'after' family drawing

The following sib is the eldest daughter in a family of five; the youngest brother has Down's syndrome.

'*Before*' (no illustration)

1 Siblings are placed in order of age, one after the other
2 Mother is drawn close to the eldest daughter

'*After*' (no illustration)

1 Work is now drawn in a creative, metaphorical style
2 Attention is brought in a positive way to the younger brother, who is placed higher than the other siblings and has the word 'kiss' written next to him
3 The parents are drawn together and the children are placed separately below them

The next sib is the eldest in a family of eight children. She has two handicapped siblings but the youngest sister, aged 3, has Cornelia de Langue syndrome, with many developmental disabilities.

'*Before*' (no illustration)

1 Only the siblings have been drawn
2 The children are divided into two separate groups

3 The youngest sib is less well-defined than the others (appears blob-like)
4 The oldest girl is clearly the largest figure

'*After*' *(*no illustration)

1 Mother and Father are now present
2 The children are now together in one row, above the parents
3 All eyes, except those of the parents and eldest daughter, are now open
4 The youngest child now has similar features to the rest of his siblings, though there is some distance between him and the last brother

In this, the final example, our sib is the eldest daughter in a family of three children.

'*Before*' (Fig 7.7a)

1 Four family members are drawn
2 They appear to be joined together as a group by connecting arms

'*After*' (Fig. 7.7b)

1 The arms no longer 'hold' on to one another
2 Another family member has been drawn in

Here are some of the changes noted by comparing the 'before' and 'after' family and figure drawings of the children.

1 Changes were seen in the larger size of 'figures' presented in the drawings which were made after the tenth session, in comparison to those drawn before the first meeting (e.g. Fig. 7.5c/7.5d)
2 In the second set of drawings, empty faces were given facial details – also facial expressions changed (e.g. Figs.7.5a/b, 7.6a/b)
3 Proportions of body parts changed (e.g. Fig. 7.5a/b)
4 The presentation of a 'parentified' child figure in the first drawing which changed to a child figure in the second drawing
5 The appearance of an additional child figure in the second family drawing, representing the handicapped child. A change in the appearance of the handicapped child was noted. (e.g. Fig. 7.7a/b)
6 The style and position of figures on the paper differed in the drawings (e.g. Fig. 7.5a/b).

Most prominent on further examination and comparison of the figure and family drawings were the positive changes in their quality and content. This would appear to show that, during the process of working in the group, the children's self-confidence improved, as did their ability to express their feelings. In general we saw more acceptance of the handicapped sibling –

(a)

(b)

Figure 7.7a and b 'Before' and 'after' family drawing

this was shown when, in the second work, the handicapped sibling was drawn as a part of the family, whereas in the first drawing he had either not been drawn in at all, drawn separated from the rest of the family, or had been represented by a figure without a clear face or body. In the second drawing he was placed together with the other children in the family and showed a resemblance to them. We saw that the 'final figure drawings' of the children showed differences in size, facial expression and body image. The drawings were more complex and detailed, both creatively and expressively. Figures were also more centred on the page or placed towards the left side of the paper and were in general more grounded (fewer floating figures). The changes appeared in all the drawings with no relevance to age difference or participation in a specific work group.

DISCUSSION

In all of the three groups, importance was attached to the considerable length of time allowed for work on the discovery and expression of feelings such as hate, anger, jealousy and fear. Shame and uncomfortable feelings around the subject of handicap was shown by the sibs' wide use of denial and closely guarded secrets. This could have played a prominent role in preventing those sibs over the age of 11 from coming and participating in the groups and may also contribute to their drop-out rate. Eighteen sibs took part initially and a total of twelve finished. However, it became noticeable during the development of all three groups that the members were increasing their ability to overcome their feelings of shame, and their willingness to speak more freely within the group about their 'secrets' was evident. It would appear that being part of a peer group offered an atmosphere of support and encouragement allowing for the building of self-confidence and the courage to face up to realities connected to their situation. The meetings became a place where the expression of feelings, discussion of common problems and a place to listen and be listened to were the accepted norms.

It was extremely interesting to observe how the stages of group development within the three groups (in relation to the model presented by Yalom (1970)) showed themselves through the choice of characters for the improvisations, and to compare how the different psycho-social roles (according to Erikson's theories, Erikson 1977) were expressed via the varying subject matters of the mini-dramas by the different age groups. The younger group members (groups 1 and 2) were more involved with the subject of 'The Family' and the interactions of different members, whereas the third group, comprising the older members, found interest in the subject of 'The Individual in Society', and the matter of 'how *I* am affected by my sib's handicap' was a central theme.

The technique of using the dramatic metaphor enabled the group members to find their own individual pace in relation to when and how they chose to relate to their problems – whether to remain at some distance and remain within the 'dramatic reality' or to come closer to facing their difficulties by moving into the 'everyday reality' (Jennings 1987, 1990, 1993). Doris, the same girl who had cried during the home interview, said, 'My closed sack with the heavy weights in it has opened a little now. It still has weights in it, but it's much lighter today.' Paula, the intellectual of the group, said, 'I'll take the present of courage with me, so I can start talking to my "outside" friends too.' 'Wow, we did a lot of work,' was proudly announced by numerous members. 'Yes,' agreed another, *but we didn't talk about our handicapped brothers!'*. Two others looked at her, then smiled knowingly at each other, saying in quiet unison, *'But Pinocchio was our brother!'*

CONCLUSIONS

The changes apparent at the end of the work process show primarily the importance and necessity of support groups for the social and emotional development of healthy children who have handicapped siblings. Acceptance and confirmation of their own feelings were assisted by listening to other group members. The knowledge that, 'There are others like me,' helped a great deal in bringing them closer to expressing themselves. The creative metaphor, with its distancing techniques, really bypassed our sibs' defences and gave them access to create the foundations for change. Working creatively in new and different ways enabled them to explore new perspectives. Dramatherapy is just what the sibs need to help them begin expressing themselves and allow them, when ready, to link up with their own life experiences.

It was clear from discussions with the sibs that neither they nor many of the parents were aware that healthy children could have emotional difficulties because of the handicap of a family member. It is felt to be of the utmost importance that our colleagues in child development, psychological services and in special education continue their work, not only with the special child and his parents, but with all the family members, including healthy siblings. Training courses in dramatherapy for professionals who run such groups would clearly be an added help and would greatly contribute to the growth of all those involved.

REFERENCES

Bax, M. (1990) Brothers and sisters. *Developmental Medicine and Child Neurology,* 32: 1035–1036.
Erikson, E. (1977) *Childhood and Society.* London: Paladin.

Gersie, A. (1987) Dramatherapy and play. In S. Jennings (ed.) *Dramatherapy Theory and Practice, 1*. London: Routledge.

Hanochi, N. (1986) Summary of Zeider's (1985) paper for Mercaz Akim [Israeli Society for Retarded Children], Israel.

Jennings, S. (ed.) (1987) *Dramatherapy Theory and Practice, 1*. London: Routledge.

———— (1990) *Dramatherapy with Families, Groups and Individuals*. London: Jessica Kingsley.

———— (1993) *Play Therapy with Children: a practitioners' guide*. Oxford: Blackwell.

Lahad, M. (1992) Six-piece story-making and dramatherapy. In S. Jennings (ed.) *Dramatherapy Theory and Practice, 2*. London: Routledge.

Landy, R. (1993) *Persona and Role Play*. New York: Guilford Press

Lee, D. (1991) Stories that Heal. In Work Book, Conference on Psychology, Health, Immunity and Disease, 4–7 Dec., Orlando, Florida.

Mills, J. C. and Crawley, R.J. (1986) *Therapeutic Metaphors for Children and the Child Within*. New York: Brunner, Mazel.

Murray, G. and Jampolsky, G.G. (eds.) (1982) *Straight from the Siblings: another look at the rainbow*. Millbrae, Ca., Celestial Arts.

Scheff, T.J. (1986) Concepts in drama therapy: the beginning of a theoretical model. In R. Landy (ed.) *Drama Therapy, Concepts and Practices*. Springfield, Ill.: Charles Thomas.

Segal, E. (1974) 'Psychoanalytical thought and methodology in dance-movement therapy', *Dance Therapy – Focus on Dance* VI:27. Washington, D.C.: American Dance Therapy Association Registry.

Snoonit, M. (1984) *The Soul Bird*. Israel: Masada Press.

Wheeler, S. (1993) Article in the *Independent*, Tuesday 17 August.

Yalom, I. (1970) *The Theory and Practice of Group Psychotherapy*. New York: Basic Books.

Zeider, Y. (1985) 'The regular siblings of the exceptional child'. Lecture given to Akim [Israeli Society for Retarded Children], Israel on 2 December 1985.

Chapter 8

From adolescent trauma to adolescent drama

Group drama therapy[1] with emotionally disturbed youth

Renée Emunah

Adolescence is a tumultuous life stage. An onslaught of changes revolutionizes the adolescent's sense of identity and challenges the adolescent with multi-level developmental tasks. Additionally, drives and unresolved conflicts from earlier stages of development re-emerge (Erikson 1968). Many adolescents, especially those in dysfunctional family situations, are unable to master effectively the multiple challenges and resort to acting-out behaviour, delinquent activity, substance abuse, withdrawal, or even suicide.

This chapter will explore the use of group drama therapy as a vehicle for helping adolescents, particularly those considered emotionally disturbed, to express and contain internal turmoil. The dramatic mode becomes a container within which the trauma of adolescence can safely be explored and mastered. The ways in which the psychological dangers inherent in this life stage can be converted into opportunities for significant intrapsychic and interpersonal growth will be examined.

The ideas and examples presented in the chapter are largely drawn from my work over twelve years at the youth centre of a psychiatric hospital. The centre served adolescents between 12 and 17 years old. Many of the clients were considered to be emotionally disturbed and had various psychiatric diagnoses, though the term 'adjustment reaction to adolescence' became increasingly prevalent in describing clients' conditions. This term was not only more innocuous than diagnostic labels indicating pathology, but also affirmed the tempestuous and disturbing nature of adolescence as a life passage.

My groups of five to nine clients met twice-weekly. Some members remained in the group (and at the facility) for only one month (totalling eight sessions); others continued for up to six months (totalling forty-eight sessions) of drama therapy treatment. Given the brief hospital stay of many of the clients, much of my focus was on finding creative ways of engaging the group and circumventing or making constructive use of resistance (Emunah 1985).

My approach focused on interactive techniques and the dramatization of fictional but realistic scenes. The fictional mode fostered an atmosphere of safety and permission, while the realistic nature of the scenes grabbed the group's attention. Issues and themes relevant to all group members were explored, enabling the group to experience a sense of commonality and universality. This sociodramatic approach (Moreno 1943, Sternberg and Garcia 1989) was integrated with playful work designed to elicit the group's spontaneity and healthfulness, as well as with in-depth personal, psychodramatic enactments with groups whose membership had been consistent over several months.

Based on my own experience and research (Emunah 1985, 1990, 1994), and that of other drama therapists working with this age group (including but not limited to Dequine and Pearson-Davis 1983, Shuttleworth 1981, Jennings and Gersie 1987, Furman 1990, Johnson and Eicher 1990, Pitzele 1991), I believe that drama therapy has a unique and critical role to play in helping young people through the tumultuous life passage known as adolescence.

The chapter begins with an overview of developmental and social factors contributing to the upheaval experienced in adolescence. The relationship between adolescent trauma and adolescent drama is then explored by focusing on four significant factors:

1 the connection between acting out and acting;
2 the interplay between emotional expression and containment;
3 the experimentation with roles; and
4 the impact of collaboration and intimacy.

THE TRAUMA OF ADOLESCENCE

The late childhood, or latency, period has been described by Erik Erikson as a 'moratorium'; in contrast to earlier and later developmental challenges, this period is characterized by relative stability and freedom from major internal conflict. But the personal and social equilibrium attained during latency is dramatically disrupted by the onslaught of adolescence.

The onslaught is instigated by striking physical, sexual, cognitive, psychological, and social changes. The adolescent's body undergoes a spurt of rapid growth along with sexual maturation and hormonal fluctuation. The adolescent becomes concerned with bodily appearance and anxious as the inevitable comparisons between one's own evolving body and that of one's peers are made, and as a new concept of body image and identity is sought.

Thinking and reasoning capacities also undergo rapid development (Piaget 1952). The adolescent becomes capable of abstract thinking and of introspection. Adolescent thought is no longer tied to concrete reality and to the present, but can more fully encompass the future. The heightened consciousness leads to contemplation of future scenarios and possibilities, consequences of past actions, hopes and ideals, and finally to existential dilemmas and moral choices (Gilligan 1982, Kohlberg 1981).

Psychologically, the adolescent undergoes a difficult period of individuation, in many ways reminiscent of the struggle for identity and autonomy faced by 2-year-olds, who attempt to define themselves via opposition and rebelliousness (the infamous 'no!'). Parallels have been drawn between Margaret Mahler's formulation of separation–individuation in very early childhood and the adolescent process (Mahler, Pine and Bergman 1975, Esman 1980, Kramer 1980). The sub-phases within separation–individuation correspond to various stages within adolescence, with the final phase, *rapprochement*, having the most dramatic parallels. The adolescent, like the 2-year-old undergoing *rapprochement*, experiences an intense conflict between assertion and dependence. When the adolescent turns back to the parent for security, support, and a sense of closeness, fears are evoked of 'regressive engulfment and dedifferentiation, leading to renewed assertions of autonomy and individuation, or desperate searches for substitute attachment objects' (Esman 1980: 287). As with the 2-year-old, the anxiety and insecurity evoked by what Blos (1968) calls the 'second individuation' phase in life are often manifested by approach/avoidance behaviour, tantrums, and acting out.

Rebelliousness is a particularly typical manifestation of the conflicted desire for independence. The adolescent resists and defies rules imposed by authority figures as a means of professing a newly developing sense of self. The assertion of differences from others – typically parents – and similarities to particular peer groups gives a semblance of new identity and independence. The desire for independence is fraught with ambivalence: independence implies not only freedom but responsibility and loss – responsibility for decision-making and loss of the protection of childhood.

The loosening of ties to infantile object relations is accompanied by loneliness, sadness, and confusion. Blos (1962) considers the adolescent experience of separation from emotional ties to family and entrance into a new stage of life 'among the profoundest in human existence'. In the shift of allegiance from the parent as the primary love object to the self and to the peer group, the adolescent is obsessed by the need for affirmation by his or her peers. Interactions with peers carry tremendous weight, leading to fluctuating moods and often a deep sense of isolation.

The 'storminess' of adolescence (Erikson 1968) is not only the result of the complex and overwhelming new challenges, but of the fact that drives and unresolved conflicts from earlier stages re-emerge and demand resolution. Adolescence has been called a second edition of childhood because, according to Blos, 'the significant emotional needs and conflicts of early childhood must be recapitulated before new solutions with qualitatively different instinctual aims and ego interests can be found' (Blos 1962:11). Unfortunately, families often have difficulty empathically fostering, containing, and guiding this process.

All major life transitions and upheavals contain the potential for disturbance, as well as for personal growth. The therapeutic potential inherent in the adolescent life stage has been, according to Blos (ibid.), underestimated. He believes that the emotional turmoil of adolescence can offer the opportunity to resolve important childhood conflicts and to surmount prior emotional obstacles. Erikson points out that adolescence is not an affliction but a "normative crisis", that is, a normal phase characterized by increased conflict and fluctuation in ego strength, and yet also a high growth potential' (Blos 1962: 11).

This state of both high risk and high growth potential makes adolescence a prime time for psychotherapy. Creative arts therapy is an obvious choice of treatment given that:

1 the internal chaos and emotionality experienced in adolescence demand external expression and acknowledgment;
2 there is a heightened creativity during adolescence (Blos 1962); and
3 aesthetic sensibility, as one type of conceptual thinking, develops during adolescence (Spiegel 1958).

Creative arts therapy offers a vehicle for eliciting and encouraging the strengths and healthful aspects of the adolescent's developing self, and for reducing the risks inherent in this life stage.

A 1989 report of the Carnegie Council on Adolescent Development estimates that 7 million young people – one in four adolescents – are extremely vulnerable to multiple high-risk behaviours and school failure, and another one in four adolescents may be at moderate risk. 'In other words, half of all adolescents are at some risk for serious problems like substance abuse, early, unprotected sexual intercourse, dangerous, accident-prone lifestyles, delinquent behavior . . . ' (Hersch 1990). Contemporary Western society has not been very helpful: the lack of community, of extended family, of meaningful avenues for expression or ways of demonstrating worthiness and of ritual all contribute to adolescent alienation.

The 'storminess' of adolescence is less likely to result in permanent deleterious conditions when intervention is offered during the storm; in fact, the storminess itself provides a positive force for emotional growth. Arts modalities can match the intensity and complexity of the adolescent's experience, and provide a non-threatening and constructive means of communicating tumultuous feelings and thoughts (Emunah 1990). When communication occurs in an intimate and empathic setting with others, in the form of group therapy, alienation is reduced. The sense of universality

(Yalom 1985) and community which develop over time sustain and reinforce the healthful experience.

FROM ACTING OUT TO ACTING

Acting out is a common manifestation of the internal turmoil experienced by the disturbed adolescent. It can be a cry to be seen, heard, and understood, paradoxically accompanied by defiance and revolt – against authority figures, 'helpers', and even the self. The language of acting out is dramatic rather than verbal; it is action-oriented. Both a rational, verbal response by an adult to acting-out behaviour, and attempts at encouraging the acting-out teen to revert to a rational, verbal mode are usually ineffectual. The dramatic mode corresponds more closely to the language of acting out. In fact, when acting out is 'translated' into acting, the result is often a powerful form of communication and therapy.

Acting-out adolescents already possess keen dramatic abilities: acting out tends to be dramatic, expressive, energetic, focused, compelling, and provocative. Acting-out adolescents are good actors, provided the characters being portrayed are themselves. An approach to therapy in which acting-out adolescents can express themselves in their own language – but within a safe, contained structure – and at the same time experience success and reward for their self-expression, is warranted. Drama therapy provides such an approach. In drama therapy, adolescent acting out is converted into acting, and the stage becomes a laboratory setting in which real life can be explored with safety and distance (Emunah 1985).

Acting offers an outlet for a wide range of emotions, at the same time requiring distance or separation from these emotions (Emunah 1983). The actor who is in a rage on stage is at that moment actually in touch with his or her own rage, at least in 'method acting' (Stanislavski 1936); even many of the same physiological conditions (as a person in a real rage) are experienced. But rather than complete immersion in the rage, in which nothing else but feeling exists, the actor is aware of him- or herself. Strong feeling is not suppressed but mastered. The dual level of consciousness in acting is reminiscent of spiritual practices in which one maintains a level of disengagement, or higher consciousness, rather than becoming completely 'caught up in the action'.

The translation, or conversion, of acting out to acting is a matter of adding to the former a degree of consciousness. Acting out is defined as a psychological defence mechanism by which an individual discharges internal impulses through symbolic or actual enactment (Blatner 1988a, Kellerman 1984, Ormont 1969):

Since the rationale for this defense mechanism occurs largely outside of consciousness, the individual experiences no sense of mastery or growth of self-understanding through the behavior. If the drive toward action could be channeled, the person might be able to make better use of the feelings.

(Blatner 1988a: 1–2)

Insight about the defensive nature of acting out is not necessary for the drive toward action to be channelled. The channelling of the drive can precede the more gradual unravelling of the underlying emotions and conflicts, thereby averting non-constructive behaviour in the interim.

The following example illustrates the conversion from acting out to acting:

Tony was a small but tough and angry 15-year-old with poor impulse control. Another boy, Daron, rushed excitedly into the room and knocked into Tony, probably accidentally. Tony yelled out, 'What the f— are you doing, you mother-f— bastard,' as he kicked Daron. Daron was about to strike back when I shouted, 'Freeze!'

Both boys stopped, rather startled. 'What the f— do you want?' Tony said, glaring at me. 'We're going to replay what just happened, as actors,' I said, knowing that if more than a few seconds went by there was little chance they would go along with my plan; the energy of the moment had to be capitalized upon. 'Yeah, sure, I'll play him and show him what it's like,' retorted Tony. 'I didn't mean to bump into you, man,' claimed Daron. 'You're so touchy. What's your problem?' 'Okay,' I interrupted, 'Tony, you come rushing in as Daron did, only the point where you crash we'll have to just pretend – no real contact. Daron, you get as mad as Tony just did – but without any hitting. Then Tony will respond with what Daron just said – "I didn't mean to bump into you . . . "'

The re-enactment was nearly as realistic as the real-life scene preceding it. The role-reversal facilitated some distance and perspective. Then we replayed the scene as it initially happened, with Tony and Daron playing themselves. We paused the action to examine each boy's internal reaction. During the third replay, in which we no longer interrupted the action, Tony responded differently: 'Daron, man, watch where you're going. You know I'm touchy about being bumped into.' 'Sorry, Tony,' Daron said. 'I was going too fast, 'cause I was excited about something. Guess what?'

Behaviour that was out of control was now in control. A dual level of consciousness, in which one observes oneself rather than remaining in a state of blind reactivity, was achieved. Equal in significance to the bit of self-mastery, insight, and behavioural change that these brief enactments facilitated was the reaction of peers watching the scenes. Three teens walked into the room during the enactments, saying, 'Is that real or are you guys acting?' When the scenes ended, Tony and

Daron proudly reported that they were acting. 'It looked so real, man' – 'That is really bad' ('bad' in American slang means good!) – 'You guys are good actors,' were the responses of the audience. And then, 'I want to try a fight scene,' and, 'Let's do some more acting!'

EXPRESSION AND CONTAINMENT

Even when the scenes enacted in drama therapy are not replays of actual life scenarios, the adolescents' creations are generally autobiographical (Blos 1962). The degree of distance between self and product during adolescence tends to be minimal. Dramatic enactment – encompassing a wide range of scenes from the imaginary to the psychodramatic – facilitates both expression and containment of inner pain, conflict, confusion and turmoil, as well as of excitement, longing and hope.

Dramatic enactment offers not only emotional release and catharsis, but also containment and a sense of internal control. The expression of feeling is obviously critical at a time when one is bombarded by strong and conflictual emotions. At the same time, the attainment of a sense of mastery over emotion is a primary psychic task of adolescence (Blos 1962). The interplay and balance between expression and containment are central components of drama therapy (Emunah 1983, 1994).

In the context of a drama therapy group, adolescents spontaneously elect to enact real-life feelings. In a guessing game in which one person leaves the room while the others decide on an emotion or attitude to portray when the person re-enters, typical selections are: hostile, rebellious, resistant, angry, depressed, confused. The choices often reflect actual moods in the room on that particular day. It is not uncommon for a group that greeted me with hostility and resistance soon to express their feelings and fears via the game, thereby averting resistance to me or to the process. The expression of hostility or resistance in the game is gradually exaggerated, resulting in cathartic release, along with humour and self-awareness. The allowance to 'play oneself' also promotes a sense of acceptance and tolerance. Most importantly, the feelings, attitudes or behaviours are contained within the safety of the game and the structure of acting. The adolescents find they can be masters of their own feelings, often even to the point of relinquishing those feelings when the game is over.

More complex dramatic processes, such as sustained scene-work, also afford the experience of expression and containment. For example, teenagers may improvise a dramatic and emotional scene revolving around a familial conflict. The teenagers may not have an outlet for the expression of these strong feelings in real life, because such expression could result in retaliation by unstable parents; the teenagers may have learned early in life not to express feelings directly. Or the expression of strong feelings in real life may tend rapidly to escalate into acting out. In the scene, however, the feelings remain contained – under the auspices of acting.

During the enactment of an emotional scene (regardless of whether the content of the scene is fictional or based on actual events), the drama therapist is constantly assessing the client's tolerance for emotional expression. Expression and catharsis are encouraged, but only to a point the client (and the other members of the group) can safely handle. When the drama therapist senses that the client has reached his or her tolerance of emotional expression, she facilitates the necessary distancing and containment. The risk of expression past this point is that the client becomes overwhelmed, which could lead to acting out, dissociation, or a delayed destructive or self-destructive response.

Providing some distance does not mean ending the scene (though this is one obvious option). Interventions can be made within the dramatic mode, with the client still maintaining contact with his or her present state of emotionality. The objective here is for emotional containment and mastery to be integrated with emotional expression, rather than for containment to imply aborting feelings to regain self-control.

The following are some examples of the ways in which the drama therapist can 'pause' and then redirect the enactment to facilitate containment and help the client achieve some distance. (These examples are not formulas, and need to be utilized with discretion, intuition, and careful reflection on the part of the therapist. The use of he/him/his is purely for ease of expression.)

1 In a scene involving a childhood trauma, in which the client is playing the role of himself as a child, he can be asked to become his current age, and then – from this vantage point – talk to the child he was.
2 In a scene (in which the client is playing himself) that has become too charged, the client can be asked to leave the enacted interaction in order to enact a phone call or visit to a close friend, with whom he can talk about what just happened.
3 In a scene about communication, the client can be asked to switch roles with his fellow player.
4 In a scene in which the client feels overwhelmed with or confused by multiple feelings, he can be asked to identify and then have others in the group play out all the different feelings he has at this moment.

The dramatic processes cited thus far in this section are process-oriented. Dramatic processes can also be product-oriented, typically involving work towards a performance or video project. Even when an outside audience will not be involved, the drama therapist can choose to highlight the aesthetic component to dramatic work. The group creates dramatic pieces that communicate their inner worlds in a powerful and artistic fashion. For example, teenagers may create a multi-media rock video exploring rage and despair (Emunah 1990), an original performance dealing with substance abuse, or a sequence of scenes about their dreams.

The aesthetic process of giving form and shape to a dramatic piece elicits internal resources and develops a sense of mastery. Expression becomes associated with creativity rather than with volatile acting out. Adolescents learn that they can be actors rather than reactors. The secondary processes inherent in creativity (Arieti 1976), in which inner material is synthesized with a rational structuring and organization, help the adolescent regain internal equilibrium (Emunah 1990). The decision-making, editing, and refining of the creative work elicit the director within, a director that can be an asset not only to creative endeavours, but to life challenges.

The heightening of the aesthetic component to dramatic work also facilitates expression and communication. Feelings that cannot be easily articulated are nevertheless powerfully communicated – both to others (the therapist, the group, and/or an outside audience) and to the self – via an artistic form. The externalization of an internal experience allows it to be better understood and assimilated. Issues and feelings are identified and clarified, but not reduced or simplified; nuances, complexities, and subtleties are conveyed. The clients find that their experiences – in all their fullness – can be witnessed and comprehended by others.

A LABORATORY FOR ROLE EXPERIMENTATION

Jacob Moreno, the founder of psychodrama, believed that our self is essentially composed of the many roles we play (Moreno 1946), a view to which most drama therapists and psychodramatists adhere.[2] In the process of expressing ourselves through many roles, we begin to see ourselves clearly. Drama therapist Robert Landy states: 'It is in the doing and seeing and accepting and integrating of all the roles, the "me" parts, that the person emerges intact' (Landy 1990: 230).

Substantial role experimentation during adolescence, which includes a shifting and evolving sense of self, is appropriate and healthy. Erik Erikson (1968) considers 'role confusion' (as opposed to 'role diffusion') a normal developmental aspect of adolescence. It is important that adolescents have the opportunity to integrate roles from past stages in their lives and to experiment with future roles. The psychological potentiality in adolescence to resolve issues from earlier developmental stages and the cognitive capacity in adolescence to envision future possibilites make this stage of life a prime time to explore roles. Moreover, the multiple changes experienced during adolescence require a kind of role fluidity which can be supported via role experimentation.

However, role experimentation can be very frightening and threatening for adolescents, especially for adolescents who do not have a reassuring, accepting, and supportive home and peer environment. These adolescents in particular need help with the process of exploring, expressing, discovering and expanding role possibilities. Many crave a stable sense of identity, and wish for that identity to ward off the turmoil in their internal and external worlds. The reawakening of the past and the awakening of the future compound the turmoil and can lead to a yearning for coherence and reassurance in the present.

The danger is that, rather than healthy role experimentation, the adolescent in turmoil will resort to role restriction. Two potentially deleterious forms of role restriction are extremism and overconstriction (Breger 1974, Freud 1958). In extremism, the adolescent overly attaches him- or herself to some new group or identity in an attempt to make a revolutionary break from dependency or from past attachments and identities. In overconstriction, the adolescent conforms too soon to an adult role which is considered to be socially acceptable. Essentially, the adolescent forces him- or herself to fit a prescribed role rather than experimenting with many different roles.

Drama therapy provides a laboratory setting in which adolescents can experiment with numerous roles, without long-term commitment or consequence. In dramatherapy, one not only takes on roles, but also discards, revises, and transforms roles. The improvisational mode allows for the role fluidity which is a developmentally critical aspect to adolescence. The engagement in a dramatherapy process, in which one can embody without surrendering to or merging with any given role, circumvents a premature, permanent solidification of identity.

The fact that one is 'only acting' is liberating; play and pretend offer a protective shield from the real world. In this safe and permissive context, familiar roles can be explored, latent roles can be unearthed, idealized roles can be examined, feared roles can be practised. Past roles can be reviewed, discarded, or integrated. Future roles can be tried on and previewed. The structured, laboratory setting reduces adolescents' fears of diffusion, ridicule, or typecasting. All parts enacted in a dramatherapy group are respected and accepted. This process of role experimentation and expansion brings about a sense of freedom and possibility, offsetting the propensity during adolescence towards extremism or overconstriction.

The drama therapist facilitates not only the embodiment of roles, but also the letting go of these roles, or the 'de-roling' process, once the scene ends. It is important that adolescents do not feel stuck in their roles, or overly consumed by any given role. The process of de-roling, in which the distinction between the scene and real life is underscored, relates to the issue of expression and containment. The drama therapist insures that the adolescent does not 'get lost' in either an emotion or a role; her interventions promote the fine balance between expression and containment and between role embodiment and role detachment.

Over time, adolescents in drama therapy develop a sense of 'identity cohesion', as they come to accept, own, and be masters of the wide range of roles that encompass their beings. The experience of being the conductor, or director, to all these roles – so that any given role is not larger than themselves but rather a part of themselves – facilitates the sense of cohesion.

Role experimentation in drama therapy with adolescents generally begins with social roles. The roles are fictional rather than personal, but they are relevant and familiar. The fictional mode provides the distance necessary at the early stages of the process, but the realistic content grabs the group's attention. Teenagers play 'a dad', rather than their own father, a best friend, a teacher, a determined student, a rebel. They play authority figures, defiant teenagers, frightened children, drug addicts, adults with rewarding careers. The generalized roles evoke personal responses. And these discussions gradually lead to the enactment of scenes in which the group members play themselves, as well as their parents, siblings, therapists, teachers, and peers. They play themselves in various hypothetical and real current situations, themselves at various past stages of their lives, their potential future selves.

In playing hypothetical scenarios involving conflict and decision-making, or scenes involving future roles, the adolescent's evolving capacity to confront ethical dilemmas and to envision future possibilities is exercised and supported. In playing scenes involving childhood roles, the potential in adolescence for reworking and resolving earlier conflicts is strengthened.

Idealized figures are examined in drama therapy. Teenagers whose main aspirations are to become wealthy drug dealers have the opportunity to try on this role and way of life. In the early stages of a group process, glorification may take over and any attempts on the part of the therapist to facilitate a deeper level of probing will be premature. But over time, as the group members come to trust one another and the therapist, and as the acting evolves from superficial to authentic and multilayered portrayals, exploration is natural. The characters undergo in-depth interviewing, replaying of earlier events in their lives, 'doubling' (in which group members voice internal thoughts and feelings), and dissection of unconscious motivation. In numerous drama therapy sessions with delinquent adolescents, group members have discovered on their own that the draw to the role of drug dealer is the longing for power. This discovery is typically followed by an exploration of different kinds of power, and the brainstorming and enactment of other ways of achieving a sense of power.

Positive idealized figures, including heros and heroines that offer hope, also come to life in the drama therapy session. The characteristics that make these figures important are examined, and then incorporated in diverse ways, including playing oneself infused with the desired traits.

Many dramatic processes facilitate the examination of self-perceptions, including the ways in which one feels perceived by others. Teenagers may be interviewed as significant other people in their lives (e.g. a parent, sibling, best friend), who speak about them. For example, Tony, the client mentioned earlier, role-played his younger brother Michael. 'Michael' was then asked questions (by the group, who played interviewers) about brother Tony. Thus, Tony's perceptions of the way he is perceived by Michael were explored.

Adolescents often experience a disturbing discrepancy between outer projections and inner feelings. Many drama therapy techniques help adolescents identify and express the way they believe they are perceived by others and the way they perceive themselves or 'feel inside'. For example, a group may be asked to create two masks – one of their personas and the other of their internal view of themselves.

Psychodramatist Peter Pitzele refers to much of his work with emotionally disturbed adolescents as intrapsychic psychodrama (Pitzele 1991). He describes viewing the faces of his clients as masks, and viewing the masks as roles. He then sets out to meet the mask, often through dramatic engagement, in the hope that the world beneath the mask will eventually be exposed. 'If I can meet the mask with my spontaneity, then like some questor seeking to gain admittance to a secret world, I may pass to the interior' (ibid.: 18).

A technique which I utilize frequently to help adolescents explore facets of themselves is to ask each person to create a sculpture by 'moulding' other people in the room into particular positions. Generally, three people are moulded, each depicting an aspect of the sculptor. This exercise can be developed by:

1 having the sculpture 'come alive';
2 asking the sculptor to take over the embodiment of one of the roles (and eventually to embody all three roles);
3 creating modifications in the original sculpture and live interaction among the three parts. This latter stage might entail revamping the sculpture to a configuration that is more representative of one's current or hoped-for state, or facilitating greater integration among the parts, or even adding a new part (Emunah 1994).

During the exploration of self-perceptions, adolescents receive immediate feedback from their peers. For example, group members may respond to one person's sculpture by saying, 'Yeah, I know that part of John,' or, 'I've never seen that side of you. I didn't know you had a spiritual side . . . '. The experience of having others see and accept the many parts of oneself cannot be overestimated; it stands among the most significant aspects of psychotherapy.

Even more important than the experience of acceptance is that of empathy. The live enactments in drama therapy communicate nuance and feeling in such a way that empathy is heightened. Those watching easily find aspects with which they identify or by which they are personally moved. Empathy among the adolescents themselves fosters a sense of mutuality and connectedness and facilitates the integration of new roles.

Case example

A frequent shift noted in adolescent drama therapy is from concealing pain via the adoption of a tough, impenetrable persona to gradually exposing the vulnerable self underneath. The following example, again of Tony, illustrates this process.

Tony exhibited an independent and invulnerable persona in dramatic scenes and in real life. He came from an alcoholic family. His parents had divorced when he was 8, and at 14 Tony was sent to live with his physically and emotionally abusive father. After one beating, Tony ran away from home. He lived on the streets for several weeks, until he was caught breaking a store window. After being evaluated, he was sent to the psychiatric hospital at which I worked.

One day in the drama therapy group Tony was cast by another boy as a father. As usual, he played the role in a highly authoritarian, cruel, and abusive fashion. At one point, he screamed, 'Get out of my house, you dumb, no-good bastard, before I beat the shit out of you.' Reversing roles, Tony responded to his father with, 'Sure, man, I don't need you anyways. Or anyone. I'm out of here.' And out he walked. Not only did he exit the scene, Tony literally exited the room.

I called him back. I knew the scene was very real for him. I also knew that at any minute he would dismiss the scene as acting, and the painful feelings aroused by the scene would be expressed indirectly, probably in the form of an outburst or fight later on. Attempting to keep him in the reality of the scene, I said, 'You're out of the house. You're walking the streets. These are the streets.' I motioned to the performance area of our room, thereby underscoring the need to stay in the room. Looking now toward the group, I asked, 'Who can play Tony's inner thoughts as he walks?' Two teenagers who strongly identified with and admired Tony, Leonard and Marie, jumped up. Following him as he walked around the performance area, they muttered, 'Good thing I'm out of there, man,' 'I don't give a damn about being there anyway,' 'I'm fine on my own.' Momentarily joining them to lend support, I added, 'I was smart to get out when I did. I know how to protect myself from getting hit by him.'

Then I asked the remaining members of the group, 'Who can be the thoughts and feelings behind these thoughts?' Daron and Robin entered the scene and began walking behind Leonard and Marie. 'Where should I go? I got nowhere to go,' Daron voiced. Robin listened for a while and finally spoke two words: 'I'm scared.' When I asked her to repeat these words, she said them with yet a deeper level of feeling.

As if released from their earlier stance, Leonard and Marie spontaneously joined Daron and Robin: 'This is kind of scary, man.' 'I wish I had a dad who loved me.' Tony stopped walking and looked up at me. 'This is real, man.'

I nodded in agreement, and suggested he join the chorus of inner feelings. I called upon David, the remaining member of the audience, to take over Tony's walking role. 'This is scary,' I heard Tony say softly in his new role. 'I got a lot of pain inside me.' Almost like a Greek chorus, the others echoed his words, supporting, encouraging, and affirming him. 'And I got to face it alone. The only way I'm gonna make it is by being tough. I gotta act strong. But inside I feel scared. And inside I'm real sad.'

Tony looked scared and sad. For the first time since his admission into the hospital, his face was soft with sorrow. The feeling of being frightened was not only a response to the content of the scene: I believe he was also afraid of being seen in a vulnerable role. My first priority was for him to experience acceptance by others of this new role. I knew that at any moment the tough persona could reassert itself.

We got into a circle and I invited the responses of the group. 'I know what Tony felt like, 'cause I've been there,' Leonard initiated. 'Scared inside, but acting tough, cause you gotta make it.' 'Yeah, I like to act like I'm okay, because I don't want my dad to know I care how he talks to me,' Marie chimes in. 'I think it was real good that you could be so real, Tony,' said David. 'It made me feel closer to you.' Daron added, 'It felt good to hear you say things that I feel sometimes too.'

At the following session, Tony opted to play the role of a father again, only this time he played the kind of father he would some day like to be. He spoke to his son in a soft, gentle voice, as he offered encouragement and praise. His facial expression was tender and loving. In the discussion afterward, Tony said, 'If I don't watch it I may grow up to be like my dad. I'm not really like him, but sometimes it seems I am because I act angry and mean like him. There's another part of me too. I'm not too sure what it's like. Maybe it's a little like the role I just played.'

The significance of empathy in psychotherapy has been stressed by many, particularly humanistic psychologists and self psychologists (Rogers 1951, Kohut 1977). In drama therapy, the empathy imparted by the therapist and the fellow group members as the outer invulnerable shell is shed facilitates the development of self-acceptance and esteem, and contributes to the overall therapeutic process of mastering internal turmoil via external, creative expression. The client literally experiences being seen (witnessed) and mirrored (often in the form of 'doubling') by both therapist and peers. The emotional, interactional, and dramatic processes in drama therapy foster and nurture the empathic climate. In this climate, clients are enabled to unearth, express, and tolerate denied pain and repressed roles.

GROUP COLLABORATION AND INTIMACY

In the reliving of the *rapprochement* sub-phase of separation–individuation, adolescents need a holding environment (Winnicott 1965) in which their turmoil can be tolerated. During this period of separation from primary love objects, adolescents need an environment that particularly supports the development of a peer group which, according to Blos, helps 'unify residues of split good and bad object representations' (Kramer 1980). The externalization of the split good and bad object representation on to the peer group helps bring about intrapsychic integration and independence from primary love objects (Blos 1976, Kramer 1980).

As the ties to the family are loosened, many adolescents experience a profound sense of loneliness and alienation. The new clan and attempted source of identity, the peer group, is fraught with conflict and uncertainty, and provides only sporadic relief from the pain. For the many adolescents who have not had a healthy bond in their childhood years with their family, and/or have not formed a healthy bond with a peer group, feelings of pain, loss, and isolation can be particularly intense.

Group therapy addresses the adolescent's developmental and social need for intense interaction with others of one's age, as well as the adolescent's longing to belong. Close ties with peers are naturally fostered in group work. The group becomes a forum in which one can solidify relationships with peers and express the pain of loss of primary familial ties and the ambivalent desire for independence – with others who are undergoing the same experience. Acceptance and 'consensual validation' (Yalom 1985), two primary curative factors in psychotherapy, are intensified in group therapy, because one is seen and heard not only by a therapist but by many people, and, in the case of adolescent group therapy, by people in one's same stage of life.

In group drama therapy, clients actively experience the universality of their dilemmas, reducing the sense of alienation and 'differentness' that plagues many adolescents. The dramatic games and scenes intentionally involve realistic enactments, rather than either highly imaginary scenes or re-enactments of particular real-life events. That is, the scenes are fictional (for the most part), but highly relevant, focusing on shared concerns within the group. Issues germane to all group members, such as relationships with parents and peers, are explored. The enactment of common themes and experiences generates a sense of kinship and connection between group members.

Peer interaction, an essential component of healthy adolescent development, is highlighted. Many of the structured games and 'warm-ups' to scenes are designed playfully to facilitate a high level of social interaction, trust, and collaboration. Competitive and individually-oriented games are avoided. The techniques are also designed to be failure-proof, age-appropriate, non-threatening, and engaging.

Once the group experiences its many layers and levels of commonality, and once a high level of trust and empathy is established, group members are also ready to tackle psychodramatic work in which specific real-life issues are revealed and explored. The disclosure of secrets, followed by empathic understanding by the group, offers an enormous sense of relief for the adolescent client. In drama therapy, the client experiences the support and empathy of the group not only by their verbal and non-verbal responses during discussions, but by their role-playing.

For example, 14-year-old Marie disclosed to the group that she had been sexually molested by her uncle when she was 11. Marie had already shared this information with several adult social workers and counsellors, but never with her peers. Marie directed a scene in which she confronted her uncle on the abuse. Robin was cast in the role of Marie. Via her role, Robin demonstrated her understanding of Marie's rage, pain, fear, and shame. When Marie later took over the role of herself, all the other group members 'doubled' for her, demonstrating their understanding and support of her tumultuous inner feelings.

Even though most members of this group had not experienced sexual abuse, each person felt connected to Marie's work. Tony, for example, had not been sexually abused, but he knew about physical abuse, humiliation, and shame. In the session following the one in which Marie shared her story, other group members enacted scenes in which they confronted family members about traumatic or unresolved aspects of their childhoods.

In drama therapy, the scenes can progress not only from the dramatic to the psychodramatic, but also from the psychodramatic to the dramatic. Individually oriented work is often followed by collective, group-oriented work. For example, in the scene described earlier (pp. 162–3) between Tony and his father, the progression was from a fictional scene about *a* father and *a* son to one that was really about Tony himself. Soon after that session, the group collaboratively worked over a number of sessions on the creation of a video show about hiding and revealing pain. The show involved a montage of poems and monologues, dance and music, artistic masks, and excerpts of dramatic interactions. The process of brainstorming ideas, making aesthetic decisions, refining and editing the final product entailed a high level of interaction and collaboration. Intimacy in this group was achieved by creative endeavours (such as the video project) and fictionalized scenes, as much as by the disclosure and enactment of directly personal material.

CONCLUSION

From a developmental standpoint, turmoil is expected during adolescence. For adolescents who come from dysfunctional families, this turmoil may better be described as trauma. Familial conflict and instability exacerbate the turmoil created by the substantial developmental challenges of adolescence, leading these teenagers to become overwhelmed. A common adolescent response to being overwhelmed is acting-out behaviour. Drama therapy can be utilized as a preventive measure, helping adolescents deal with powerful emotions and conflicts, in the hope of circumventing acting-out behaviour. Drama therapy can also be a treatment of choice for acting-out adolescents.

In drama therapy, the acting-out adolescent discharges destructive impulses via the process of acting. Communication occurs within his or her own dramatic and action-oriented language, but under the safe, contained auspices of dramatic acting and the guidance of a drama therapist. The overwhelming emotions underlying the acting-out behaviour are given outlet. Relief and catharsis are experienced as the adolescent expresses emotions and unravels the multiple aspects to his or her turmoil and pain. Concurrent with emotional expression is emotional containment. While the former brings relief and catharsis, the latter develops ego strength and an internal locus of control.

Once the adolescent experiences relief and mastery through the process of expression and containment of emotion, he or she is psychically freed to begin to tackle one of the developmentally critical tasks of this life stage: experimentation with roles. Drama therapy provides the permission to sample, preview, review, discard, and develop roles – an opportunity that all adolescents need! The exploration of diverse roles expands awareness about who one is, who one has been and who one is becoming. A sense of both clarity and possibility is experienced. Role restriction, a potentially deleterious reaction to adolescent turmoil and trauma – which can have severe repercussions in later life – is circumvented. In place of role restriction, the adolescent encounters the multifaceted nature of identity and the human capacity to renew and transform one's way of being in the world.

The intense and painful alienation so often experienced by adolescents is alleviated by participation in a highly active and interactive group. Commonalities are evidenced from the beginning of the process via the enactment of scenes that deal with shared issues. Even as the scenes progress from the more general to the more specific, from the fictional to the actual, and from the group to the individual, the sense of universality prevails. Once dramatized, the varying circumstances of individual stories are less important than the feelings they evoke, and these feelings are often ones with which others in the group are familiar. As one witnesses the trials and triumphs of others, empathy is heightened. And empathy, a great antidote for alienation, brings the group to a deeper level of cohesion and intimacy.

The dramas unearthed in the drama therapy session remind both clients and therapist of our common heritage and humanity, as we travel through the passages of life. Some of these passages are smooth sailing, and others – most notably and notoriously adolescence – are tumultuous, demanding support. Adolescent dramas evoke empathy – for at the same time that they help unravel, contain, and heal – the traumas of this consequential part of the life journey.

NOTES

1 The phrase 'drama therapy' as opposed to 'dramatherapy' (one word) has been used in this chapter in accordance with US style.
2 Psychodramatist Peter Pitzele suggests that we regard ourselves as a dynamic collective of roles, 'an "Our Town", a mythological realm, in which may be found characters or beings in various stages of development, some mutually communicative, some isolated, some nascent, others moribund' (Pitzele 1991: 16). Taking the view of self as a collective of roles a step further, drama therapist Robert Landy believes that the notion of self is superfluous and mythological. Rather than self, the roles we play are themselves the 'containers of all the thoughts and feelings we have about ourselves and others in our social and imaginary worlds' (Landy 1990: 230). Landy claims that in the absence of a self there still exists a 'primary dramatic process of identity'.

REFERENCES

Arieti, S. (1976) *Creativity: the magic synthesis*. New York: Basic Books.
Blatner, H. (1988a) *Acting In: practical applications of psychodramatic methods* (2nd edn). New York: Springer.
―――― (1988b) *Foundations of Psychodrama: history, theory, and practice* (with A. Blatner) (3rd edn). New York: Springer.
Blos, P. (1962) *On Adolescence: a psychoanalytic interpretation*. Glencoe, Ill.: The Free Press.
―――― (1968) The second individuation process of adolescence. *Psychoanalytic Study of the Child*, 22: 162–86.
―――― (1976) Split parental imagos and adolescent social relations: an inquiry into group psychology. *Psychoanalytic Study of the Child*, 31: 7–33.
Breger, L. (1974) *From Instinct to Identity: the development of personality*. New Jersey: Prentice-Hall.
Dequine, E. and Pearson-Davis, S. (1983) Videotaped improvisational drama with emotionally disturbed adolescents. *The Arts in Psychotherapy*, 12: 71–80.
Emunah, R. (1983) Drama therapy with adult psychiatric patients. *The Arts in Psychotherapy*, 10: 77–84.
―――― (1985) Drama therapy and adolescent resistance. *The Arts in Psychotherapy*, 12: 71–80.
―――― (1990) Expression and expansion in adolescence: the significance of creative arts therapy. *The Arts in Psychotherapy*, 17: 101–7.
―――― (1994) *Acting for Real: drama therapy process, technique, and performance*. New York: Brunner/Mazel.
Erikson, E. (1968) *Identity: youth and crisis*. New York: Norton.
Esman, A. (1980) Adolescent psychopathology and the rapprochement process. In

R. Lax, S. Bach and J. A. Burland (eds) *Rapprochement: the critical subphase of separation–individuation*. New York: Jason Aronson.

Freud, A. (1958) Adolescence. In *Psychoanalytic Study of the Child*, 13: 255–78.

Furman, L. (1990) Video therapy: an alternative for the treatment of adolescents. *The Arts in Psychotherapy*, 17: 165–9.

Gilligan, C. (1982) *In a Different Voice: psychological theory and women's development*. Cambridge, Mass.: Harvard University Press.

Hersch, P. (1990) The resounding silence. In *The Family Therapy Networker*, 14: 19–29.

Jennings, S. and Gersie, A. (1987) Dramatherapy with disturbed adolescents. In S. Jennings (ed.) *Dramatherapy Theory and Practice, 1*. London: Routledge.

Johnson, D. R. and Eicher, V. (1990) The use of dramatic activities to facilitate dance therapy with adolescents. *The Arts in Psychotherapy*, 17: 157–64.

Kellerman, P. F. (1984) Acting out in psychodrama and in psychoanalytic group therapy. *Group Analysis*, 17(3): 195–203.

Kohlberg, L. (1981) *The Philosophy of Moral Development*. San Francisco: Harper & Row.

Kohut, H. (1977) *The Restoration of the Self*. New York: International Universities Press.

Kramer, S. (1980) Residues of split-object and split-self dichotomies in adolescence. In R. Lax, S. Bach, and J. A. Burland (eds) *Rapprochement: the critical subphase of separation–individuation*. New York: Jason Aronson.

Landy, R. (1990) The concept of role in drama therapy. *The Arts in Psychotherapy*, 17: 223–30.

Mahler, M., Pine, F. and Bergman, A. (1975) *The Psychological Birth of the Human Infant*. New York: Basic Books.

Moreno, J. (1943) The concept of sociodrama. *Sociometry*, 6: 434–49.

—— (1946) *Psychodrama*, vol. 1. Beacon, NY: Beacon House.

Ormont, L. R. (1969) Acting-in and the therapeutic contract in group psychoanalysis. *International Journal of Group Psychotherapy*, 19: 420–32.

Piaget, J. (1952) *The Origins of Intelligence in Children*. New York: International Universities Press.

Pitzele, P. (1991) Adolescents inside out: intrapsychic psychodrama. In P. Holmes and M. Karp (eds) *Psychodrama: inspiration and technique*. London: Tavistock/ Routledge.

Rogers, C. (1951) *Client-Centered Therapy: its current practice, implications, and theory*. Boston: Houghton Mifflin.

Shuttleworth, R. (1981) Adolescent dramatherapy. In R. Courtney and G. Schattner (eds) *Drama in Therapy*, vol. 2. New York: Drama Books Specialists.

Spiegel, L.A. (1958) Comments on the psychoanalytic psychology of adolescence. *Psychoanalytic Study of the Child*, 13: 206–308.

Stanislavski, C. (1936) *An Actor Prepares*. New York: Theatre Arts.

Sternberg, P. and Garcia, A. (1989) *Sociodrama: who's in your shoes?* New York: Praeger.

Winnicott, D. W. (1965) The theory of the parent–infant relationship. *The Maturational Processes and the Facilitating Environment: Studies in the Theory of Emotional Development*. New York: International Universities Press.

Yalom, I. (1985) *The Theory and Practice of Group Psychotherapy* (3rd edn). New York: Basic Books.

Chapter 9

Images and action

Dramatherapy and psychodrama with sexually abused adolescents

Anne Bannister

The image which we present is, of course, the role, or collection of roles which we play (Moreno 1961). The image we receive of others may be one-dimensional if we see them in only one role, for example 'the teacher', 'the doctor'. With those close to us our received image will be multi-dimensional but will usually be incomplete and most people emphasize some of their roles and suppress others.

The image an adolescent presents, especially to their peers, is essential for self-esteem. A 12-year-old girl was convinced that she had to wear trendy clothes in order to have lots of friends. A 13-year-old boy described himself as a 'cool dude' and said that 'the look' was his most important consideration in life at the moment. Both these young people had been sexually abused and both were coping, with difficulty, with all the usual problems which adolescents face. Their home situations were still insecure, each had suffered abuse for over half of their young life, and each was determined to control at least one part of their life, their image.

In addition to the personal image which people present this chapter will also look at some common recurring images which arise in the work of abused adolescents and children. For instance, the painful image of a 'dead baby' may recur in waking moments as well as in dreams. The feelings of fear, which are usually present in abused young people, may appear as a monster image which overwhelms the young person. In contrast the need for justice is often expressed as an image of a queen, judge or godlike figure. The therapeutic group may have a collective image of justice which is expressed by all the members as an urge to act out 'court' or 'Judgement Day' scenes.

Psychodrama is a method of group psychotherapy which emphasizes action rather than words. Dramatherapy uses movement, action and sound to facilitate healing. Although psychodrama and dramatherapy are primarily used in groups this chapter will also give many examples of 'action techniques' used in a one-to-one situation with adolescents. Psychodrama can help us to look more closely at our roles, to watch others playing similar or different roles and observe reactions. We can try out new roles, from fantasy or reality, and perhaps take risks which are unacceptable in ordinary life. Moreno stated that psychodrama gave us an opportunity to make mistakes without being punished. Young people may have little opportunity to make their mistakes in a safe setting with adults who will not take advantage of inexperience.

Adolescence is a turning point, a time of action and change. Young people at times of crisis will take refuge in familiar ways of coping. Children who have been abused may react in the same way as they reacted to their abuse, even though they realize that this reaction is no longer useful. Psychodrama and dramatherapy can show that there are other, more functional reactions, more appropriate to the situation.

HOW CHILDREN COPE WITH ABUSE

Case example: Kelly ' the controller'

Kelly, for instance, fought to control every situation in her life. She had some friends, those who admired her audacity, her cleverness and her capacity to get her own way. She had enemies too, those who had suffered from her bullying, her blaming and her apparent unconcern for others. Her motto was: 'Get them before they get you.' Her aggressive image successfully deflected those of her peers who might seek to intimidate her. Most adults, on the other hand, automatically assumed she was the originator of teenage rebellion and discord.

Kelly's parents were having a hard time. They were a white, middle-class family, and although they knew that Kelly was bright she had underachieved during her last year at school and now, at 16, was jobless, dabbling in the local drug scene, and probably putting her health at risk through unsafe sex as well. They knew she had been sexually abused by an uncle from the time she was 4 until she was 14. Not surprisingly, Kelly had posed behavioural problems for some years, but this had been manageable until after her disclosure of abuse at 15. Both parents supported Kelly, and believed her, but she was amazed by the intensity of her mother's grief and her father's anger. There were marital rows. Less surprising was the uncle's denial, but the grandmother's support of her son, rather than of Kelly, was difficult for the girl to come to terms with.

When Kelly was first abused, at the age of 4, she had no control over the situation. Her uncle, who was baby-sitting, threatened to tell her parents that she was a naughty girl who had stayed up late to watch a television programme. Later he changed the threats by telling Kelly that she was the instigator of the abuse because she sat on his knee wearing only a nightdress. Desperately, she sought to gain some control over this escalating situation. Tantrums and refusal to stay with the uncle were dealt with firmly by her father. Attempts at being 'sick' so that her parents would not go out were thwarted by mother administering medicine, hot-water bottles and soothing words before she went out with her husband.

Accordingly, Kelly coped by accepting that she had instigated the behaviour, that she was 'a bad girl', and by seeking to control as much of the rest of her life as she could. Her younger brother suffered from her bossiness, teachers described her as wilful, but Kelly was coping with an impossible situation in the only way she knew how.

Case example: Cynthia ' the victim'

For Cynthia, however, the situation was quite different. She was the eldest of three girls. Her mother had become ill after the birth of the third child and so Cynthia soon became a surrogate mother to both her sisters. Her mother died when Cynthia was 6 and from that moment she felt responsible for her sisters' welfare. Her family were members of a strong religious group which was popular in the black community where they lived. Her father received much support from members of this church so he was able to continue to work, with their help. Of course Cynthia still felt that she had to take her mother's place, and when her father began to abuse her sexually she resignedly accepted the role. When she was 10 she began to protest because she realized that this did not happen to other girls in her community. Father threatened to abuse her younger sisters instead. From that moment Cynthia took on her victim role.

Cynthia's plight was exposed only after she had given birth to her father's baby at the age of 14. Her health visitor was suspicious of Cynthia's refusal to name the baby's father and, on questioning the 12-year-old sister, she learnt that the father had been abusing her also for several years.

Cynthia and Kelly were at opposite ends of a spectrum of coping behaviours. Kelly had to take control, even to the extent of identifying with her aggressor. Cynthia became victimized and may have gone on to be further abused in relationships with other adults. By the time they reached adolescence both girls had become fairly fixed in these behaviours even though they were now dysfunctional and causing further problems for them.

HOW DRAMATHERAPY AND PSYCHODRAMA CAN HELP

Pitzele (1991) describes the image that disturbed adolescents present as 'a mask'. He recognizes that these are 'coping masks' and he accepts this, not seeking to destroy the mask, but trying to explore the persona behind it. By respecting the 'bored', 'don't care' or 'dunno' mask he encourages the young person to explore the feelings that lie behind it. The members of the psychodrama group can assist each other in these explorations. It must be difficult to hold on to a 'bored' mask in such a group.

Young children try constantly in their play to increase their repertoire of roles. Emotionally deprived children may have been given little opportunity to play and little encouragement to try out roles. By adolescence most young people have an assortment of roles which they can use at will, according to circumstance. An abused child, however, is likely to stick with the role which seemed safest at the time of the abuse. Sometimes, as the author has illustrated elsewhere (Bannister 1992), this can lead to a false assessment of an abused adolescent, as someone who has learning difficulties or is 'slow'. Dramatherapy gives the opportunity to practise new roles and increase role repertoire.

Children who have had many changes in circumstances, different carers and different homes, sometimes miss out on essential rituals and rites of passage that other, more secure children may have experienced. Both dramatherapy and psychodrama can recognize this need and can provide affirming experiences to counterbalance the threatening and demoralizing effects of earlier life trauma.

Kelly ' the controller'

In keeping with her controlling role Kelly rejected any kind of therapy out of hand. She had been interested in drama at school and had been encouraged by a young drama teacher who was also involved in a local experimental theatre group. Kelly was flattered to be asked to join. During the following year she played many roles and her parents noticed a more introspective side to her which they had not seen before. She wrote an epic poem about a girl who had suffered abuse which the director adapted so that the drama group could perform it. A young dramatherapist who was a member of the group asked Kelly if she would assist her with a group that she was running for young offenders. These boys and girls, aged 14 to 15, had come to the attention of the probation service because they had committed petty crimes. Kelly was by now 18 years old.

The male probation officer who also ran the group was frequently cast by the young people in stereotypical male roles. He played an aggressive, drunken father, a controlling policeman and so on. In protest at this he instigated group discussion on gender issues. The discussion turned to sexual harassment as several of the girls in the group talked of incidents at school or at home. The group then decided to act out a scene of rape that was currently in the news and this was done, following through to the court scene and sentencing.

Everyone played several roles and scenes were repeated as most of the group members wished to play the judge. Afterwards Kelly talked with the two workers about her own experience and how she realized she had been able to express her fears as well as her anger in the previous drama group. She realized that some of the young people in the adolescent group had suffered similar experiences to her own and they too had reacted in controlling ways. She had begun to practise different roles in her life, as well as in the group. Perhaps inadvertently at first, drama had begun its therapeutic work.

Cynthia ' the victim'

Cynthia's father was found guilty of incest against her and her sister. He received a prison sentence. All the girls were taken into care and Cynthia's baby was adopted. She had wanted to keep it very much but realized that, at 14, with no parental support, this was probably not viable. She accepted her fate and continued to look after her two younger sisters in their care situation. A perceptive social worker recognized her vulnerability. Although her sisters were beginning to respond to the love and care of their foster mother, Cynthia could only respond by giving even more of herself. She agreed to see the psychodramatist who assessed that Cynthia was not yet ready to work in a group. She was quite unable to protect herself against exploitation by other adolescents. In addition she would have been the only black member of an all white group. The therapist decided to work individually with her for the time being.

Cynthia waited for the therapist to tell her what to do. Her own creativity had been stifled and she would have been too embarrassed to initiate any action herself. The therapist noticed that she was interested in a collection of small (3-inch) dolls that represented adults and children, males and females. She was asked to choose dolls to represent her family. Carefully, she selected the appropriate black dolls, not forgetting the smallest baby-doll to represent her own child. By removing herself directly from the action Cynthia was able to work psychodramatically with the dolls and she began by expressing her grief.

The loss of her baby opened up a deep well of tears for Cynthia. Never had she allowed herself to cry before. At first she kept herself separate from the action. She was only crying for the doll-girl who had lost her baby. Soon she was able to cry for the doll-girl who had lost her father, and was sad, even though he abused her. Eventually the floodgates opened and she filled her own well with tears for her dead mother. For eight years she had not recognized her own pain in her efforts to comfort her sisters and her father.

After the tears came the anger, which had also been deeply repressed.

The expression of grief seemed to liberate Cynthia's body and she stamped around the room kicking cushions and throwing toys about. A tantrum by a big 14-year-old can be a powerful sight. The anger was directed, safely enough, at the workers and the system that had persuaded her to part with her baby. It moved on to her father as she raged about his betrayal and how he had persuaded her that it was her duty to take her mother's place in every way. She found the final betrayal of his abuse of her sister particularly hard to bear. Finally she was able to continue her grief about her mother's death by an expression of anger about being abandoned by her.

The therapist asked Cynthia now if she would like to be a member of a group for girls who had been abused. By this time the group had two other black girls as well as five white girls. The group would give Cynthia an opportunity to practise her new ways of behaving. She completed twelve sessions with the group and, with another group member of her own age, she went back to school to complete her education.

THE USE OF RECURRING IMAGES

The dead baby

Cynthia had begun to work on her pain by remembering the recent loss of her baby. This was a real event but it may have had particular poignancy for Cynthia because of the loss of her own childhood. She had begun to lose touch with her childhood when her mother became ill. After her death, and especially after the abuse by her father, her inner child disappeared, or 'died'. The image of a dead baby appears frequently in therapeutic work with abused young people. Perhaps all young people mourn the passing of childhood but for an abused child there must be an unconscious recognition that their inner child was not nurtured or allowed to grow naturally.

Sexually abused children may become prematurely eroticized, may become overly cynical and mistrusting or may even seek to abuse power themselves. All these traits are more typical of adults than of children and young people. It seems that youngsters understand their need to behave and react in more childlike ways. It is as if they need to mourn the premature death of their childish persona and to nurture the growth of a new child.

Case example: Julia

One young woman, Julia, illustrated this need in a very dramatic way. The therapy room was used for young children as well as adolescents. It contained a dolls' house and furniture and a dolls' cot with twin baby-dolls in it. In addition it held large floor cushions, plenty of drawing materials, some tiny 3-inch dolls, animal puppets and modelling material. The dolls for younger children were deliberately left in the corner of the room when adolescents were seen since experience had shown that they would often be used spontaneously.

Julia was 14 and had been living in long-term foster care for six years. She and her older sister had both been abused by a stepfather and by their two older stepbrothers. Julia had been abused for about four years until her sister, who was then aged 10, had told a teacher what was happening. Julia's mother had herself been abused by her father and did not want to release the children for adoption but unfortunately she was not able to protect them. Although she and her husband were now separated, her stepsons, who were now young men in their 20s, frequently stayed with her.

Julia enjoyed storytelling and she was very adept at this. She often started the sessions with a story which she would proceed to act out. The room also contained a 'dressing-up' box and a large mirror and Julia enjoyed draping herself in flowing chiffon robes and adding jewellery. Her favourite roles were very strong, powerful ones, the queen or the pop-star. She told a story about a beautiful, wise queen who had twin girl children. The children were cared for by a faithful nurse and also by a manservant. Julia draped herself in purple chiffon and added silver belt and shoes for her role as queen. The twin dolls played the babies and two rag-dolls played the servants. Unlike most younger children Julia did not spontaneously reverse roles and become a baby or a servant. She remained fully in control in her role as queen throughout the story, which was continued for about six sessions.

The manservant was really a monster in disguise and one day the queen came home to find the faithful nurse very distressed because the monster had killed the baby. Julia, as queen, spent time reassuring the nurse that the death was not her fault. She then reverted to narrative and said that the manservant had changed into a monster and had, with the help of two other monsters, overcome the nurse. As queen, Julia then planned and carried out an elaborate funeral for the baby at which hundreds of people mourned her death. Throughout this story and enactment the twin baby had been rather cursorily cared for by the nurse but in reality had been very neglected by Julia. The therapist asked what was to become of this baby. Julia looked confused and, after some thought, said that she, the queen, would care for her personally.

This was the start of a long process whereby Julia, as queen, cared for the baby and allowed her to grow and become a wise princess. The nurse (who had been given the same name as Julia's mother) was, at first, given care and attention. Eventually the queen began to express her anger at the nurse for not seeking help. It was at this stage that

Julia decided to personalize the story and she began to express, for the first time, her anger and frustration with her mother. Julia was asked to describe the qualities of an ideal mother and she did so, stressing protection, strength, understanding and support. The therapist asked her to reverse roles with the 'ideal mother' and to speak to the doll representing herself. She did so and told 'herself' that she would always believe her and protect her. She was reversed back into her own role and, using the nurse doll, the therapist repeated the words of the ideal mother so that Julia could hear them.

The discussion between Julia and the therapist then seemed much calmer. Julia had been able to express anger against the parent who had not abused her and she was then able to accept fully that her mother was not able to be an ideal mother in the circumstances. This discussion seemed very different from Julia's earlier superficial comforting of the nurse/mother character.

Case example: Patrick

Patrick's image of the 'dead baby' was a much more violent one. He was 13 and had been abused by a man who posed as a family friend. Patrick used the dressing-up box to clothe himself in a pirate outfit, complete with sword. He chose a baby-doll from a selection in the corner and pretended to cut its head off and then to cut off its limbs. He spent a long time on this, shouting and stamping and swinging his sword. He repeated the action several times, adding even more violent embellishments each time. He then set out every doll in the room, naming them as parents, grandparents and other members of an extended family. He then proceeded to slaughter them all, screaming that they deserved to die because they had not saved the baby. In a subsequent session Patrick said he would like to become 'a sword' and as a sword he felled a monster teddy bear that he had noticed in an adjoining room and had asked to use.

Clearly Patrick had identified with his abuser in some ways and the sexual symbolism of the sword was obvious. The therapist reminded Patrick about all the people who had been slaughtered in the last session. He renewed his attack on the teddy, stating that he was paying him back for killing the baby. However, the teddy refused to be killed by the sword. With great energy Patrick lifted up the teddy, after knocking it down, telling the therapist that the teddy was impossible to destroy. The therapist asked whether anyone could help but Patrick shook his head. Patrick was re-enacting his own drama and was able to admit his complete vulnerability. In fact he may not have been able to 'put up a fight' since the abuser had offered many emotional and material bribes that he knew were attractive to Patrick.

The therapist drew Patrick's attention to some puppets in the room. She asked whether they could help. Patrick picked up a crocodile and considered it. 'What else would you need to destroy the bear?' the therapist asked. 'Courage,' replied Patrick. 'Maybe the crocodile has some,' suggested the therapist. Patrick took up the theme. In addition to the crocodile he picked out a badger who was wise, a lion who had strength and a fox who was clever. He reversed roles with each of the puppets to see how it felt. Together the puppets and the sword demolished the teddy bear. The therapist pointed to the extended family dolls which lay around the edges of the room. 'Perhaps they have learned that they needed some more courage, wisdom, strength and cleverness to outwit the bear,' she said. Patrick took up the suggestion, re-enacting the whole scene, with the family dolls watching, and learning.

Case example: Jean

In contrast to Patrick, Jean was a quiet, thoughtful 16-year-old. After several sessions she began to speak of a classmate who had died at the age of 6. She said she had only recently remembered this girl, whom she thought was named Jane. She felt frustrated that she could not remember any detail about Jane except that they were friends at school and one day the teacher had announced that she had died. Jean agreed to re-enact the classroom scene. She played herself, and then the teacher. The therapist asked her to reverse into herself again. Jean began to cry quietly. She said she felt extremely sad. The scene was ended and in a subsequent session Jean acted out a dream of being lost in a wood where she had been led by her father. Her father had been her abuser. Whilst she role-played herself wandering in the wood she suddenly said that she was looking for Jane. She cried again as memories resurfaced and she realized that 'Jane' had not really existed. She was the 6-year-old Jean who had 'died' or 'become lost' when her father had begun to abuse her.

The image of fear

Case example: Hyacinth

Small children who have been abused often use the image of a 'monster' which may not directly represent their abuser but will almost certainly represent the fear which they had for the abuser. This monster may take the form of a television character or a popular cartoon. In adolescents and adults the image of fear is more varied.

Hyacinth, a black African 15-year-old, said that fear was the strongest feeling she had. Even though her father had returned to Africa she still woke up in the night fearful that he had returned. She was asked to draw her fear and she drew a large face with a beard and short curly hair. Over it she drew prison bars, saying that she was too afraid to look at her fear unless it was contained behind bars. Much of the work with Hyacinth was concerned with very practical counselling about how she and her mother and siblings could protect themselves should her father return. By role-playing imaginary sequences in which he returned to physically and sexually abuse her, Hyacinth was able to face the fear, to recognize its reality, but also to prepare a defence against it so that she could be more assertive. It was important for Hyacinth that her mother, who was also afraid, should join in the sessions. Together the two women, mother and daughter, were able to devise a strategy which helped them to move from victims to survivors.

Case example: Moira

Moira was a 14-year-old white girl who found it difficult at first to take part in any creative activity. She seemed to be afraid to move from her seat so role-playing was not on the agenda. She never raised her voice above a whisper and would not draw since she was afraid the therapist would say that the drawings were 'wrong'. She was not interested in the small dolls, the dressing-up box or the puppets. The exception was a small blue bear with only one ear. (The image of the wounded animal is also a common one with children and young people.) She picked up Bluey and absentmindedly stroked him as she quietly replied to the therapist's comments. The therapist noticed that Moira's whole body position was protective of herself. She frequently used expressions such as, 'I'm afraid you won't like it.' Because her voice was almost inaudible the therapist asked her if she liked writing. Fortunately Moira responded enthusiastically and spent several sessions writing letters (not to be sent) to her mother, her grandmother and her sister. She managed to express much sadness and feelings of resentment.

She was not able to write any letters, or make any statements, about her stepfather, who had abused her. Slowly the therapist worked towards helping Moira to look at this. It was clear that fear was preventing Moira from looking more closely at what had happened to her. The therapist asked her if she could look at her fear and choose someone who could be her ally as she did this. Moira chose Bluey, the blue bear whom she had cuddled throughout the sessions. She was asked to imagine that her fear was in a corner of the room. She immediately said she could see it, an octopus-like creature, squelching and heaving. It was large, at least a metre across, and there was no way that Moira was going to move any closer to it.

The therapist asked how 'fear' could be controlled. To her surprise

Moira said that Bluey could sing. The therapist invited him to do so. Moira picked him up and in a very clear voice began to sing a song from *Oliver*. Apparently her school were putting on a performance of this and, although Moira did not have a part in it, she had learnt the songs. The therapist joined in, feeling surprised and pleased that for the first time Moira had suggested a creative intervention. She asked whether the bear could use his voice to shrink the octopus and Moira thought that this was possible. She began softly and was encouraged to direct the full force of her voice at the octopus until it began to shrink. Moira was able to visualize the shrinking of her fear until it disappeared completely. In subsequent sessions she was able to look more closely at the abuse she had suffered.

Case example: Janice

Many young people will use the image of protective bars or a fence to hold back the fear, as Hyacinth did.

Janice said that she wished to build a wall and to make sure it was in place before she could look at her fear. She picked up cushions to represent bricks in the wall. She named each cushion as a self-protective quality which she possessed herself, or as a friend or family member who could support and protect her. She walked up and down behind the wall which was too high to see over. She said she felt as if she were demonstrating outside a nuclear establishment.

The therapist encouraged her to draw placards to wave on the 'demo'. She drew two: 'DOWN WITH DRUGS' and 'DOWN WITH PORNO'. Her abusers were drug users who had taken pornographic pictures of Janice to sell to raise money to feed their addiction. As she waved the placards she chanted the words, 'Down with drugs, down with porno,' and then, 'Down with dragondrugs,' and 'Death to the dragon.' She described the dragon of fear who lay behind the wall and the therapist encouraged her to remove the bricks from the wall, one by one, until she was surrounded by cushions. She named each cushion as she removed it and as she did so the therapist placed a tiny plastic dragon on the far side of the wall. Janice laughed as the last cushion was removed and she saw the size of her fear. She jumped up and down on top of it and then wept, for the first time in the sessions, and talked about her genuine fears about the pornographic pictures.

The image of justice

From the age of 8 or 9 children develop a conscience and a strong sense of morality. 'It isn't fair' is a frequently repeated phrase for children in the age group 9–12. Abused children are often coerced into victimization by an adult perpetrator's subterfuge and rationalization. Consequently the children do not necessarily appreciate fully how their trust has been betrayed until later when they feel able to look at what has happened to them. It is often at adolescence, then, when young people are able to realize that they are not guilty of causing their own abuse, that their sense of justice and fair play can be expressed.

Case example: Lucy

The justice role may be expressed as a fair and wise king or queen, as we saw earlier when Julia played the queen who had twin daughters.

> Lucy, a 17-year-old with learning difficulties, drew a picture of herself at 3 years old, wearing a crown. She said she was a king. The picture she drew was horrifying; the king was administering justice in a vengeful and violent way by killing other children. Lucy said the children deserved to die. She added a devil figure to the picture, stating that 'the devil was good and he decided who lived or died'. This picture opened up the possibility of work with Lucy on her extreme guilt and feelings that she was completely bad, a 'devilish person'. Lucy had, in fact, abused younger children, and so her self-perception had been reinforced by other adults who were alarmed by her behaviour. Before producing the drawing she had completely refused to discuss her abusive offences or her memories of her own abuse.
>
> Theoretically Lucy could have been asked to play the role of herself as 'king' at 3 years old so that she could realize how little choice she had at that time. However, it is not wise to risk re-abusing someone by asking them to take the role of themselves as victim. In addition the circumstances of Lucy's own abuse were particularly horrific. The therapist therefore stayed with the drawing and asked Lucy to play 'god' now and to look at the scene in the drawing and make a judgement about how much choice the 3-year-old king actually had. Lucy thoroughly enjoyed the 'god' role since it fitted in with her coping mechanism which was one of extreme control. She passed a judgement that the little king had no choice but to commit violence because that behaviour was all that the 'devil' and family members had shown him. She became angry with all those people who had made the king 'do things'. Still in role, she was encouraged then to empathize, first with the victims she had drawn and then with herself at 3 years old.
>
> It took many sessions with Lucy continuing to play 'god' before she could fully accept that she had had no choice about her behaviour at the age of 3. She found it difficult to accept that she had not always been in total control. Her learning difficulties had made her even more

vulnerable so whenever she was subsequently abused, emotionally, she had tightened up her control mechanisms. Eventually she was able to understand how and why she had protected herself and then to understand further that she did now have a choice about her behaviour. She was at last able to empathize with the children she had sexually abused. Role play was then used to practise future non-abusive behaviour.

The group as an image of justice

As we have noted, in the group of which Kelly was a member, court scenes are popular amongst adolescent groups, especially with groups for young offenders and with young people who have been abused. The judge is a role which controlling youngsters find comfortable. Sometimes the court scene is played to prepare young people for a court appearance as a witness when they have been sexually abused. Then the drama is a rehearsal so that the court appears less alien and frightening. At other times abused young people ask to replay the court scene, within their therapy group, so that they can 'put right' what they see as errors of judgement when their abusers were not found guilty or when their sentences were very light. Although some abused youngsters are depressed or upset when their abusers go to prison, especially if they are close relatives, many abused people react in a different way. If the abuser is not convicted or is not jailed they feel that the court did not take their hurt seriously, or that they were not fully believed. Children whose coping behaviours are controlling often appear unhurt or emotionally intact to a casual observer. Because they are not obvious victims their damage is severely underestimated. Lawyers sometimes pick up on this and juries are told that the victims 'are not seriously damaged'. Sometimes judges make similar comments when passing sentence.

Adolescents to whom this has happened often act out their pain by disruptive or violent behaviour. Often the violence is turned against themselves and they may mutilate their bodies, their hair, or their clothing. They may develop eating problems and will often have an unrealistic view of their own body image. By acting out the judge role, particularly in a group setting, the adolescent can regain some control and can explore options within the safety of the group.

Case example: Gill

When a group of abused adolescent girls decided to act out a court scene Gill asked to be the judge. She set up a scene which owed a great deal to her own predicament. A rapist had attacked a 14-year-old girl who was in a children's home. The offender had been a worker at the home. Gill constantly interrupted the 'defence and prosecuting counsel' to give them directions about the culpability of the girl, advising them that she was already sexually experienced and therefore she had not suffered much. Gill had been taken into care because of abuse when she was 7 and had been further abused by a foster father and subsequently by the care-worker. The scene she was re-enacting was very similar to the one she had experienced in court. After sentencing the offender to a few months in prison Gill finished the enactment and the group sat down to share their feelings about the scene.

Gill remained in control, apparently ignoring the comments by all the other group members. They were all horrified that the girl's ordeal should have been so misunderstood and that the offence should have been minimized. Gill listened carefully but did not agree with anyone. The groupworkers noticed that Gill's behaviour began to change from that session. Her appearance was the most striking difference. She changed from aggressive boots and spiky hairstyle to a softer look and for the first time she began to show some sympathy and support for other group members. Although she had nominally played the judge herself, in fact she had allowed the group to be the judge of what had happened to her and their fair and supportive comments had helped her to see that she had not been the instigator of her own abuse and that her suffering was recognized.

THE GROUP PROCESS

Group therapists working with adolescents who have been abused must be especially careful to create conditions of safety. Time spent in encouraging group members to make contracts about their behaviour will be rewarded by greater ease of decision-making for groupworkers if agreements should be violated. Boundary-making, for young people who do not have appropriate boundaries, is essential, so group rules should be adhered to. A sense of justice and fair play is vital, though, so sanctions should not be imposed without discussion and representation. Jennings and Gersie (1987) describe groups for adolescents as needing 'firm boundaries with some realistic flexibility'.

It is most important that abused people should not feel further abused within the group. This aim takes precedence over an individual's need for a cathartic reaction. The groupworker has a responsibility to the whole group, so if an adolescent acts out in a way which is painful for others then the worker needs to acknowledge this and spend time afterwards in promoting self-healing.

One way is to ask group members to connect with a part of themselves which is helpful, which can protect them when necessary. As the young person thinks about this they are then asked to become that part and to share with the group the ways in which they protect their vulnerable parts.

This sharing and respecting of coping mechanisms can increase self-esteem and reduce guilt. It can also increase self-understanding and can help the young person to reject some coping procedures which are no longer necessary.

The kind of exercise described above, in the case of Gill, would not be suitable for a newly formed adolescent group. As Willis (1991) points out, adolescents fear too much self-disclosure happening too fast. A newly formed group would be happier working through story or images. It is important to note that Gill was directing 'a story' about a fictitious girl who had been abused, and at no time did it become explicit with the group members. It is usually unnecessary to 'interpret' story or metaphor to children or adolescents. Sometimes young people will point out the similarities in their own experience to the therapist and the work may be more effective when this happens. However, Hellendoorn (1988) states that the possibility of leaving concealed what is at the same time revealed enables the young person to communicate things which cannot be said aloud.

Case example: Sam

Sam, at 12, was the youngest member of a group for sexually abused girls. Somehow this made her try harder to be grown up so her clothes and mannerisms were the most outrageous. The group had agreed to use 'drama' in the contract for work so each week they chose to enact a scene or a story. Reports in newspapers had been covered, scenes such as pop-concerts or parties had been tried and most recently the group had acted out an updated version of the Cinderella story, inspired by a cinema visit. Sam said Cinderella was 'rubbish' but she would like to act part of the Snow White story. The group said they could not remember it well but Sam was insistent.

She cast herself as Snow White and asked a quiet, attractive girl to play Snow White's mother, 'who is killed when she is stuck with a needle'. A poignant scene ensued when the mother pricked herself with a needle and died. Snow White's father, the king, had to tell his daughter about her mother's death. One of the groupworkers was chosen to play the king. It was obvious that Sam was moved by the sympathetic way in which she was told about the death. Sam then chose the other group-worker to play the wicked stepmother and enacted a scene where the stepmother sends Snow White into the woods to be killed. Snow White, of course, is reprieved by the woodsman who leaves her in the wood. Sam then moved to the scene where Snow White is cleaning the dwarves' house and the stepmother appears, dressed as an old woman, and gives her a poisoned apple. Thanks to the care of the dwarves Snow White recovers, only to fall into a death-like sleep when the stepmother reappears and sells Snow White a comb, with which she pricks her head.

Sam stopped the action at this point and one of the groupworkers suggested that the group might like to show what they thought about the wicked stepmother. The group used a large teddy bear which was often the recipient of their anger and they demonstrated their feelings about the stepmother by kicking, thumping and stamping on it. Sam joined in the assault, stabbing the teddy with a 'hitting stick'. This is made from rolled-up newspapers and is a useful 'prop' for active groupwork.

Afterwards the group talked about feelings and Sam shared that the person she was really angry with was her mother. It was not necessary for her to share more but the workers surmised that she had, in the fairy story, shown the aspects of her life which were causing her most concern. They knew from her history that Sam had suffered abandonment and neglect. Although her sexual abuse was the reason for her inclusion in the group she was most disturbed about the fact that when she was about 2 or 3 her mother had become addicted to drugs – pricked by the needle. Mother had then exposed Sam to many dangerous situations, she had been forced to steal to pay for mother's drugs and she had been raped by mother's boyfriend - as dangerous as the poisoned apple and the comb. The interpretation was unnecessary but the workers were better able to understand Sam's anger and her current worries.

CONCLUSION

In this chapter we have looked at dramatherapy and psychodrama used in groups for adolescents. We have also looked at psychodrama used in one-to-one sessions with young people. A basic rule of psychotherapy is that the therapist must have respect for the client. This is even more important when we look at sections of the community which have not been respected. Over a decade ago feminists pointed out that women had often not been respected in therapeutic work and had been treated as 'faulty or deficient men'. More recently racial awareness has helped us to realize that those of a minority culture may also be treated as 'different therefore deficient'. Those with learning difficulties or physical disability are still heavily discriminated against in the community and therefore by some in the 'helping professions'. The voice of children and young people is only just beginning to be heard. Groups like the National Association for Young People in Care (NAYPIC) and children's rights and advocacy groups are beginning to make their mark.

Therapists with children and young people must be aware of the adult tendency to prescribe for youngsters, without proper consultation. Those working with abused people must always have good, experienced, consultants who can advise when a therapist is in danger of inadvertently re-abusing in any way. A common pitfall in this area is the failure to work with, instead of against, the resistance that clients, especially adolescents,

often bring to the work. Kellerman (1991) writes about a group of adolescents he worked with. They were silent and antagonistic and yet they
continued to attend the sessions. A therapist with less respect for the
group would have given up but Kellerman continued to attend, as they
did, and eventually was rewarded as he learnt of old pent-up aggression
which was being contained within the group. Soon the members were able
to work through this, with great mutual benefit.

The necessity for adolescents to be 'held' and contained by the therapist
is stressed by Holmes (1990) in a description of an interview with a
'resistant' adolescent. Blatner (1973) stresses this too and points to
Moreno's own words: 'We don't tear down the protagonist's walls,
rather, we simply try some of the handles on the many doors, and see
which one opens.'

Although dramatherapy and psychodrama can be seen as a kind of play
therapy for all ages this is not disrespectful or patronizing to adolescents
and adults. Western society often demeans play activity, or categorizes it as
sport or competition, but 'play' is an essential part of growth and a natural
healing mechanism which children use. Therapists can, with their own
creative skill, encourage this to help children, adolescents and adults,
including, of course, themselves.

REFERENCES

Bannister, A. (ed.) (1992) *From Hearing to Healing: working with the aftermath of child sexual abuse*. Harlow: Longman.
Blatner, H. (1973) *Acting-in: practical applications of psychodramatic methods.* New York: Springer.
Hellendoorn, J. (1988) Imaginative play technique in psychotherapy with children. In C. E. Schaefer (ed.) *Innovative Interventions in Child and Adolescent Therapy*. New York: Wiley.
Holmes, P. (1990) Why should I talk to you? In A. Bannister, K. Barrett and E. Shearer (eds) *Listening to Children*. Harlow: Longman.
Jennings, S. and Gersie, A. (1987) Dramatherapy with disturbed adolescents. In S. Jennings (ed.) *Dramatherapy Theory and Practice, 1.* London: Routledge.
Kellerman, P. F. (1991) *Focus on Psychodrama*. London: Jessica Kingsley.
Moreno, J. L. (1961) The role concept: a bridge between psychiatry and sociology. In J. Fox (ed.) *The Essential Moreno.* New York: Springer (1987).
Pitzele, P. (1991) Adolescents inside out, intrapsychic psychodrama. In P. Holmes and M. Karp (eds) *Psychodrama: Inspiration and Technique*. London: Routledge.
Willis, S. T. (1991) Who goes there?: group-analytic drama for disturbed adolescents. In P. Holmes and M. Karp (eds) *Psychodrama: Inspiration and Technique*. London: Routledge.

Part IV

Developmental framework

Shall I be mother?

The development of the role of the dramatherapist and reflections on transference/countertransference

Di Grimshaw

Clammy hands all around me
Ones that say they care
And the thing that really gets me is
The hands which should, aren't there.

Lisa

INTRODUCTION

We each have a mother. One biological mother. The mother–child relationship is different in every case. Most of us pass through childhood and emerge seemingly able to cope with the next stage. Others are not as fortunate, and require help to ease the passage, and, in extremes, to emerge at all. If the mother–child relationship is unsatisfactory, the emergent child is likely to show varying degrees of insecurity, mistrust and aggressiveness.

The unfortunate child has experienced parenting which is not *good enough*. The question is, does the therapist attempt to provide what is missing?

This chapter was conceived as a general exploration into the role of the dramatherapist. Taken in isolation, however, this inevitably gives rise to more questions whilst answering precious few. With this in mind I have attempted to compare and contrast the role of the dramatherapist with that of the mother.

The mother–child relationship is considered within the framework of object relations and includes an exploration into the nature of the mother as portrayed in fairy stories.

The stages of developmental play are examined in relation to the child's emotional growth; and how these might be encouraged not only by the mother but also by significant others the child encounters.

Finally I attempt to explore how a dramatherapist might enter into a child's dramatic world not primarily through the medium of drama but by engaging her own 'inner child'.

STOCK CARS AND HANDS

Where do I start in sharing my own experiences, personal and professional, in support of my belief that *the* most valuable resource a dramatherapist has is herself? I did not want to write my autobiography, for this is not the nature of the book, yet it has to be autobiographical. It is one journey.

I started with an image. A car. I did not want a car. If I am to mark my journey into the field of dramatherapy with children and young people, I would much prefer to travel by more poetic means. On horseback would be ideal. Furthermore, I did not understand the car image. It made no sense whatsoever. The image niggled, insistently. Worse still, the car was an old banger, nothing smooth or refined.

Then I came across an image I had drawn in therapy some months previously. The image depicted my 'safe space'; my bedroom as a child. On the sheet I had scribbled 'Saturday nights – hearing and smelling the stock cars'.

As a child I often visited the stock-car ground with my father – a *smörgåsbord* of sensory experiences: acrid smell, roar of engines, flood-lights, excited crowds and the sweet taste of Dandelion and Burdock. I held my father's hand, gripping tightly and shrieking. The air itself seemed alive and I was safe.

Years later, whilst visiting my family, I returned to the ground with my brother. We marvelled at the desolation. A vacant place. There were no more stock cars. Only this. I felt a sadness for the children who would never know this. Not to know these thrills and the safety of *that* hand.

Some children rarely experience *that* hand. Others have it for a brief time. Some are almost crushed by the oppression it represents, and we all learn to some extent how to hold on to it for our own survival.

THE FIRST HAND

The hand of the mother (primary carer) stretches out to hold her baby, soothing and reassuring. The baby knows instinctively what his needs are and begins to initiate the touch.

The mother gently bathes her child, holds him to her breast and feeds him.

Later these hands will reach out in encouragement when he takes his first steps. He will retract his hand as a sign that he is angry with her. At other times he will fight her with his hands clenched. He learns to trust.

In *The Continuum Concept* (1977) Jean Liedloff portrays the infant's first days of life through the senses of the newly-born. It is an imaginative and distressing account of a baby born in a maternity ward.

The child is thrust from the warmth and comfort of the womb (in which he expected to spend his life, having no knowledge of anything other) and, after being wrapped in a dry, lifeless cloth, is placed in a box. He wails and wails. No one comes. He hears the wails of others like him. The sound means nothing to him. He is alone. Exhausted, he falls asleep.

On awakening and discovering the nothingness again his body is racked with desire. This is unbearable. He screams and is lifted, eventually, from the box. He experiences the hands, and is no longer alone. His cold, wet nappy is changed for a dry one. Returned to the box it is as though the hands had never been there, or the wet nappy. There is no conscious memory, no hope.

Lifted again and held to the breast, all the agony he has experienced is non-existent. The taste and texture of the breast, the warm flowing milk, and his mother's heartbeat. He sucks until he is full; satisfied, he dozes off.

On waking he is in hell, for there is no memory of the breast, only a yearning, an intolerable longing to be touched. His body stiffens in terror and he shrieks as if being tortured. His mother is sure he does not really need anything, he has been fed and changed, yet his distress is real. She leaves him, reluctantly, following her own mother's advice not to pamper him.

René Spitz documented in great detail the effects of infant separation from the mother (Spitz 1945). He observed different groups of infants raised in environments with varying degrees of maternal presence. In particular he studied a group of infants raised in an institution where primary needs such as hygiene and nutrition were meticulously met, whilst human contact was almost non-existent. As a result, no emotional bond was established. All these infants showed symptoms of withdrawal and anxiety. Some lost the will to live.

The psychoanalyst Germaine Guex was fascinated by patterns she observed in her patients, such as anxiety, aggressiveness, and an insatiable need for love and acceptance, which reveals basic emotional insecurity (Guex 1950).

Guex suggests that the root of emotional insecurity cannot always be attributed to actual abandonment by the mother. The patient may never have been separated physically from the mother for prolonged periods. Instead, it is the outcome of the mother's emotional response, which is understood by the child as abandonment. The child feels unloved and, like a mixture of Wednesday's child and Thursday's child, proverbially speaking, is full of woe and has far to go.

Very few professionals working therapeutically would dispute the statement that the roots of a person's emotional life are buried deep in the earliest childhood years, and are fed in particular by the interaction between the infant and his mother.

Almost a century ago Freud understood that the mother gave something essential to the baby, to enable healthy physical and emotional growth. This we have come to understand as mother-love. Absence of or dysfunction in this bonding process between mother and infant have been shown to have devastating effects for the infant.

Object relations theory (Klein 1932) provides us with an understanding of the infant's inner world from the moment he is born.

The child's inner world is described in terms of a dramatic relationship, the conflict between love and hate. The infant projects on to the 'bad' object (the bad breast in Kleinian terms) the bad experiences – feelings of persecution, anxiety, fear; and projects and then introjects 'good' experiences from the good breast – feelings of security, acceptance and satisfaction – to create a positive internalized object.

In time the infant learns that he is separate from his mother, and he experiences her as an other: an other containing love and hate within one, not two, separate entities. The conflicts co-exist giving rise to ambivalence (Freud 1912).

An awareness of this ambivalence will develop only if the child has an experience of 'good enough mothering' (Winnicott 1965) which has been able to tolerate the child's contradictory impulses. Only when the child is aware of this ambivalence is he able to tolerate these impulses – to direct and control them. A child who has not had 'good enough mothering', as Spitz's observations show (Spitz 1945), understandably finds the impulses overwhelming.

Fairbairn also saw the infant within a context, but whereas Klein described the child's impulses as instinctual, he recognized the impulses within a social context (Fairburn 1952). The infant has a basic need for human contact.

The child knows that *the* hand is there and by this hand primarily he will encounter the world.

If the child's needs are not met, he will learn to deny these needs. They are repressed, withdrawn, hidden. The child defends against the exposure of unmet needs, thus avoiding yet another disappointment, for this is what the child has experienced. Denial of unmet needs is often expressed by projecting unacceptable/difficult feelings onto others.

The child is presenting a 'false self' (Winnicott 1964) to the world. The hidden unmet needs are turned inwards on the child, which he experiences as hopelessness. There is a split.

THE LOVING MOTHER, THE EVIL STEPMOTHER AND THE WITCH

Fairy stories provide a rich seam, both for exploring emotional conflicts and for developing a child's resourcefulness in coming to terms with unmet needs.

These stories may have 'happily-ever-after' endings, usually when the handsome and loving prince rescues the young woman in distress. What happens before this?

Cinderella's mother dies (parents' disappearances in fairy stories have frequently been attributed to death; modern stories may have a number of reasons for absence), leaving her daughter exposed to the cruel acts of a jealous stepmother and stepsisters. Her father is apparently unaware of his daughter's abuse.

Little Red Riding Hood's mother sends her young daughter into a wolf-ridden forest. The abusive nature of Hansel and Gretel's stepmother prevails over their pitiful father's love for them and he agrees to lead his children to starvation. How do these children survive such traumas? Were they recipients of 'good enough mothering' during infancy? Are we to take this for granted?

According to Fairbairn, everyone at some level withholds unmet needs from the world outside (Fairburn 1952): we all experience to some extent a split; likewise, everyone must have had some degree of mother-love from somewhere, even if not from the biological mother, otherwise the infant would not have survived (Spitz 1945).

The extent to which Cinderella could make sense of her traumatic ordeal and the realization that she was not responsible for her stepmother's feelings and behaviour would depend on the parental acknowledgement Cinderella had in her early upbringing.

The Cinderella story becomes more interesting still as we are introduced to the fairy godmother. She is to play a pivotal part in Cinderella's passage through adolescence.

The fairy godmother bears witness to Cinderella's misery, she offers her a helping hand, which is gratefully accepted.

The metaphoric quality of drama allows a child to enter a world of wolves, princesses and witches yet the themes of power, envy, greed, loyalty, companionship and loneliness are very real. Bettelheim has studied children's stories in relation to developmental psychology (Bettelheim 1977). He believes stories appeal to children because they address the difficulties encountered in growing up, and provide a new dimension to children's attempts to resolve the inevitable confusions, conflicts and frustrations they will face. The child is encouraged to engage imaginatively with good and evil, love and hate, right and wrong.

The female characters in many children's stories are made particularly easy to identify. The real mother is usually described or referred to in favourable terms: a source of warm love and protection. Then with mother absent, if all seems lost, a fairy godmother will provide help, and of course hope. The stepmother, on the other hand, is variously portrayed as deceitful, spiteful, untrustworthy and even murderous. The witch and the stepmother are in effect one and the same character. This bad/evil character is often disguised so as to lure children into a false trust.

The witch in the Hansel and Gretel story deceives the children into entering her candy house. They were starving to death and she offered them delectable, irresistible sweets especially prepared with children in mind. How could they refuse?

Just as the 'good enough mother' is understood to tolerate the co-existence of love and hate within herself by the child, so the contradictory feelings are contained within the vehicle of the story. These feelings are often personified by the female roles.

There is a special bond formed between the storyteller and the listening child. The narrator provides the means of transport, her protégé leaps aboard. The child is rapt through exposure to a fertile make-believe world of possibilities. Stories, a form of projective play, invite the child to engage emotionally and creatively and to empathize with the hero or heroine.

In addition, stories are often read or told to children at bedtime. The adult's presence at this time is hopefully comforting for the child, as the transition from day to night can be a frightening one. The story bridges day and night as it crosses the domains of good and evil, love and hate, right and wrong.

LOOKING WITHIN

Drama in schools is a powerful means of exploring social issues such as bullying, drug abuse and sexual and racial prejudice.

Using the metaphor of an interview, with a sinister and unpredictable twist, pupils on a teaching practice experienced discrimination, hostility and humiliation. The drama was brought to an abrupt end as emotions intensified dangerously. Afterwards the group were able to share and compare some feelings provoked by the drama, to bring the issues out of the metaphoric situation, and to begin questioning personal prejudices. Although the drama was contained within the metaphor of an interview some young people became very involved in their characters. The feelings of rejection, anger, aggression were experienced as *real*.

The rationale was that if bullies/aggressors could experience bullying themselves it would be so painful they would never again bully. What was naively overlooked at the time was that some children possibly bullied more as a consequence, because they realized the power they could wield over their victims and the fear they could incite. For some children having experienced humiliation, bullying may be perceived as the only course of action: projecting anger and hatred on to others. Humiliating others may be a physical 'cloak' hiding the real emotional powerlessness felt within.

The power of drama lies in its quality of accessing repressed feelings. Therein however also lies its potential for abuse.

I had no background information on the young people; several were likely to have suffered abuse in some form, therefore some may have interpreted the drama session as another abusive encounter.

STORMING TOWN HALLS

In our final production at drama school we performed Peter Whelan's *The Accrington Pals*, a harrowing true story of war, sacrifice and the struggle for truth. As preparation, some students visited the northern town of Accrington, set in the heart of Lancashire. The recollections of the town's 'elders' of horrifyingly large Allied losses suffered during the Battle of the Somme were vivid and passionate. So, too, were feelings towards the authorities who withheld this information from the townsfolk. Only after the town hall was stormed by outraged women was the truth finally admitted.

During performances people sobbed in the audience, at times so loudly that it became quite disconcerting for the actors. How could it be that drama stirred up such powerful emotions?

The Accrington Pals is a dramatic representation of a real historical event. It may have been a cathartic experience to members of the audience, yet the nature of the situation did not allow for exploration of these feelings. The grief and loss felt by the women of Accrington were accentuated by the knowledge that those at the town hall did not care. For members of the audience there will have been some whose grief and pain at losses in their life had never been truly acknowledged or even witnessed by another.

Churning up gravel, skidding around a track, or storming town halls seem to epitomize the early stages of my journey.

Events, encounters and enlightenments have served to help refine methods and approaches, but the underlying philosophy on children remains unchanged.

My philosophy is, as Gibran expresses so beautifully in *The Prophet* (1926), the belief that our children do not belong to us. Our role as adults is to be there for the child, to provide not only food, warmth and shelter, but to teach the child to love. Only when a child feels loved, can he love.

The child learns acceptance, respect and tolerance. He understands himself to be an individual valued for his own qualities; his thoughts, ideas and feelings.

DRAMA WITH YOUNG PEOPLE

In working with non-school attenders, drama became the predominant means of expression within the discussion group.

Anger and mistrust were the most prevalent feelings amongst those present: anger with parents/carers, teachers, social workers, probation officers and the police. Underlying this often explosive energy was a sense of inadequacy, a hopelessness: 'No one ever listens to me/no one cares about what I want/ I can't be what they want me to be/nothing that I do or say will make any difference.'

Drama provided a container for the anger and frustration (obviously actors could not be allowed to hit one another). The group searched and found words to express themselves, they were able to hear and to be heard.

Many cultures use dramatic ritual to mark transitions in life (Grainger 1990), such as marriage and death; and in some cultures, the passage from childhood to adulthood. Adolescence is often a chaotic and confusing time, containing as it does separation from parents/carers, development of sexuality, explorations into personal relationships and many other challenging facets of teenage life.

Specifically, drama in the form of ritual (wherein such issues are collectively acknowledged and addressed) can provide a vehicle to help the more general rite of passage into adulthood.

A RUDE AWAKENING

Wishing to work specifically with young people, I became a residential social worker. I had never imagined that physical, sexual and emotional abuse were so widespread. The 'adults' employed to support these young people were, certainly in my case, and for many others, little more than adolescents, living through our own chaos and trying to survive in that volatile place ourselves. I felt largely inadequate working within an environment which seemed to perpetuate the chaos instead of responding to the real needs of the young people in our care.

I grew angry and frustrated, felt unheard and unsupported. My anger was partly fuelled by specific causes, a chronic lack of training (with the exception of control and restraint techniques) and inadequate ongoing support. Mostly, though, the anger was nebulous in nature, directed towards those who made or did not make decisions, whose agenda seemed to contain anything other than actively enabling the young people to address issues in their own lives, make decisions and effect real change. Quite simply, those in management were out of touch with the clients and staff.

On one occasion, a substantial number of residential and field social workers 'stormed' the headquarters in protest at the sacking of a colleague.

The 'crime' she had committed was one of self-defence against a very angry child who had attacked the social worker with a fire extinguisher. The colleague was reinstated, the child's real needs, which undoubtedly had some bearing on the violent outburst (one of many), remained unmet. Several questions arise from this series of events. How does a worker respond to physical attacks from young people in her care? How can the worker be supported in helping the young person express his violent/angry feelings in a way that is less destructive, in a way that may offer a resolution? How could a worker be so supported that she could tolerate the child's feelings, without feeling threatened or helpless and thus becoming defensive?

I moved on to work in a regional centre for young women believing it would provide an opportunity to undertake long-term work rather than crisis intervention. The centre offered a secure unit and its own school. I was warned before my first shift in the secure unit about the emotional wrench I would feel when I locked the bedroom doors. When the time came it was done hurriedly and with sheer relief. I felt at times we were all sitting on a time bomb. Occasionally the tension would abate, allowing us to relax and actually enjoy one another's company; barriers would slowly come down and trust between young women and staff could develop.

Despite these minor inroads, trust was very fragile and easily threatened. Conflicts arose among the staff group which, with hindsight, were clearly exacerbated by the emotional turmoil of the client group, and feelings of frustration and inadequacy on the part of the staff.

Drama is a means through which we can feel (again) without being overwhelmed or engulfed by these feelings. It provides a safe, containing vessel in which to express the feelings, and to allow healing to begin.

One particular shift at the centre was fraught with tension. Three of the young women were arguing over missing, allegedly stolen, clothes. Knowing the likelihood of a physical confrontation and the consequent need for control and restraint techniques (the prospect of which, despite the extensive training, still filled me with apprehension), staff had to intervene.

Four members of staff accompanied the young women over to the secure unit, with the 'promise' of a just resolution. The secure unit was the only space available which would ensure privacy. The doors remained unlocked.

An amicable chat was clearly out of the question. Instead we set a time limit of half an hour. I asked each of the young women to choose a worker, and indicated a space away from the others, to share what they were feeling and why. They had ten minutes to do this, then we would come back together. I had no idea what the next stage was; somehow they needed to talk with one another. We met again. The atmosphere had eased a little, perhaps as some of the feelings had already been shared and believed. We discussed the next move.

The workers sat around a table, and the three young women stood behind them. A dialogue followed, where feelings of mistrust, jealousy and hurt were shared. The women could add new material by touching the shoulder of their 'double', but they could not speak directly to each other.

The 'thief' acknowledged guilt and was forgiven, and within the time allowed we returned to the unit with a just resolution.

CLAMMY HANDS

Lisa, a 15-year-old resident, was an inspirational poet. Her creations were simply constructed, powerful and personal. She wrote about the events leading up to her being taken into care, and the siblings the authorities refused to allow her to visit. One of her poems, reproduced on p. 189, forms the basis for this chapter.

The poem is about her rejection by her mother and the pain and confusion this caused Lisa. She taught people like myself much about our role. We could not replace her real mother, yet ours were the only hands available to her.

Lisa, like many of the young people I have met, was particularly conscious of 'clammy hands': hands that cling, hands that are really there only to have their own needs met.

The clammy hands in Lisa's poem say they care, but is that care merely a façade to hide the carers' underlying motives in the work? Too often the carer/worker is unable to be emotionally present for the young person.

Unlike Lisa, some children and young people who have experienced abandonment seem to have, as Guex observed in her patients (Guex 1950), an insatiable need to be accepted and loved. Some are very practised in denying their own feelings and needs in return for love and acceptance, however unworthy that 'love' is. This can place a child or young person in a very vulnerable and potentially abusive situation.

Donna, a 14-year-old girl, absconded from the children's home and became acquainted with three young people. Although she had never met these people previously Donna willingly agreed to return to their home. She found herself a victim of the most appalling, sadistic abuse. Donna was systematically beaten, sexually abused and humiliated.

The psychiatrist who cared for Donna believed the only reason for her survival was her well-developed and fortified defence system. Donna had experienced prolonged episodes of emotional neglect and physical and sexual abuse. These episodes began shortly after her first birthday. Donna's means of survival was to switch off to physical and emotional pain (to dissociate), in exchange for 'love'.

Anne Bannister has observed, in her work with sexually abused children, the ability to anaesthetize not only against physical suffering, but also against sensations such as hunger (Bannister 1989). Dissociation is a form of denial; repressing or cutting off unmet needs and feelings from the world outside.

As children and young children are potentially vulnerable to exploitation by adults, an awareness of the messages consciously and unconsciously being communicated is vital.

In one home for young women, all but one of the management staff were male. Although there was a policy on sex discrimination in existence, it seemed to have superficial relevance to some.

After reporting an incident of sexual harassment that I had witnessed I was frustrated though unsurprised to find my colleague chose not to pursue the allegation, for fear of losing her job. As a single parent, her continued employment was understandably more important to her. The needs of her children took precedence over her own treatment. Retraction of her statement was met with relief by management. For myself, I saw it as a grave failing of the system, with serious consequences for the young women in our care. What messages were we giving to these young women? I did not want to be a part of a system which supported the notion of male dominance and the belief that gender, age and position presume righteousness.

Alice Miller speaks out fiercely against the opinion that age brings wisdom, and proposes that, in order to be aware of what is happening around us, we must first know what is happening within us (Miller 1990). We must be able to *feel*. Allowing oneself to feel and respond honestly to a situation is for some a terrifying prospect. It is a step into the unknown. It seems so much easier to switch off, to rely on hierarchies and 'accepted', if not 'acceptable', ways of being.

In the early stages of this journey one of the unconscious forces at work is a need to be accepted. Acknowledgement of this frightening drive is a painful and slow process. For myself, the primary requisite for this process to begin was to find my own 'space'.

AN OTHER'S HAND

This all-important space was provided by a visiting psychotherapist who offered individual therapy to some residents. Staff also requested time with the psychotherapist, and this was readily agreed to by the management. Perhaps it was thought that there would be fewer emotional demands made of them as a consequence. Whatever the reason, I was grateful for the opportunity.

Within these sessions I had the space to explore work-related issues, my own skills, vulnerabilities and needs. I felt empowered. I was able to express previously repressed feelings of anger and frustration, without being engulfed by them, to move through them, and begin to make sense. The psychotherapist was also a psychodramatist and often we looked at an event using role-reversal, doubling and sculpting.

The support and unity of colleagues at that time was vital. We were discovering a new language which enabled us to focus on the feelings evoked by the work, without skating over them. As a consequence, we could propose positive changes borne out of constructive criticism and genuine care for the client group.

'Feelings groups' were established for the residents and staff, as a forum for airing disagreements and misunderstandings, but also for giving positive feedback and thanking others for time spent together. There was much hope around. 'Storming the town hall' was not, after all, the only means by which we could be heard.

Unfortunately, changes in attitudes and perspectives take time and commitment, and all too often power is employed as an easy option ('Do as I say because I am your mother/father/teacher/manager/bigger than you/ older than you'). In short, anything other than giving an honest response.

The psychotherapist suggested that I might be interested in attending a conference on something called dramatherapy. Within dramatherapy I discovered that different strands of understanding, theories, experiences and instincts could be tied together. Instead of churning up gravel and skidding around a track I now felt I was at least on foot, though often plodding, and occasionally sinking under the weight and responsibility of my endeavour to become a dramatherapist. I realized also, with trepidation and excitement, that I was in a position to truly offer my own hand.

The first years of the infant's life are considered the most important for both the growth of the individual and the development of the personality. Yet the individual is *continually* growing.

I have encountered many people whom for a time I have 'connected' with. With some it has been their hand that I have reached out for, with others they have reached out for mine. We have shared feelings that have been acknowledged, and words that have been heard. We may not have offered advice, and for the most part we may not have wanted it. Instead we had someone who was able to stay with us throughout our confusion or distress, and to give us the time and space to find our own solutions. It is through and by these connections that the inner needs can be acknowledged, allowed the space they deserve, and ways found to re-own them. Defence mechanisms block the making of these connections, because to make a connection is dangerous. It is threatening.

One person I 'connected' with was a woman called Jo. Jo had willingly given up a lucrative business career in search of something more rewarding. She chose to work voluntarily with ex-offenders. Jo described healing thus:

As you grow up and get hurt, you build a wall around yourself, which is like a person. Each brick is made of very thick armour-plated glass. They interlock in an intricate pattern. Over time you lose the plan of how they fit together. So eventually you see other people's feelings but you can't feel back. You're protected, you can't feel, you can't give and you can't receive. Only when there's trust, can the pattern be worked out.

This blocking of the adult's emotional life, according to Alice Miller, and the adult's subsequent difficulty in understanding and responding to the feelings of children, can be attributed to the adult cutting off his/her own childhood because of unmet needs and/or traumatic experiences that have passed, unwitnessed (Miller 1984). In order for any adult to be emotionally present for the child – whether parent, social worker, teacher or drama-therapist – it is first essential that the adult be emotionally present for their own 'inner' child. Gibran believes that only something which lies within the depths of our own knowledge can be revealed to us by another (Gibran 1926). If we block out our own feelings, urges, needs, prejudices, thoughts, creativity, how can we possibly help another acknowledge their own?

After the bond with the primary carer, other bonds or 'connections' are made. These usually happen in a natural, unassuming way, such as a relationship with a special teacher or favourite aunt or uncle, someone the child feels comfortable with. Perhaps the therapist is attempting to emulate a special teacher. Should the therapist attempt to emulate anyone?

The roles of teacher and therapist share common ground in terms of respecting, listening to, and empathizing with the child; however, the tasks differ. The task of the teacher is to facilitate the child's understanding of his outer, interpsychic, world. A good enough teacher is able to engage the child by providing stability, acknowledging achievements, encouraging the child to take risks, recognizing the child's abilities and dis-abilities. The task of the therapist is to help the child's understanding of his inner, interpsychic world.

Carl Rogers claims there are three core qualities necessary for any client-centred therapist (Rogers 1951). These are genuineness, non-possessive warmth and accurate empathy. These qualities are also applicable to the teacher. Aspy and Roebuck (1983) studied the effects on educational and personal developments of students in relation to these qualities possessed by teachers, and found a favourable correlation (Aspy and Roebuck 1983). The qualities relate to greater gains in academic subjects, fewer disruptive problems, increased motivation and fewer absences.

THE THERAPIST'S HAND/SHALL I BE MOTHER?

A child may be referred to therapy initially as the result of a behavioural symptom, such as aggressive outbursts, inappropriate sexualized behaviour, or the child's becoming phobic or withdrawn. The referrer's measure of success in therapy may be a decrease in the frequency and/or intensity of the behaviour. For some children, focusing on the perceived problematic behaviour and finding a satisfactory resolution might be sufficient. For most children, however, the presenting behaviour is an indication of a deeper conflict. Boersma, Moskal and Massey believe that the treatment of some presenting symptoms, such as school-phobia, by desensitization techniques is often inappropriate, as the therapist fails to recognize the child's unconscious and the possible hidden root of the fear (Boersma *et al.* 1991). They illustrate how a child's phobia of the wind could be located in the child's unconscious fear of parental separation. Bowlby believes that children often develop reactive fears and depression if the mother–infant bond is understood by the child to be precarious (Bowlby 1969, 1973).

As a dramatherapist it is my aim to acknowledge and explore these deeper conflicts with the child, to encourage the child to search for his own resolutions, and thus to work towards inner healing.

Guntrip, an associate of Fairbairn and Winnicott, supports Fairbairn's understanding that every personality experiences a schizoid split at some level (Guntrip 1971). He emphasizes the importance of trust within the therapeutic relationship as a prerequisite for healing of the schizoid personality; healing of the different parts of the self, the hidden and the visible so that a 'true self' may be present in the world (Winnicott 1964).

A child who has experienced good enough mothering and has been brought up in an accepting, respecting and loving environment is less likely to be obstructed/blocked in making connections with others. He will have a sense of emotional security. The child will not be immune to, nor should he necessarily be 'protected' from, difficult or painful emotions. *The Girl who Loved the Wind* (Yolen and Young 1987) is a story of an overprotective father and his daughter, who grows restless and unhappy in her comfortable yet unrealistic home. She feels imprisoned. The little girl discovers the wind and how sometimes it is sad and harsh, and other times it is sweet and beautiful. She allows herself to be carried away by the wind; to live in the real world, to experience joy and pain; to live life to the full. As long as the child is emotionally secure enough she will struggle with painful and difficult feelings, and with the event/incident provoking them, and in time find a satisfactory solution. The event is integrated into the child's psyche sufficiently to prevent lasting trauma.

A child who has not experienced good enough mothering will have great difficulty in integrating some experiences. Such experiences will be mentally filed away under sections marked 'Does not make any sense', 'Danger', 'Guilt', or 'Hurt'. In time, defences arise to protect from further experiences, such as 'Do not trust', 'Beware of women/men', 'Never become vulnerable'. Often an individual can pass unnoticed through childhood, adolescence and into adulthood untrusting, unable to form meaningful relationships, withdrawn and isolated.

Sometimes however the behaviour of a child may cause enough concern to an adult to seek professional support.

A dramatherapist could be employed to offer this support. The factors at play within the therapeutic relationship are potentially contradictory. A child or young person finds himself in a room with a stranger. He may have met her briefly before with his parents/carers. He may have been told that this stranger was here to help him, to listen to him, to make sense of his life and the problems he is facing. He doesn't have any problems. He is sick of people interfering, and wishes they would leave him alone. To be left alone to do what he wants, even if it hurts others and himself in the process. That's how it is. He may, on the other hand, have been told nothing about the stranger. Only that he *has* to attend these sessions as part of his treatment of care programme.

The dramatherapist is aware of her task, to acknowledge and explore the hidden, unmet needs of the child.

As it is the task of therapy to locate, acknowledge and explore the hidden child, the 'inner' child, it seems reasonable to base the therapeutic relationship on the primary bond with an other. This is not a new theory. Winnicott put forward the theory that what takes place in the therapeutic relationship is an attempt to imitate the natural process that characterizes the mother–infant relationship (Winnicott 1965). The basic principles of tolerance, acceptance and respect found within a good enough mothering relationship are the basis for the therapeutic relationship. Eichenbaum and Orbach support Winnicott's theory, emphasizing the importance of consistency and ability to 'hold' the client, to tolerate the *whole* client, thus offering a new kind of 'psychological umbilical cord' (Eichenbaum and Orbach 1983). Keeping with the metaphor of this chapter, the therapist is offering an other hand to the child.

Virginia Axline states clearly that the most important element in therapy is the relationship established between the therapist and the child (Axline 1989). The therapist strives genuinely to accept the child *as he is*, to witness and reflect back his feelings; to trust in the child's ability to facilitate change in his life, given the opportunity to do so. The therapist is emotionally present for the 'inner' child.

According to Suttie, no amount of technical skill, theoretical knowledge or thoroughness on the part of the therapist will compensate for the absence of a sympathetic understanding, and the ability to empathize with the child, both the presenting child and the 'inner' child (Suttie 1988).

How can a dramatherapist empathize with/be emotionally present for the child?

In order for the dramatherapist to be emotionally present for the child in therapy, she must allow *her own inner child* to be present. This child is held safely within the therapist's psyche. The therapist must truly believe that the child in therapy will be able to meet the needs of his own 'inner child' if he is facilitated to do this by someone who has, herself, met her own 'inner child's' needs. Anne Bannister believes all children are capable of healing themselves, if only adults will allow them to do so (Bannister 1992). When adults have actively prevented children from healing, when they have aggravated the wounds, then the therapist has to facilitate the child's self-healing process.

It is not the task of the therapist to gratify the child's needs, and to follow this assumption implies that the therapist knows what is best for the child. The therapist accompanies the child on his journey, not her own. Within the therapeutic space it is the child's needs which take precedence; the therapist is not there to have her own needs met. She is conscious of having clammy hands.

The dramatherapist's role can be further compared to the role of the mother in the area of creative play. The infant begins to play initially within the primary relationship providing it is secure enough. A child will naturally engage with play in order to externalize what is within, in an attempt to make sense of it. He will use play to explore his surroundings in relation to himself.

Casement recognizes the non-intrusive presence of the mother, who is willing to be included in her child's early playing, yet also willing to be excluded (Casement 1990). The choice belongs to the child. It is often the mother's background presence providing the security that allows the setting for creative play to develop.

There are many theories and frameworks within which play has been observed and defined in terms of its nature and purpose. As a drama-therapist, Sue Jennings's description of play as a developmental process (Jennings 1987) reflects my own personal and professional experiences of play. Developmental play comprising three stages – embodiment play, projective play and role-play – also resonates with object relations theory.

In the infant's early life he encounters the world primarily through his senses – the texture of the breast, the warmth of milk, the sting of a wet nappy, a comforting hand.

The infant begins initiating contact with the outside world. He begins exploring his impact on the world of water, of faeces, food and sand. He learns to imitate human sounds and facial expresssions. This is embodiment play.

When the child can predict to some extent the objects around him (can their physical presence be relied upon?) he will begin to engage in projective play, projecting feelings and meanings on to objects. Objects take on a symbolic meaning. The mother is the child's first 'object'.

Embodiment play may develop into projective play. Stories can also be understood as projective play in the narrative as feelings are projected on to imaginary characters. The play allows for a distance between the child and his feelings.

A child will, in time, relate to the symbolic object, becoming someone or something in response. He is entering into a world of role-play. He has a sense of self: who he is in relation to others and his environment.

The mother, or primary carer, also exists within a context, just as the child. She brings with her to that relationship her own attitudes, experiences and feelings. Feminist psychotherapists Eichenbaum and Orbach expound object relations theory by exploring the nature of this being, the mother, not as an object but as a subject, active within the primary relationship (Eichenbaum and Orbach 1983).

It follows that the dramatherapist also is not an object. She too brings into the relationship feelings, attitudes, and beliefs. The dramatherapist is responsible for addressing her own material so that she may be emotionally present for the child. This journey of self-exploration I understand to be an endless one. As Winnicott wisely employed the phrase, a *good enough* mother, the term can also be applicable to the therapist.

A child entering dramatherapy is likely to feel rejection towards, mistrustful of and angry with the therapist. These feelings may not be overtly communicated. How they are communicated depends on the child's coping strategies. How they are received will depend on the therapist's.

Case example: Jake

Jake found emotional isolation a means of survival. He needed to survive feelings of rejection and grief, permanent threats to him. Jake's mother had left the family home seven years previously. Under-developed for his 14 years, Jake appeared to be a lost child, yearning for physical warmth and affection. Yet it was impossible to get close to Jake. He seemed to be surrounded by a transparent wall. It was possible to see him, but not to touch him. Jake was found inciting attacks on younger, more vulnerable residents. He found he could manipulate others into arguments and conflicts then safely withdraw to watch the ensuing scene erupt. Jake was directing his own dramas, only no one else was aware of being directed.

Jake's early work in the dramatherapy sessions revolved around three imaginary yet familiar creatures. They were Jake's own creations, the main character and two auxiliaries, clear representations of good and evil. Jake's stories told and retold the same drama, this conflict. Each time the main character became the battleground. He was alone in his despair, *yet he always survived.*

Jake is a creative individual who has drawn upon his ability to help him cope with his life. Alice Miller writes of creativity as a defence mechanism which allows for survival, yet masks rather than reveals the 'inner' child (Miller 1990).

I sensed Jake's mistrust of me in the early sessions. He expressed an indifference towards his mother: 'Why should I care about her, she doesn't care about me?' I am also a women, and Jake's experience of women to date is that they are untrustworthy and rejecting.

One session Jake discovered my collection of stones and pebbles. He became animated and, for the first time since meeting, he looked me straight in the eye. Jake, I discovered, also had a stone collection. The following week he brought his transparent boxes filled with an array of shades, shapes and sizes of different stones.

We began to explore the stones, one by one, describing the many layers of almost three-dimensional colours. Jake came across a blue tiger eye. He held the stone in his hands, exploring its contours as he was reminded of a toggle from a blue duffle coat he no longer had. The coat was worn by a confused and frightened 7-year-old who watched his mother leave him, and he didn't know why. Jake sobbed as he recalled his memories. 'She didn't want me.'

The stones allowed Jake to engage in a sensory experience, which, like embodiment play, accesses unconscious, 'bodily-held' sensory memories. Jake had expressed some of the hurt and despair of the trauma. He had experienced, as the audience watching *The Accrington Pals*, a catharsis. Unlike the audience, these expressed feelings could be witnessed and validated. His 'inner' child was cautiously stepping into the therapeutic space.

During the duffle coat session I experienced a powerful urge to throw my arms around him. I resisted. As quickly as the urge had emerged, it disappeared, replaced instead with a sense of emotional withdrawal. Suddenly I felt rejected. I did not hug Jake, and I found the task of emotionally staying present for Jake extremely challenging.

From this dramatic, non-verbal communication the following questions arose: were the despair and hopelessness I experienced my own unresolved material which, when triggered by Jake, felt overwhelming for me? could I hold my own 'inner' child within? did I then respond to Jake's transference of rejection by withdrawing myself?

In the next session I shared my dilemma of wanting to comfort him in his grief, yet feeling that that was something *I* needed to do, and not necessarily Jake's need. He responded immediately by saying, 'No one *ever* hugs me but my dad.'

Jake displayed many characteristics belonging to a schizoid personality – fear of intimacy, a sense of futility and powerlessness. However, having a label does not heal.

Jake has now begun to explore his relationship to power through a metaphor. As a child Jake recalled his father telling him the story of 'The Tinderbox'. For Jake the precious content of his tinderbox is power.

Jung believed that a child's use of imaginative expression in the presence of a therapist may enable him to release intense unconscious symbols at a critically emotional time (Jung 1964).

Jake's journey continues along its path, only now the 'inner' child has a companion, a tinderbox containing Jake's own power.

THE CHILD'S HAND

It seems only fitting, following this stream of questions and uncertainties, to close with some thoughts on the child.

Society seems reluctant to acknowledge the impact of childhood experiences on the adult. When children and young people are labelled 'the criminal element', 'delinquents' and 'thugs', it is usually the parents, and in particular the mother, who are deemed responsible. If the mother is a lone-parent, society's condemnation falls even more heavily on her shoulders. When will we understand that raising the next generation is *the* most important role any adult can undertake, and that men and women will one day receive the support and acknowledgement due.

At times it is necessary to 'storm the town hall' in order for the child to be heard. Other times, the voice is a whisper heard only by an other:

> The little boy watched, wide-eyed, as the emperor's procession passed by. A cascade of colours, a cacophony of sounds. He clung tightly to his father's hand as he whispered, 'The emperor is wearing no clothes.' His father smiled. He knew his son spoke the truth.

CONCLUSION

'Shall I be mother?' was a personal exploration into the role of the dramatherapist through its comparison with the role of the mother.

By considering the mother–child relationship it would seem that qualities encompassed by the 'good enough' mothering relationship would be highly valued by the dramatherapist. However, the dramatherapist cannot *be* 'the child's mother'.

The question 'Shall I be mother?' was originally directed towards the child in therapy. Put another way, is it the task of the dramatherapist to offer reparenting? Having considered the role of the mother it becomes apparent that many other individuals can contribute towards the task of 'mothering'. During the chapter I refer particularly to teachers and social workers. However, with respect to the role of the dramatherapist it is crucial to understand her task, that of facilitating the child's self-healing through his own creativity.

In order for this to be possible it is essential that the dramatherapist is able to engage with her own 'inner' child. This 'inner' child allows the dramatherapist to be emotionally present for the child in therapy. Thus the question 'Shall I be mother?' must first be asked by the dramatherapist herself with respect to her own 'inner' child.

NOTES

Throughout this chapter both the primary carer and the dramatherapist have been referred to as female. Much as I would like to challenge the belief that the primary carer and the dramatherapist are usually female, unfortunately I cannot. I question why it is still generally the female parent who provides the primary bond, and strongly dispute the argument that only the mother can fulfil the child's needs. Why too is it so difficult to find male dramatherapists working with children in this country? There are presently three times as many female dramatherapists as there are male. (Information provided by the British Association for Dramatherapists, 1993.) Is dramatherapy in this country, and in particular dramatherapy with children, becoming the domain of females, following other professions such as infant and primary teaching and nursing? What messages are we communicating to our children and young people about the differences between the genders?

REFERENCES

Aspy and Roebuck, C. (1983) *Freedom to learn for the Eighties.* Oxford: Charles Merrill.
Axline, Virginia M. (1989) *Playtherapy.* Churchill Livingstone.
Bannister, Anne (1989) The effects of child sexual abuse on body and image. *Journal for the British Associaton for Dramatherapists,* 12 (1): 37–43.
Bannister, Anne (ed.) (1992) *From Hearing to Healing.* Harlow: Longman.
Bettelheim, B. (1977) *The Uses of Enchantment.* New York: Vintage Books.
Boersma, F. J., Moskal, R. and Massey, D. (1991) Acknowledging the wind and a child's unconscious: creative therapy with trance experience. *The Arts in Psychotherapy,* 18: 157–65.
Bowlby, John (1969) *Attachment and Loss.* Vol. 1: *Attachment.* London: Hogarth Press.
——— (1973) *Attachment and Loss.* Vol. 2: *Separation: Anxiety and Anger.* London: Hogarth Press.
——— (1980) *Attachment and Loss.* Vol. 3: *Sadness and Depression.* London: Hogarth Press.
Casement, Patrick (1990) *Further Learning from the Patient.* London: Routledge.
Cattanach, Ann (1992) *Play Therapy with Abused Children.* London: Jessica Kingsley.
Eichenbaum, L. and Orbach, S. (1983) *Understanding Women.* Harmondsworth, Middlesex: Penguin.

Fairbairn, R. W. D. (1952) *Psychoanalytic Studies of the Personality*. London: Routledge.

Freud, S. (1912) *The Dynamics of Transference*. SE 13.

Gibran, K. (1926) *The Prophet*. London: Heinemann.

Grainger, Roger (1990) *Drama and Healing: the roots of drama therapy*. London: Jessica Kingsley.

Guex, Germaine (1950) *La névrose d'abandon*. Paris: PUF.

Guntrip, Harold (1971) *Psychoanalytic Theory, Therapy and the Self*. New York: Basic Books.

―――― (1975) My experiences of analysis with Fairbairn and Winnicott. *International Review of Psychoanalysis*, 2: 145–56.

Jennings, Sue (ed.) (1987) *Dramatherapy, Theory and Practice*, 1. London: Routledge.

―――― (1990) *Dramatherapy with Families, Groups and Individuals*. London: Jessica Kingsley.

Jung, Carl (ed.) (1964) *Man and his Symbols*. Harmondsworth, Middlesex: Penguin.

Klein, M. (1932) *The Psycho-Analysis of Children* (rev. edn). London: Hogarth Press.

Laplanche, J. and Pontalis, J. B. (1988) *The Language of Psychoanalysis*. London: Karnac Books.

Liedloff, Jean (1977) *The Continuum Concept*. New York: Alfred A. Knopf.

Masters, Brian (1985) *Killing for Company*. London: Jonathan Cape.

Miller, Alice (1984) *Thou Shalt Not Be Aware*. London: Pluto Press.

―――― (1987) *For Your Own Good*. London: Virago Press.

―――― (1990) *The Untouched Key*. London: Virago Press.

Rogers, Carl (1951) *Client-Centred Therapy*. London: Constable.

Rogers, Carl (ed.) (1983) *Freedom to Learn for the Eighties*. Oxford: Charles Merrill.

Schaefer, C. C. (ed.) (1988) *Innovative Interventions in Child and Adolescent Therapy*. J. Wiley & Sons.

Spitz, R. A. (1945) Hospitalism: an enquiry into the genesis of psychiatric conditions in early childhood. *The Psychoanalytic Study of the Child*, 1: 53–74.

Suttie, Ian D. (1988) *The Origins of Love and Hate*. London: Free Association Books.

Winnicott, Donald W. (1964) *The Child, the Family and the Outside World*. Harmondsworth, Middlesex: Penguin.

―――― (1965) *The Maturational Processes and the Facilitating Environment*. London: Hogarth Press.

Yolen, J. and Young, E. (1987) *The Girl who Loved the Wind*. New York: Harper & Row.

Chapter 11

Families and the story of change

Simon Dermody

INTRODUCTION

This chapter explores how dramatherapy processes offer a universal language for change to families in distress. Integrating ideas from the Systemic, Transgenerational and Strategic Family Therapy schools, it offers a dramatherapy model for the assessment and treatment of families presenting with a range of difficulties. Case illustrations are used to exemplify the specific application of this model.

THE ART OF THE THERAPIST–JUGGLER

When I meet a family and they begin to share their story with me, I quickly start to feel like a juggler. A juggler's task is to keep airborne a number of juggling sticks simultaneously. The therapist–juggler who works with families 'juggles' a stepfather's view on parenting, a mother's protectiveness of her son, a child's feelings about a recent divorce, the concern of a grandparent over how family patterns have changed in modern times. All of these juggling sticks are passed over into the willing and outstretched hands of the therapist, who is expected to begin to keep them airborne successfully.

The image of the therapist-as-juggler helps me in my efforts to hold these differing and equally valued individual perspectives on the 'family story'. More importantly, it makes it easier for me to generate an overview, or 'meta-perspective', on the plurality of worlds that create the family psycho-system.

The idea of the family as a psycho-system views the family as a *system of individuals*, each with their own unique psyche, intimately connected by hereditary, attachment and life-cycle events over time.

The family is a psycho-system of two, three, four or more generations, who progress *simultaneously* through the human life cycle. Each generation negotiates its way through its own life-cycle phase at the same time as the other generations: grandparents are coming to terms with ageing whilst adults/parents are struggling with the multiple responsibilities of their roles; and as children play their way through childhood, tortured teenagers endure the exquisite turmoil of adolescence.

This combination of generations synergizes to create its own, particular family 'psycho-ecology' which seeks to maintain a delicate emotional balance as it evolves interactively through time.

My attempts to help families change whilst maintaining their balance or psycho-ecology have occupied much of my work over the last ten years. This approach has been made possible by the gradual application and integration of dramatherapy and play therapy methods within the more verbal and conceptual traditions of the various family therapy schools (Dermody 1988). Most useful to my work with families has been the gradual introduction of the *symbolic-expressive* language of play and drama. The richly symbolic language of play/drama has offered all the family, adults, adolescents and children alike, a therapeutic milieu within which they can actively explore and discover the new possibilities of change.

DRAMATHERAPY, PLAY THERAPY AND FAMILIES

Dramatherapy as a discipline has evolved over the last thirty years primarily within the context of groups (Jennings 1987). Evolving from such a background and therapeutic tradition has given dramatherapy a sound theoretical framework within which to develop dramatherapy practice with groups. Integrating group theory and group psychotherapy with theatre and drama techniques has enabled dramatherapists to develop sophisticated group practice with a huge range of clients.

More recently, Landy and others have begun integrating the theoretical frameworks of individual psychotherapy with the enactive and symbolic techniques of dramatherapy (Landy 1992). A new model or paradigm for individual dramatherapy is thus, at this present time, being evolved and established. This currently emerging model is helping to feed the developing enthusiasm for dramatherapy one to one, which continues to grow.

Throughout the same period, the practice of dramatherapy with part or whole families, certainly in this country, has been very limited indeed. A recent attempt to publish a *Dramatherapy Journal* 'special' produced only two papers on the subject (Dermody 1992, Walsh *et al.* 1992). Prior to this, publications by dramatherapists on the subject were almost exclusively from the pen of Roy Shuttleworth (Shuttleworth 1987).

Dramatherapy as a discipline has shown a curious reluctance to enter the field of work with families. This is a lost opportunity, I believe, for the profession and for families. The practice of dramatherapy offers a unique therapeutic language to clients. This is true of dramatherapy work with groups, individuals and *client families*.

There is a clear historical explanation why dramatherapy has not entered the field of family work. The 1960s, 1970s and 1980s were the three decades which saw dramatherapy emerge as a distinct discipline, with its own unique identity and approach. These three decades paralleled the passage of the therapeutic group as the dominant and most accepted context for collective therapy to be practised. Already established as a theory and method for therapeutic change, and, even more important, recognized and sanctioned as a 'legitimate' therapeutic force, group therapy was able to parent the new-born dramatherapy through its creative childhood and adolescence. This was a mutually agreeable arrangement, for which, for many years, dramatherapy was, I suspect, quite grateful.

I fancy, rather, that things have changed somewhat in the last few years, with dramatherapists ever more eager to demonstrate what they uniquely do. At the same time, dramatherapy as a discipline is quite rightly very keen to define what is *different* in its practice, rather than what is similar to other disciplines.

Certainly drama and theatre trace their cultural origins in the community and group experience, and dramatherapy will always be a powerful therapeutic force in groups. There does now also appear to be an opportunity for dramatherapy to extend its practice into a whole range of areas, including work with families. The creative, universal and above all *symbolic* language of drama adapts itself with great plasticity to all human living and work contexts: the family, the business organization, the school, the work team, the couple, the individual, the team sports context. It can be argued that only the group, the individual and the family are the truly *therapeutic* contexts for practice, and the others are dramatherapy applied in a secular setting. However, all of these social and human contexts are open to practitioners who are seeking to extend their practice over and beyond the dramatherapy group.

WHY *FAMILY* THERAPY?

Curiously enough, the evolution of family therapy as a distinct discipline in its own right also spans the decades of the 1960s, 1970s and 1980s. It is, however, fair to say that family therapy did not achieve legitimacy as a therapeutic discipline until the end of the 1970s.

I remember that, when I first started working in the field of mental health in the mid-1970s, any form of 'talking therapy' in the NHS occurred in a group setting. It was only when I began specializing years later, in the field of child and adolescent work, that I discovered that therapists were now seeking to bring about change with whole families present.

To me it is a curious fact that, whilst dramatherapy has very much avoided developing a theoretical and methodological base for work with families (only one dramatherapy training programme, in Torquay, offers a module on 'Dramatherapy with Families'), family therapy has over the years shown great interest in the metaphorical and symbolic language of play and drama (Watzlawick 1967, Shuttleworth 1987, Cade 1983, Erickson 1980).

Family therapy evolved from the individual psychoanalytic tradition, initially in the USA and then in England and Italy. It was developed by innovative thinkers who asked the question: where do we go from here? It seemed obvious to them that, if the source of much human suffering lay in disturbances in attachment, and these disturbances were maintained by continuing dysfunctional family patterns, positive therapeutic change could be achieved through working with the whole or part of a family. This shift from an individual to a 'family systems', interactive, model of human behaviour seems to be part of a wider scientific and cultural process of the 1970s and 1980s (Bateson 1980). This movement began to focus on the *complex pattern of interrelationships between individuals*, as well as on individuals themselves. If you like, on the interpsychic as well as the intrapsychic.

From the start, family therapists such as Virginia Satir and Carl Whitiker sought to work within the natural drama of the family. They used a range of dramatic techniques to enable family members to play and experiment with their learned and ascribed family roles. Whitiker's 'therapy of the absurd' reflected the surreal, theatrical language of Ionesco, Beckett and company, so influential at the time. Early pioneers such as Salvador Minuchin often put family members into 'enactments'. These were carefully selected and stage-managed family role-plays, which aimed to challenge some of the dysfunctional patterns in client families (Minuchin 1977). Throughout the evolution of the family therapy movement in the 1970s and 1980s, the creative tensions between the metaphorical language of play, drama and enactment have continued to be explored by many family therapists.

A THEORETICAL FRAMEWORK

Before going on to outline a working method for dramatherapy with families, let me offer three currently influential ideas in family therapy which I believe can be useful to the dramatherapist who works with families.

The idea of the *family script* (Byng-Hall 1985) offers an historical, transgenerational view of the family. This enables a perspective on patterns over time, which become visible over generations of family life and change. An example of a transgenerational pattern would be a father, himself a second-born son who enjoyed a special intimacy with his father, who reproduces that relationship with his own second son. Such a pattern would be replicative; patterns in the family script are either *replicative* or *corrective*. An example of a corrective script would be a woman who experienced an unhappy relationship with her mother, and sought to parent and mother her own daughter in a very different way.

Allied to this idea of the family script is that of *family mythology* (Byng-Hall 1979). Family myths are conceived of as a powerful set of unconscious family beliefs which organize thinking and ascribe family roles to individuals, within and across generations. These family myths accrue over generations of time and are fed by accounts of events which take on a legendary significance. Accounts or stories of these events are usually apocryphal or embellished moments of family history, which are used to reinforce the family myth. For example, the family of an anorexic client I worked with had a powerful, disabling family myth about the 'disaster' that might occur if they showed feelings openly and experienced emotional intimacy. This disabling myth (unconscious family belief or mind set) was reinforced by a legendary event that happened in the father's family in a previous generation. He described a legendary event from his family of origin, when his parents and brother had a 'terrible row'. This description of the event reinforced the current family myth that emotional expression and openness between family members was dangerous and destructive. His own wife and two daughters had paid a terrible price for this. One daughter had left and cut off from the family (Bowen 1978). The other daughter had spent most of her time helping her parents avoid conflict, defusing situations and often detouring feelings through herself (Palazzoli 1978).

The emerging role of self may often collide with the family 'scripted' role, producing stress at key developmental moments, such as adolescence.

A second idea of potential use to the dramatherapist in work with families is the notion of the *family as a system*. The usefulness of the natural metaphor of the family as a system helps keep in mind how delicately attuned and interrelated is the psycho-ecology of the family. Any natural organism/system, be it a beehive, a tree, or a family, shares universal principles of operation; self-organization (structure and boundaries), self-regulation (balance/harmony), and self-transcendance (growth and development) (Tatham 1990). Of crucial therapeutic significance is: *change in one part of a system means change in another part of the system.* When a second child is born to a family, it influences the psycho-social development of the first child. A daughter or son going into puberty raises the profile of sex in a family, often influencing the sexual balance and intimacy between spouse/partners. The powerful feelings of loss associated with children leaving home frequently amplify the mid-life identity issues of middle-aged parents/spouses. And so on.

Also connected to this idea of the family as a system are the twos (dyads) and threes (triangles) that are the natural units of family. Every family has natural dyads, mother–son, father–daughter, mother–daughter, father–son, brother–brother, sister–sister, brother–sister, in any combination. Then there are the natural triangles: mother–father–son, father–mother–daughter and so on. These are the archetypal family relationships, because they are the natural, biological, human relationships that characterize our species. Nature sets an agenda for each of these archetypal family dyads and triangles; they each have psychological business to do with each other, fathers with sons, mothers with daughters etc. This natural psychological agenda, set within these archetypal family roles, has universal themes. These themes are reflected and mirrored worldwide in myth, legend, theatre, drama, art, music, religion and poetry. All human symbolic culture is then a rich repository of therapeutic source material for work with families, as it reflects the universal family dilemmas. In world theatre, the storylines and relationship configurations from Greek tragedy through to Sam Shephard chronicle the essentially unchanged themes of the archetypal family relationships. When you meet a family, if you focus on the twos and threes, much will become clearer.

The third idea of potential use to the dramatherapist in work with families is the notion that *all therapy is strategic* (Watzlawick 1973). That is to say, the therapist takes responsibility for managing progress towards change. The idea of the therapist consciously manipulating therapeutic change may not be of immediate appeal to the self-styled 'client-centred' practitioner who values therapeutic 'genuineness' and 'integrity' above all else. Such qualities of client-centredness, genuineness and integrity are essential for all good therapy. But the therapist who works with families, however holistic and egalitarian-minded, needs always to be aware of his position in the therapeutic field of complex operations we call 'change'. Families are complex, seductive and multilayered psychosystems, and the dramatherapist who works with them needs to develop a strategic attitude of mind that *anticipates the change that change will bring*.

DRAMATHERAPY WITH FAMILIES: ASSESSMENT

Free play

When I work with families, I like to introduce, at the outset, the experience of *spontaneity and play* as integral to the process of therapy. This is relatively easy to do if young children at the play age are present.

It has always struck me as something of a misnomer under the Trade Descriptions Act for family therapists to claim they are doing *family* therapy, when most of them base their whole approach almost exclusively on words and sophisticated ideas. Young children, often the focus of the 'problem' pattern, are almost immediately asked to sit to one side and are handed a piece of paper on which to draw. They are then ignored for forty-five minutes until they quite understandably become active in other ways, in an attempt to become involved.

I learned about this therapeutic wastage, the marginalization of children, when watching a clinical psychologist colleague interviewing a family. The father, mother and two eldest children sat for an hour whilst the father (a man under extreme stress) tried to articulate his views of the problem, frequently silencing other members of the family in the process. Meanwhile the youngest son, aged 7, sat on the floor drawing with the ubiquitous pen and paper. At the end of the session my colleague said goodbye to the family and picked up the large sheet of paper left by the little boy. In the centre of the paper was an image of a man, clearly the father, surrounded by an army of artillery, tanks, rockets, grenades, all of which were pointed directly at him and about to go off! This one image encapsulated with great intensity the explosive level of feelings in the family and the embattled position of the father as two of his children approached the leaving home age.

I use this vignette to suggest the rich imagery that spontaneously emerges in 'child's play', and which is available to the dramatherapist willing and able to employ a symbolic and poetic therapeutic language in work with families.

Assessment and stagecraft

The family, then, is a complex, multilayered system with a richly symbolic psycho-ecology all of its own. How do we provide this psycho-system a therapeutic space, within which to enact its story?

In the beginning, I find it useful to compare family assessment with the early stages of rehearsal for an improvised play (Johnstone 1981). We are inviting the individual family members to enter the empty, potential space (Brook 1972) and fill it with improvised themes from their family story. They know their story; at this point we do not. In order for us to learn about it, we create a safe, neutral, free play space within which they can 'discover' their story.

At this point in the therapeutic stagecraft we need to offer a minimum, safe structure within which the family can freely improvise. I find the following sequence a useful developmental paradigm:

Joining/boundary-setting
Warm-up
Spontaneity
Improvisation
Symbolic expression
Story-making
Role-taking

Filling a room with all or any of this combination of toys – puppets, dolls, hats, masks, cushions, animal figures, a sand tray, cars, lorries, ambulance, pens, paper, paints, dollshouse and a table – invites spontaneity. Children of course respond instinctively to a play space, and lead their more reluctant parents and teenage siblings into the symbolic field of spontaneity. They often show an interest in a toy or puppet as soon as they enter the therapy room, and I immediately invite them to pick it up. This invitation can be extended into a general invitation to the family to explore the room and its contents in *free play*.

At this point, observation of both the *process* and *content* of family play develops significance. At the level of process, who pairs off with whom? Which child plays with what parent? Who is isolated? Which children play interactively? All of these process questions help the therapist focus on *family organization, family structure, family pattern*.

At this initial stage, the content of family play, the imagery, symbols and themes contained within it, may only be hinted at and glimpsed. I always offer to keep any scribbles or drawings produced at this point.

It may be useful now to discuss the practice of the use of video, co-therapy or a team approach in dramatherapy work with families.

Family therapists routinely work in a video suite and video-record their sessions. This became standard practice in family therapy, out of deference to the emotional and interactional complexity of families. It was recognized that so much information was being communicated at any one moment by a family that, unless video was used to enable routine post-session review, much would be missed and lost.

Dramatherapists beginning work with families will probably have to struggle hard to get access to sophisticated video facilities. I would, however, encourage you, for the reasons already given, in every effort to find and use video. In addition to the recording of family–therapist interaction, in the later stages of therapy a dramatherapist can utilize much more creative use of video. For example, I frequently sit through recorded sequences of play, story-making and enactment with part or whole of the family watching themselves, and discuss their observations, comments and reflections. In this way video can be used as a self-reflective exploratory medium, which can introduce the possibility of change.

There are many advantages in having either a co-therapist or a team to do therapy with families (if you can find either in these hard-pressed days of economic accountability!). The advantage of a team or co-therapist is that they offer another pair of eyes and ears with which to observe and attend to the complex patterns of playful and dramatic interaction in which the family are engaged. While your focus may be drawn to a mother and child at play, your co-therapist or team may be observing another piece of behaviour in a different place. Each moment or image helps to build up a picture of the family's organization, structure and patterns of interaction.

These differing perspectives of therapist, co-therapist or team offer a richness of views of the family; if you like they form a therapeutic system which observes, mirrors and reflects the family as a system.

A period of joining – you with the family, the family with you, the family with the space – can, then, last anything from fifteen to thirty minutes. On average, most of the family sessions last around one and a half hours, which allows time for a mid-session break, when the team can consult and the family can have a drink.

I tend to judge the length of the first period of free play from the level of interaction between the family members and the materials in the room. During this period of free, unstructured joining play, much information is made available already; and assessment is very much about the release of information.

Family puppet story

I like then to invite the whole family freely to select from a range of hand puppets one or two each, and ask them to touch and practise some simple movements with them. Then the family are invited to make up a family puppet story, a technique pioneered by the American art therapists Irwin and Malloy (1975). The family need to be left to discuss some ideas for their puppet story, and to make decisions about themes for the plot and roles for the puppets they animate. A small low table can serve as a performance area for the puppet story. Alternatively a row of chairs can be used, with the family sitting on the floor behind the backs of the chairs out of sight, puppets held up as they enter the action.

My observation is that families access the puppet story method quite freely. It is a loosely structured, improvisational story technique that utilizes the safely distanced, symbolic language of puppets (Scheff 1981). By introducing the narrative schema of *story*, it offers the family a metaphorical framework within which to improvise themes from their own family story, safely disguised and distanced. Even at this early stage of assessment, relevant patterns, themes and motifs from the family story will be revealed and enacted on the puppet stage. It is at this moment that the family's own physical, verbal, behavioural and feeling patterns are symbolized and transformed through the metaphorical language of the puppet story.

The first family to whom I offered this technique had come to therapy in difficulty with adolescent separation/independence gaining. The eldest child, a 16-year-old son, had taken seven Paracetamol and appeared generally unhappy and confused about his life. The rest of the family were sympathetic but equally confused about what to do or what might be done to improve things. In their puppet story, the 16-year-old son chose a bear puppet. In the story the bear wandered aimlessly around, going from one place to another, and from one puppet to another, trying to find things to do to fill his day. The compulsive, purposeful but fruitless searching of the bear produced an overwhelmingly sad and poignant image.

The bear's 'aimless wanderings' were a symbolic, deeply personal statement for the son, articulating and expressing his own acutely felt adolescent turmoil and angst. It was also the first strong indication to us as a team of the poverty of experience in the family script around male adolescent initiation, what we now call independence gaining. The symbolic narrative of the puppet story confirmed and developed our thinking about the family script. We were able to do more work on the transgenerational father–son patterns. This revealed the father's own difficulty in finding his way through the teenage years, and his protracted search for his own adult identity. Work in this area seemed to help the family.

It is this imbalance in the delicate psycho-ecology of the family that can become dysfunctional over time. If, for example, the father–son relationship, as in the above family, is not resonantly attuned or cathected, the psycho-ecology of the family system over generations can become detuned and out of balance. Therapy in this context can be seen as a way of helping the family rebalance its inner psycho-ecology.

Family spectograms

This can be a very useful way of building up more information about family organization and structure. It can also elicit some very creative right-brain material which the dramatherapist can work with later in the therapy.

Genograms or family trees are 'big' in family therapy. Family therapists do a lot of genogram work! The genogram is a relationship map which depicts the wider extended family over a minimum of three generations. It identifies the family's organization and structure, and also enables therapists to focus on any particular relationship.

I like to use the technique in a creative and participatory way, and ask each member of the family if they would like to draw a family tree showing who they think is important in the family (Figure 11.1). Who they include or omit is always revealing, and gives important information about who is close or distant from whom. I ask them to imagine each family member as an object or animal, and so create a *family spectogram* that generates many symbolic images of the family. (A 6-year-old stepdaughter drew her stepfather as a steam train! A father drew his son as an iceberg!) We then stick all the individual family spectograms together into a large canvas and attach it to the wall of the room. This family spectogram canvas serves as a symbolic, relational backdrop to all the subsequent work undertaken by the family. Its symbolic material can later be worked

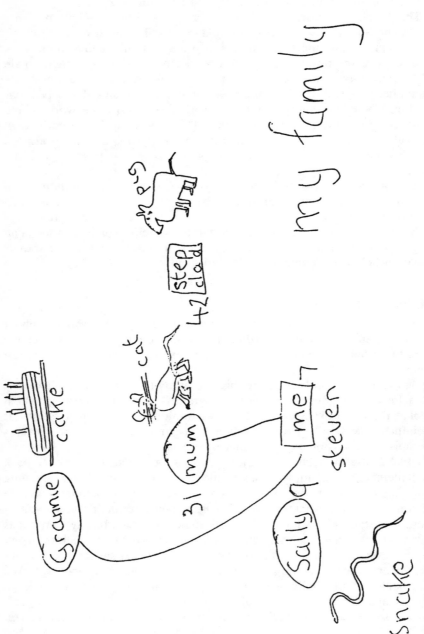

Figure 11.1 Family spectogram of a 7-year-old boy

with, using a wide range of dramatherapy methods including storytelling, story-making, story enactment, maskwork, sculpting and role plays.

The imagery and symbolic material released in the family spectogram helps create a symbolic language and therapeutic culture unique to the family. It is an external representation of the family's internal imaginative worlds. These images and symbols imbue all the therapeutic work, and can be a constant point of reference to which family and therapist can return. They are if you like the base elements from which therapy can be constructed, because they bridge the inner world and experience of each family member, and the interactive conflux that is the family system. From them any relationship, dilemma or experience can be explored in a safe enough way.

Micro- and mini-sculpture

At the early stages of family work, another way of exploring symbolically the relational structure of a family's organization is to use sculpture methods. I believe families engage more comfortably with the micro- and mini-sculpture level in the assessment phase of their work. The tiny Spanish/Mexican family figures I use are safely distanced from the 'real' family. For mini-sculpture, I move up to larger human figures of 3–4 inches in length, or offer similar sized animal figures.

I have come to recognize that the size of the figures used for family sculpture *raises the level of intensity* or emotion in the room. It is for this reason that I wait until later sessions before offering the family the idea of full body sculpting.

At some point in the first or second session, I invite the family members to sit down around an A1-size sheet of plain white paper. They are then presented and introduced to the mini-size human figures, and then neutrally invited to arrange the figures on the paper in any way they wish. I usually say something like, 'Who wants to show me how their family is at home?' This request is made to all individuals in the family including children and teenagers, and each person takes a turn in micro-sculpting their view of the family's relational organization. As each person micro-sculpts their structural view of the family's relationships, gradually a composite picture of the family's organization takes shape in the therapist's mind. Of course, the *differences* as to who sees whom as close to or furthest from whom, is important information to both the therapist *and* the watching family members.

I develop this curiosity and new information by asking some simple 'circular' questions (Cechin 1986). Examples of circular questioning might be to ask a brother whose family micro-sculpt depicts his father and sister as far apart whether he thinks they have always been this distanced? Was there a time when they were closer? If so, when does he think they began to move away from each other? What does he think might have triggered this movement away? Does he believe father and sister will stay this far apart? What might begin to bring change between father and sister?

These questions are *neutral*, in the sense that they explore a relationship between two family members through the eyes of a third family member. The technique of asking a third family member to share their view of a dyadic relationship between two other family members can be universally applied to all the family relationships, within and across generations. This 'neutrality' can enable the safe exploration of potentially quite sensitive information. It also enables creative speculation on the causes, and on future prospects for possible change in the relationship.

Moving this technique on to mini-sculpting, particularly with symbolically distancing animal figures, can raise the level of intensity within the family about a relationship. I remember a family who shared this animal mini-sculpting method, and revealed the full level of conflict between a father and son. The mother/wife selected a bear figure and a lion figure to represent father and son perpetually in conflict. By exploring this father–son relationship with circular questions, and *staying within* the animal metaphor, the mother was able to do a number of things for herself and on behalf of the family. The mother gave expression and emotional ventilation to the intensity of the father–son conflict and her discomfort about it. She was clearly uncomfortably *triangulated* (Minuchin 1981) between the two males in her family, towards both of whom she had differing but strong loyalty and attachment. In externalizing and expressing this conflict, some relief was gained by all family members. It is my belief that families, indeed all clients, come to therapy to experience going beyond their usual threshold of emotions. To dare this they need to feel sufficiently 'held' within the therapist's integrity and the metaphorical safety of the therapy's symbolic language. This combination of micro- and mini-sculpture with animal figures can help them cross this emotional threshold.

Let me offer you a final thought on family assessment. One of the great things about our therapeutic language, play and drama, is how it invites active participation from all ages in the dialogue of change. I believe it crucially important that every family member who attends an assessment session has the opportunity to make or fashion a personal statement that comes out of their individual emotional conviction. As a consequence, I believe, they can feel that they leave something of themselves *behind* when they leave the session. I believe that if they have had the opportunity to create something through the *symbolic use of the imagination*, they are then engaged at a significant personal level within the family dialogue of change. When this personal, imaginative and emotional engagement process has happened it is more likely that they will return. If they do not, then something of significance has usually occurred for them. They go away changed in some way.

STORIES OF CHANGE

How do we use all this information and the symbols created? Where do we go from here? Already there are so many choices to make, so many exploratory options to be considered. This is always the way with families. The family is a multilayered psycho-system, and its emotional and relational complexity is compelling.

How do you take the family story forward? What symbolic dramatherapy methods will best serve the family in their explorative telling of their story? Role-play, role-reversal, doubling? Story-weaving, storytelling, story enactment? Use of masks?

As you begin to explore a way forward, let me introduce the idea of individuals becoming twos, or dyads, and dyads becoming threes, or triangles. Remember that when the Athenian playwrights introduced the part of the third character, they innovated the biggest shift in the Western theatrical tradition, perhaps the Western cultural tradition. Why was this such a quantum leap and how does it relate to work with families?

Family structure and family communication patterns are built around relationships between two or three people: the dyad and the triangle. In families, four becomes two dyads, or a triangle with one left out. If you doubt this, think about a family of four you know: your own or a friend's or a client family. Invariably in families of four, each parent establishes a 'special' closeness to one child; or one family member is excluded or self-excludes from the interaction of the other three.

Families of five become one dyad and one triangle, or two dyads and one excluded. And so on. Look for dyadic and triangular patterns of communication, within, between and across generations.

Role-play

With this in mind, I move into therapeutic work with families using the language of dramatherapy, to improvise on the *recurring themes* that families bring to the sessions. These are if you like the central motifs in the family story, which usually tie into the family script, its myths, and how these myths get the family hung up on change at certain key, developmental moments.

Let me return to the story of a family mentioned earlier, with the 'lost' teenage son, unable to find his passage through adolescence and destructively turning in on himself. We explored the transgenerational theme of the father–son relationship over three generations (the triangle across the generations of son/father/grandfather). To do this we created a linear chair sculpt, with chairs representing ages 10–25, an age-range spanning the onset of puberty to full adulthood. Built into this enactment was the option for any family member to role-play themselves at any of these ages, or role-reverse with any other member of the extended family at any of these ages. Father talked as himself aged 18, listless, lost and alienated from his own father. The son sat and watched transfixed. Gradually different members of the family moved in and out of roles, sometimes doubling for each other, to articulate ideas about the possible way forward. In this way feelings about relationships, ideas about adolescent change, and powerfully held unconscious beliefs from the family script were worked through at an experiential level. This experiencing, through sculpting, role-taking, role-reversal, doubling and witnessing, is crucial to a successful re-authoring of the family story.

I use the method of the linear chair sculpt, integrated with role-reversal, quite regularly at the post-assessment, therapeutic stage of work with families. It seems particularly useful when dealing with transgenerational issues within the family script, which often collide with life-cycle tasks like independence and leaving home.

Masks

Masks can be used in a variety of ways with families. I employ them in two principal ways when working on themes of conflict avoidance and conflict.

An ability to express and contain a healthy degree of conflict within and between family members is a testament to the balance of its psycho-ecology. Families need the creativity of negotiation and healthy expression of individual differences. The family culture that encourages differences and allows itself the safety valve of the occasional tempestuous row facilitates in a healthy and enabling way the development and progress of its members through the life cycle. In my experience, two types of families block and inhibit this healthy process: the anorexic family and some stepfamilies.

I mentioned earlier the family with the disabling myth about avoiding conflict. They were a family of four, parents and two daughters. The eldest daughter had 'escaped', and lived several hundred miles away with her husband. The youngest daughter, in her mid-20s, lived in the same house as her two natural parents, even though she had bought a flat of her own in a different town. The younger daughter had been hospitalized for being seriously anorexic several years earlier. As is so often the case in psychosomatic families, family members worked extremely hard to avoid any differences and conflict. They came asking for help to change, and then resisted every invitation to encourage them to explore their differences in a more open and forthright way. After half a dozen sessions it occurred to me that we might experiment with mask play (Baptiste 1988). The idea of mask play needs to be introduced as a gentle invitation, after a number of sessions with a family. The process of mask making needs to be explained in a simple and matter-of-fact way. Demystifying the process was the single biggest factor in this family's accepting the idea.

I invited mother, father and daughter to draw a face of themselves interacting in their typical family patterns. They thus drew their family 'persona' (Jennings 1990), which was shaped and coloured by the conflict-avoiding myths within the family script. Then, working with finger paints on large sheets of paper, I encouraged them to work in isolated parts of the room, to play and experiment with colours that could begin to express uncomfortable feelings of conflict. At the next session I gave each family member two cardboard face templates, and they worked for the whole session painting, colouring, cutting and sticking a family 'persona' mask, and a 'self' mask. We thus worked for two full sessions on mask creation. At the next session they began to hold the masks up in front of their faces for short periods, alternating the persona mask with the self mask.

Next we took a family scenario suggested by the daughter, where she could experiment with wearing her carefully made mask of self. She had created a highly colourful and striking looking mask of self, which was in deep contrast to the anodyne, grey image of her family persona mask. In the family scenario chosen, a true-life scene of mother and daughter shopping together, the daughter and mother first wore their persona masks. The scene was then replayed with the daughter wearing her mask of self. The replay was very different in feel and content; the daughter in her self mask was less compliant, more assertive and even mildly challenging of some of the mother's suggestions. This broke the ice, and began to allow more spontaneous freedom of expression and exploration of difference within this enmeshed, fearful and overcontrolled family triangle. Over the next several sessions, mother, father and daughter used mask play, substituting persona and self masks, in a variety of situations and contexts. Gradually, it became possible for the family to explore difference and permit conflictual discussion between themselves in the session *without* wearing masks. In this process their family 'persona' began to absorb some of the rebellious colour of their mask of 'self'.

I have used similar methods of mask making and mask play of family scenarios in work with stepfamilies. Often in a stepfamily you will find a parent–child or parent–teenager dyad in open conflict. This is usually a stepparent/stepchild, going through the painful, ritual process of reattachment. If this occurs during early adolescence, it can be a particularly tough tussle. In this case, I ask each family member to create a mask for each member of the family, and two of themself. The owner's two masks of self are decorated in different ways. One masks depicts their self-image; the other mask is painted as the owner believes he or she is perceived by the adult with whom they are principally in conflict. In stepfamilies this is usually the stepparent. I encourage children and teenagers to draw their view of the other family members, as positively or negatively as they do see them. Masks are then shown and put on view and discussions encouraged about how and why colours and images were created. One stepdaughter drew her stepfather's mask as a bald-headed boxer. They began to get into discussion about this pugilistic portrayal. I invited the stepfather to speak from behind the boxer mask and discuss his stepdaughter's perceptions of him. The ensuing dialogue was creative in two principal ways. It allowed the stepdaughter to express for the first time some of the pent-up frustrations and anger she was feeling towards her stepfather. (Out of loyalty to her mother she had suppressed these feelings, thus preventing the process of reattachment from following its natural course.)

As she began to allow herself to give vent to these feelings, her stepfather started to give her feedback about who he really was, which was necessary for her to begin to see him in a 'new way'.

Story

> The story is the theatre's greatest operation.
>
> Bertolt Brecht

I often work with story in my work with families. I mean story in the sense of a dramatic narrative, either improvised or from a found source such as a play text, a myth or a folk tale. In essence, the story (either improvised or found) creates a reflecting dialogue between itself and the family story. The therapeutic story, through its interaction with the family story (what the family are and how they live), is a symbolic catalyst for change, pointing a way forward to the next narrative step in the family's story. The interaction of the therapeutic story with the family story inevitably generates *alternative stories* (White and Epston 1993) and new possibilities of change.

I use story-making, storytelling and story enactment methods in my family work.

An example of story-making came quite early on in my work with a single mother and her two daughters, aged 7 and 9. In the spontaneously improvised family puppet story in session no. 1, themes of limit-setting, controls, boundaries and school refusal emerged. These were also the overtly stated reasons for referral, in relation to the youngest daughter. Using the story-making method (Lahad 1992), I invited the family to draw a 'Getting-up Story' in six boxes. In the 'Getting-up story', mother portrayed the youngest daughter as refusing to get up, or not getting dressed and constantly making her mother and sister late on school mornings. When I suggested that we try acting the story, the youngest daughter shied away, not wanting to be herself in the story. I invited the daughter and the mother to play each other. This they agreed to do. The mother was a reluctant and disobedient daughter, whilst the youngest daughter, in the role of mother, was highly critical and censorious of her. The oldest sister played herself and attempted conciliation. When the youngest daughter-as-mother proclaimed loudly, 'You are a terrible child,' mother-as-daughter broke down, instantly becoming herself and saying, 'I do say those things to her, I get so cross; it's all wrong.' This was a turning point in the work. I invited mother to the next session on her own, when she talked at great length about the very painful time for her when her youngest was born. She and the girl's father separated at this time, and mother and her new baby and young daughter became isolated. Mother went into an unhappy, deeply depressing episode in her life, impoverished, grieving for her lost partner, and cutting herself off from her own family because of the shame she felt over the marriage break-up. All this had affected the attachment process between mother and her youngest daughter, and mother began to see that some of her anger and unhappiness had been felt by her new daughter, who had responded over the years with naughtiness and disobedience, a cover for her hurt.

Storytelling to families is a well-developed practice, used quite a lot by family therapists. I either use a well-known story, such as a folk tale or myth, or improvise a story from the themes and content of the session. Storytelling usually comes at the end of a session, when giving a final intervention or message to a family. (I say more about framing final interventions in the conclusion of this chapter.)

I have often worked with families negotiating the late adolescent phase of the life cycle. This life phase is primarily concerned with the leaving-home transition, and I often tell the story/myth of the Aboriginal Walkabout. This story emphasizes the positive, initiatory, individuation themes around leaving home. It places the transition from boy to man in a deeply historical and anthropological context, emphasizing the naturalness of the human transition, and can be used well by couples who may be 'hanging on' to a teenage child, caught up in their marital dysfunction. The trick with storytelling from a found source is in the selection of the story as much as in the telling of it. The themes and relationship configurations need to fit on to the family story in a way that creatively engages the *family's dilemmas about change*. That is, in a way that shows them the next possible narrative step in the family story.

I use improvised storytelling regularly in work with couples, as part of family work. Couples' relationships can encounter difficulties at all phases of the family life cycle. The image/symbol of the Garden is a powerful and flexible metaphor for the couple relationship, with all the potent connections between nature and sexuality. Sexual dysfunction is usually the final difficulty between a couple, with the problems between them going back much further. I use the Garden as a central image in storytelling to couples, and incorporate events and developments in the Garden to synchronize with sequences in the couple's life. When storytelling as part of a final intervention, at the end of a session, I do not make connections, left to right brain, between the story told and the couple's life story (Shuttleworth 1985). To do so is, I believe, to reduce the impact for change contained within the metaphor of the storytelling (Cade 1983). The couple do the connecting for themselves, *between the sessions*.

Story enactment of a found text is a method which can be used in the middle and later stages of work with a family, when themes and an agenda for change in the family story have clearly emerged. Play texts, myths, films and books are all sources for story enactment, and can be used in one of two ways. Firstly, the characters and their relationship configurations can be taken from a found story, and the family can take on roles in an improvised enactment of the found story. Shakespeare and Greek drama are very good for this, because both explore such timeless and universal family themes. I usually introduce the main characters and their key dilemmas as the plot develops, and invite opinions on the action from family members. When they are sufficiently identified with the action of the story, and distanced from their own family story, I suggest that we improvise and role-play the found story. I often stop the action of the story enactment, challenging the family members in role to come up with alternative outcomes or alternative action to those in the known story. Recently I used some of the storyline of *Hamlet* with a reconstituted stepfamily, where the teenage son was in such open conflict with his stepfather and natural mother that the new family system was in real danger of breaking up. We enacted the Banquet Scene (improvising in contemporary dialogue), and then processed the scene out of role, exploring the emotional dilemmas of the three central characters, Mother, Son and Stepfather. By enacting the roles and discussing the relational configurations in the play, the family were able to express pent-up feelings related to their own family dilemma. From this enactment, it became possible for them to begin to shift perspectives on their problems of integrating as a new emotional system. The boy's loyalties to his natural father began to feel fully acknowledged and respected, which made the beginnings of a relationship with his stepfather possible.

CONCLUSION: SOME TACTICS FOR FAMILY CHANGE

When I meet a family who bring themselves for therapy, I find it useful to ask myself two questions. First: what phase of the life cycle is the family negotiating (Table 11.1)? Second: what are the rules that organize the parental couple?

Table 11.1 The stages of the family life cycle

Family life-cycle stage	Emotional process of transition: key principles	Second-order changes in family status required to proceed developmentally
1 Leaving home: single young adults	Accepting emotional and financial responsibility for self	a Differentation of self in relation to family of origin b Development of intimate peer relationships c Establishment of self re. work and finanical independence
2 The joining of families through marriage: the new couple	Commitment to new system	a Formation of marital system b Realignment of relationships with extended families and friends to include spouse
3 Families with young children	Accepting new members into the system	a Adjusting marital system to make space for child(ren) b Joining in child-rearing, financial and household tasks c Realignment of relationships with extended family to include parenting and grandparenting roles
4 Families with adolescents	Increasing flexibility of family boundaries to include children's independence and grandparents' frailties	a Shifting of parent–child relationships to permit adolescent to move in and out of system b Refocus on mid-life marital and career issues c Beginning shift towards joint caring for older generation
5 Launching children and moving on	Accepting a multitude of exits from and entries into the family system	a Renegotiation of marital system as a dyad b Development of adult to adult relationships between grown children and their parents c Realignment of relationships to include inlaws and grandchildren d Dealing with disabilities and deaths of parents (grandparents)
6 Families in later life	Accepting the shifting of generational roles	a Maintaining own and/or couple functioning and interests in face of physiological decline; exploration of new familial and social role options b Support for a more central role of middle generation c Making room in the system for the wisdom and experience of the elderly, supporting the older generation without overfunctioning for them d Dealing with loss of spouse, siblings and other peers and preparation for own death. Life review and integration

Source Betty Carter and Monica McGoldrick, *The Changing Family Life Cycle: a framework for family therapy* (2nd edn). New York: Gardner.

I find having these two questions in mind helps focus the early assessment sessions. Each life-cycle phase presents families with key developmental tasks. Developmental tasks can be made more difficult if they coincide with life events such as bereavement, separation, divorce, redundancy, remarriage, moving home. It is important to understand if the arrival of puberty, or entering school, or weaning, has collided with a divorce, remarriage or some other life event.

Similarly, I find it crucial in my work with families to look upon the parental/spouse couple as the key unit within the family system. Their beliefs, their patterns of communication, their psycho-ecology are what organize the family functionally and dysfunctionally. The couple's relationship is what forms the family in the first place. They set the script for the family; and their newly forming family script emerges from the combining family of origin script. They are the biological and psychological blueprint for the family, and also crucially influence its emotional culture. Understand how their communication works and you are halfway home.

I see families with various intervals between sessions. If a family is in emotional crisis following break-up/divorce or sudden bereavement, they may need to be seen weekly for a period. Usually I see families in fortnightly to monthly intervals, for sessions lasting one and a half to two hours.

Using this family dramatherapy method implies symbolic enactment in most if not all of the sessions. I also routinely finish the sessions with a therapeutic 'message'. This technique is a legacy from my family therapy training, which enables me to offer as many *positive statements and reframes* as possible on individuals' and the family's behaviour. Experience has taught me that people who are 'stuck' are more willing and able to change if a *positive intention* is attributed to their past and existing behaviour patterns. This somehow seems to offer a therapeutic absolution, enabling individuals to absolve themselves from some of their redundant patterns. We are, after all, all trying our best.

I also often caution a family from trying to change too much, too quickly. There is a therapeutic reality to this. Emotional healing following loss, separation, bereavement, divorce etc., as we all know, has its own natural recovery tempo. With families who say they wish to change, but appear stuck, I emphasize and caution *against* change. Sometimes with these sorts of problems and families a strategic and paradoxical *proscription* of change can be helpful. It is as if, by being told that they do not have to or should not change, they are reminded of the burden of staying the same (Papp 1983).

To begin to develop your work as a dramatherapist with families, you need to find a space in which to practice, and a family to see. In some ways it may be easier to join an existing team which sees families in an NHS,

Social Service or other context. With your unique dramatherapy skills, you will probably find most teams are receptive to the idea of your joining. This is how I got started, gradually introducing the concept and practice of symbolic enactment as part of the overall therapeutic approach. Eventually, a small group of us set up a Creative Therapies Clinic for families which operated with dramatherapy and play therapy as *central* to the therapeutic approach with families, rather than being integrated into an orthodox family therapy method. There is nothing to prevent you developing your practice with families now, independently, perhaps incorporating some of the ideas in this chapter into your method. With its many methods and skills, our discipline offers a therapeutic language that is in many ways ideally suited for work with families. With an experienced supervisor, to whom you could take your work, you will have a great deal to offer your clients.

I have written this chapter to offer some guidelines for those of you who want to begin to make the transition from dramatherapist to family dramatherapist. I am sure you will find it an exciting transition to make. Good luck to you.

REFERENCES

Baptiste, D. A. Jr (1988) Using masks as therapeutic aids in family therapy. *Journal of Family Therapy*, 11(1): 45–58.
Bateson, G. (1980) *Mind and Nature*. London: Fontana.
Bowen, M. (1978) *Family Therapy in Clinical Practise*. New York: Jacob Aronson.
Brecht, B. (1964) *Brecht on Theatre*. (Trans.) J. Willets. London: Methuen.
Brook, P. (1972) *The Empty Space*. Harmondsworth, Middlesex: Penguin.
Byng-Hall, J. (1979) Re-editing family mythology during family therapy. *Journal of Family Therapy*, 1. 103–16.
——— (1985) The family script: a useful bridge between theory and practice. *Journal of Family Therapy*, 7: 301–5.
Cade, B. (1983) Some uses of metaphor. *Australian Journal of Family Therapy*, 3 (3): 135–40.
Cechin, C. (1986) Hypothesising, circularity, neutrality – revisited. *Journal of Family Therapy*.
Dermody. S. (1988) Dramatherapy with families. Unpublished dissertation.
——— (1992) Metaphor with families. *Journal of the British Association for Dramatherapy*, Summer 1992: 9–11.
Erickson, M. (1980) *The Collected Papers of M. Erickson*. New York: Irvington.
Irwin, E. and Malloy, E. (1975) Family puppet interview. *Family Process*, 14 (2): 179–91.
Jennings, S. (1987) Dramatherapy with groups. In S. Jennings (ed.) *Dramatherapy in Theory and Practice*, 1. London: Routledge.
——— (1990) *Dramatherapy with Families, Groups and Individuals*. London: Jessica Kingsley.
Johnstone, K. (1981) *IMPRO–Improvisation and the Theatre*. London: Methuen.
Lahad, M. (1992) Storymaking in assessment. In S. Jennings (ed.) *Dramatherapy in Theory and Practice*, 2. London: Routledge.

Landy, R. (1992) One to one: the role of the dramatherapist working with individuals. In S. Jennings (ed.) *Dramatherapy in Theory and Practice*, 2. London: Routledge.

Minuchin, S. (1977) *Families and Family Therapy*. London: Tavistock.

—— (1981) *Family Therapy Techniques*. London and Boston, Mass.: Harvard University Press.

Palazzoli, M. (1978) *Paradox and Counter-Paradox*. New York: Jacob Aronson.

Papp, P. (1983) *The Process of Change*. London and New York: Guildford Press.

Satir, V. (1972) *Peoplemaking*. Palo Alto: Science and Behaviour Books.

Scheff, T. (1981) The distancing of emotion in psychotherapy. *Psychotherapy: Theory, Research and Practice*, 18: 46–53.

Shuttleworth, R. (1987) A systems approach to dramatherapy. In S. Jennings (ed.) *Dramatherapy in Theory and Practice*, 1. pp. 12–20. London: Routledge.

—— (1985) Metaphor in therapy. *Journal of the British Association for Dramatherapists*, 8(2).

Tatham, P. (1990) A systems view of self; and vice versa. Unpublished paper.

Walsh, S., Tregay, K., Woods, J. and Benbow, S. (1992) Using psychodrama techniques in family therapy. *Journal of British Association for Dramatherapists*, Summer 1992: 12–16.

Watzlawick, P. (1967) *The Pragmatics of Human Communication*. New York: Norton Press.

—— (1973) *Change*. New York: Norton Press.

White, M. and Epston, D. (1993) *Narrative Means to Therapeutic Ends*. New York: Norton.

Chapter 12

The labyrinth dance of adolescence
Journey through darkness and light

Yiorgos Polos

INTRODUCTION

I should like to introduce this chapter with the Greek myth of Theseus, in which a labyrinth plays an important part; I shall then develop the idea of the labyrinth and its relationship to light and darkness.

Theseus was the son of Aegeus (or, according to other versions, Poseidon) and Aethra. He grew up knowing nothing of his father, who had left signs by which he could be identified (sandals, swords) under a rock which Theseus would be able to raise when he had grown to young manhood. And so it came about that Theseus set off for Athens, to find his father. On his way, he had adventures with various monsters, and on his arrival in Athens his stepmother, Medea, attempted to poison him, but at the last moment, his father – who was about to help Medea dispatch Theseus – realized who he was.

Theseus undertook the task of ridding Athens of a terrible scourge: the city's obligation to send seven youths and seven maidens to Crete each year, to be devoured by a monster belonging to King Minos. The Minotaur, a beast with the body of a man and the head of a bull, was kept imprisoned in the labyrinth, a prison designed by Icarus.

With the help of Ariadne, sister of the monster – who gave him a thread to find his way into the labyrinth and out of it again – Theseus killed the Minotaur.

On his way home, Theseus forgot to haul down the black sail of his ship and to raise the white sail which he and his father had agreed would be a sign that he had succeeded. Aegeus, in his despair, plunged into the sea and was drowned; since then, the sea has been known as the Aegean. Theseus came back to Athens, and ruled as king. The important achievements of his reign bring us out of the world of the myth, touching on the borders of historical time.

THEMES OF ADOLESCENCE

I have referred to this myth in order to ask the following questions concerning the theme of this chapter. Is the Theseus myth related to adolescence? Is the Minotaur part of adolescence? Are there any similarities between the 'mythopoetic' process and adolescence? Is the relationship between light and darkness a specific mythopoetic process which is relevant to adolescence? In other words, could the labyrinth of life become a prison? And if so, what is the path of freedom towards adulthood?

The adolescent function resembles a second birth, one which is intellectual and cultural and which takes place outside the family. In order for this birth to take place, psychological birth must have occurred (1–3 years) and the internal libidinal 'object' must be stable. This internalization takes place during the initial stages of the omnipotence of infancy, when child and mother are one, and then during the period 5–18 months, during which the child experiences diversification and attempts to gain autonomy from the mother and a sense of his or her own resources.

According to Melanie Klein (1969), this is the period of the depressive position, during which the mother is understood as an entire 'other' object and the child begins to form a separate ego.

If we were to observe this period in terms of the qualities of light and darkness, we could say that children need not come in direct contact with the dazzling light which sharpens contrasts; this would be the light of separation from the mother, of the existence of a world beyond the mother. Children need a gentle, dim light, a light of their own, born out of the clash of contradictions within them. In fact, many people now criticize the fact that babies are born into the harsh light of clinics.

Integration of this relationship between light and darkness continues into adult life. Adolescence can be a fertile time, during which young people expand their experience of the new light and dark.

It is also during adolescence that individual sexual identity is structured. The structuring occurs when the individual has found ways which can help him or her work through anxiety and worries about sexual function and identity. It takes place at a time when boys, with their sperm, can impregnate girls and become fathers, and when girls reach sexual maturity and can bear children. Metaphorically, the boy becomes the bearer of the fire or light of human existence, while the girl is the dark hiding-place where that fire will be kept and will grow. From this reciprocal union, new light will be born.

Young people leave behind the 'ancient' light and dark of their parents – the fire-bearing power of the father and the darkness of the mother's womb – in order to work out their own reciprocal light.

It is the ability to manage fire – that is, to keep it alight and reproduce it and to keep shadows at bay – which allows young people to make the conquests of adulthood; our ancient ancestors managed fire and with the ritual cooking of food symbolically supplied blood to the brain. The brain, supplied with blood, is capable of symbolism, art, medicine, deification, conscious life, morals and especially the imposition of order upon chaos.

However, the development of human attributes brings with it feelings of failure, guilt, shame and grief.

The feeling of failure stems from our inability to realize the fantasy desires of childhood – for example, that the frog will turn into a prince. Thus many young people engage in battles with their self-image. They feel guilty, as if the light had been stolen by trickery: their bodies have grown as if by magic, and the juices of life and death have been created as if by deceit on the part of the parents, who have made no apparent contribution to the process.

The shame stems from the fact that the new image is, of necessity, obvious: it cannot be controlled or hidden. The grief is for the lost self, and also for the separation from the persons and situations associated with that self.

I am suggesting that adolescence is a process of half-light and of polarity: a search for clear light as well as darkness. In that half-light adolescents try out their new experiences, sensations and images. It is the in-between time, the half-light before dawn comes and before night falls.

Absolute light would destroy their explorations: for example, one young man was accused by his sister's partner of having touched him sexually while they watched an erotic scene on television. After this event, the young man in question felt cast from the shadows into the light of day. On the other hand, absolute darkness represents *amnesia* of the experiences and memories in the young person's existence. For example, another young man who wished to change his surname and take his mother's maiden name remembered during therapy that his paternal grandfather had also changed his name and taken his mother's maiden name, because his father had maltreated him after her death.

The completion of adolescence is the ability to pass from the half-light into light and darkness. Indeed, it is an integration of them both.

As they develop, adolescents come into contact with light and darkness by means of the interaction in the relationship between the two. In order to explore this relationship, I shall use the term *focusing*.

FOCUSING

We often employ the words 'acting out' when talking of adolescents and of the things they do. Adolescents replace words with actions, or carry out an action relating to a different context: an 'enacted transference' takes place. These actions usually result from the anxiety which the young person has failed to work out in play in childhood: they cannot take verbal form, but instead become acts.

Another term we use is 'acting in', which describes the ability to use dramatized acts in order to explore a specific life anxiety within a specific frame of reference, such as psychodrama.

The term 'acting' in the dramatherapy framework refers to the dramatization of a specific space or time, very often with a theatre structure (see Mitchell 1994, Jennings 1992, for example). The term is usually employed – mistakenly, in my view – as identical in meaning to acting out or acting in, or is limited in use to the theatre.

Acting out, *acting in* and *acting* differ from each other, and from *focusing*. Focusing is an important concept in dramatherapy; we need to be able to focus in space as a way of regulating distance, in time, in intensity of light and in concentration of theme. It is comparable to taking a photograph – does the focus need to be 'telescopic' or 'wide-angle'? Within the dramatic action, we can focus on *as if*.

What is it that determines how adolescents focus? Adolescents determine this through their own existence. Their bodies themselves are transformed.

The birth of the adolescent presupposes another birth, one which has gone before: birth from another body, that of the mother. In addition, however, in terms of fantasy, the adolescent also existed before in the desires of the father and mother, in the desires, over time, of all the previous generations.

Adolescents need to focus on experiences by means of nostalgia or through fantasy. In the same way as film directors or photographers use the viewfinder to see images, so adolescents need to focus on experiences, thoughts and fantasies relating to the past and the future. The present is significant only in terms of these discoveries. The present is a mystery, a borderline phase in which everything changes – and changes unharmoniously. Adolescents can work through this lack of harmony using focusing. Focusing is in itself an experience, but differs from the cinema or photography in not always leading to concrete results.

A film about adolescence would be one made by adolescents themselves. Perhaps this would be impossible, since adolescents are unable to distance themselves sufficiently from the phenomenon.

Bearing in mind Robert Landy's theory regarding distance in therapy using the theatre, which involves the human capacity for working through matters of concern to the individual by creating a distance from the question (Landy 1985), it could be said that adolescents are always 'at a distance' from questions which concern them. However, they are capable of focusing even on matters from which they are obviously overdistanced or underdistanced.

Adolescents' ability to focus makes it possible for them to overfocus or underfocus, as if they were able to change lenses: take, for example, an adopted adolescent with learning difficulties. He looks slightly older than he is, and is very handsome. At his current age, he is flooded with nostalgia for childhood (wanting to play or be naughty all the time etc.). He experiences the future as a fantasy: he wants to learn photography so he can be an aerial photographer. He lives very little in the present: for example, he is embarrassed when women desire him, even though he talks about it all the time.

Light and darkness – the harmony or conflict between them and the phenomena generated by their relationship – play a decisive part in focusing in adolescent development.

TRANSFORMATION

The adolescent's route towards maturity, independence and taking charge of the 'true self' is one of mastering identity and is connected with Winnicott's concept of the *true self* (see Winnicott 1971). The true self, according to Winnicott, is the source of initiative, the sense that one is real and that one's identity is genuine and not fictitious. Creative ideas and spontaneity also stem from the true self.

According to Richard Courtney: 'Adolescent maturation hinges upon the student's concept of roles. This grows from an acknowledgement of "appearance" to a realization of "truth"' (Courtney 1980: 56). He attributes to the 12–15 age-range *the appearance of the role*, and to ages 15–18 *the truth of the role*.

A process of *transformation* is thus inherent in adolescence: transformation in the adolescent's body, and the mystery that accompanies that transformation. Language becomes richer and is full of the expression of desires; the absence of language is often converted into action. For example, the scene in which a more mature woman touches the erect penis of the adolescent in the bathroom is one in which the young body of the adolescent is initiated into the adult world in terms of both fantasy and reality (as in the film *Little Big Man*, with Fay Dunaway and Dustin Hoffmann).

The true self, the true image, emerges from a process of experimenting with roles, first by imitation and using the appearance of the role, and later through the truth of the role.

The capacity to imitate is at the core of ritual and ceremony. Thus ritual and ceremony move us through emotions, thoughts and questions it would otherwise be difficult to experience.

In traditional societies, symbolic rituals were a medium for socialization, promoting social identity and consolidating adult roles.

Today, the process of attaining adulthood, which includes familiarization with the norms and values of society, has been replaced by other activities, inherent in which, as Turner tells us, are heightened consciousness and the aesthetic experience – qualities similar to those of traditional symbolic rituals (Turner 1967). For example, rituals involving motorcycles, sport, hooliganism, graffiti, styles of dressing (especially punk), late-night parties, songs, comics and magazines are all attempts by today's young people to obtain areas of initiation and acceptance in societies in which official rituals – military service, school etc. – have lost their effective role as agents of initiation. These official rituals now treat young people as units of production and not as young lives with intimations of life and death, who can be initiated into adult life only through ritual transformation.

CULTURAL BIRTH AND THE META-FAMILY

Conflict belongs to young people. When they give in to it, it is as if they are coming to terms with the destruction of themselves and those who gave them birth.

We have already seen that adolescence involves a second birth. This birth, however, takes place outside the family; it is an intellectual and cultural birth, but above all it is a *self-birth*.

The birth of the young body is connected with birth into the meta-family of the peer group. As with focusing and transformation, *regression in the peer group* gives a sense of actualization in the here-and-now.

This regression can take place if birth in the family has already occurred; it owes itself to the family, but it does not take place in the family. The meta-family – that is, the peer group – is the adolescent's transitional social object.

With the regression which takes place in the peer group, young people engage in a search for their mythical ancestor. As Aslanidis has noted, this search procedure is the mythopoetic function (Aslanidis 1985). Adolescents are not interested in their historical past: they have no spare libido to invest in their parents or the therapist.

The second birth is a rite of initiation. Initiation takes place using mythopoetic functions: for example, the young people who, dressed and behaving in a similar manner, listen to mega-death and heavy metal music.

Regression takes place in a primordial mode. The world of myth is the world of nature, the cause of our existence; it represents the unconscious mental reality, containing polarities such as the conflict between nature and culture. All this is expressed through the discourse of the myth, an entity, like language, which is primordial *per se*.

The mythical discourse is neither translation nor history; it brings the universe into the human world, like an answer or greeting.

There is a trend in the structure of the mind for humans to polarize their experience. In order to understand our experience, we divide it into opposing units such as mind–body, or science–art. The mythopoetic functions, dramatized as rituals, are a mental process of normalization within social reality, which reconcile oppositions.

Smoking in adolescence, for example, is not a habit: it is a ritual connected with the adolescent's regression in the meta-family, and its purpose is to control opposing affective states, such as anger, anxiety, depression and their opposites.

Rather than controlling these opposites by means of earlier and more primitive forms of gratification such as indulging in food or sweets, adolescents prefer ritual tastes such as smoking, sometimes accompanied by drinking.

Smoking has a suppressive effect on adolescents, acting as a drug to facilitate integration, and relieving the tension caused by emotion. Adolescents choose this solution, which is also connected with their desire to experiment with the habits of adults, so as to appear and feel 'mature' themselves.

My first experience of a day centre for young people aged 15–21 years with thalassaemia problems of individual emotional identity was of seeing the rest area. Cigarettes and coffee cups were everywhere in the areas for staff and patients. There was an intensity to the smoking which reminded me strongly of railway stations or the intensity with which soldiers smoke. It was clear that, although these young people were putting their lives at risk by smoking, they preferred that life experience as a reminder of death to the identity of 'patients'. They preferred the smoking ritual as an initiation into life.

MYTH AND THE DANCE OF CONTRADICTIONS

The mental process of normalizing of contradictions during adolescence does not stem from *analysis* of the myth, but from the *synthesis* which ordinary people have performed for centuries, using their own lives.

The myth orchestrates all levels of reality. Adolescents are interested in living the myth, not in analysing it. They live through consumerism, anti-consumerism, television, ecology etc. They are interested in living the myth of the fast-food joint, of the rock concert, of ecological campaigning, of late-night parties and so on.

Although it is this synthesis of the myth which interests them, adolescents want to live that synthesis in the purity of experience. That purity comes from the 'dance of contradictions' which exists, to begin with, in the adolescent body. This conflict may lead, not to a synthesis or to normalization of differences, but to lack of harmony, to a process of inhibition.

Mental disorders in adolescents occur when they fail to enter the half-light, but remain in the reflected light of childhood.

Some adolescents, who were never really children, are unable to stand up to the test of transformation in the half-light: they cannot regress, because they would regress into the Minotaur's labyrinth. Their body is incapable of changing lenses, of focusing; if it focuses, it does so automatically. It is unable to relax. Adolescents, and especially adolescent girls, often make love mechanically, without any element of the reciprocal in the relationship. This is particularly true of young people who are addicted to drugs or other substances.

Mental disorder may result from the struggle to be culturally and mythopoetically reborn into the peer group, thereby becoming critical members of society. Brecht wanted the audience in the theatre to acquire the ability to distinguish between fantasy and reality, to be able to stand back from his plays. This process of rebirth and critical distance is similar to the maturation of adolescence.

STRUCTURING THERAPY FOR ADOLESCENTS

Since adolescents have difficulty in focusing, transformation and cultural birth can serve as both an explanation and a guide for therapy in dealing with short-term stress, mental disorder, mental illness or adolescent breakdown (psychosis), to use Lanffere's classification (Lanffere 1992).

Intervention across the spectrum from adolescent breakdown, in which adolescents need care because their lives may be in danger, to short-term stress can be characterized by three qualities: focusing, transformation and cultural birth.

If we fail to take these qualities into consideration, then it is possible that we may discourage and humiliate adolescents through suppression, demands for behavioural compliance and normalization programmes (i.e. a medical model of treatment). Therapy by means of drama contains the three qualities as structural features, and can help in an approach to care.

We could learn a lot about mental illness by focusing our attention on our thinking about, and presence in, care for mental illness as a reproduction of our attitude towards it.

If, for example, the hostel were seen as an alternative form of focusing and not as a place for behaviour control, if medication were part of an overall ceremony which takes place inside and outside the ritual areas (hospital, home etc.), then we could put questions such as: who is conducting the ritual? what kind of ceremony is it?

The care model for psychosis involving outpatient treatment, day hospitals, hostels, vocational workshops and social rehabilitation services will fail so long as it continues to serve narrowly medical aims.

Numerous services of a different nature are needed because multilevel care is essential in the areas I have proposed: transformation, experimentation with focusing, and cultural birth.

Dramatherapy as part of the therapeutic process could have the following goals for adolescents:

1 sensory experience and body work;
2 repertoire of individual roles;
3 critical acceptance of society (through improvisation, for example);
4 enrichment of life through the creative process;
5 working through of communication issues.

The adolescent could be assessed within the dramatherapy by means of:

1 physical expression;
2 play;
3 life in the group;
4 personal creative activity;
5 theatrical convention;
6 art which 'guides the soul', i.e. which leads towards independence and autonomy.

I would like to conclude by suggesting that Theseus may well have been an adolescent who, at the outset of his adolescence, proved that he could find his father after passing the tests of adulthood (Periphetes, Sines, Pityocamptes, Skiron, Procrustes). He was also tested in the 'battle of the soul', as in the labyrinth he fought against his powerful other side, the Minotaur which devoured seven youths and maidens.

Theseus emerges victorious, but he does not succeed in keeping Ariadne, who had guided him. He also kills his father, by forgetting to change the sails on his ship from black to white.

The adolescent transition into adulthood is a complex process. Adulthood does not contain light alone and adolescence does not contain darkness alone.

What is important is the shape of the labyrinth.

BIBLIOGRAPHY

Anastasopoulos, D. (1991) Relations between adolescents and teachers. In G. Papazisis (ed.) *Adolescence: expectations and investigations.* Athens, Child Research Institute: Papazisis Editions. (In Greek)

Antinucci-Mark, G. (1986) Some thoughts on the similarity between psychotherapy and theatre scenarios. *British Journal of Psychotherapy*, 3(1): 14–19.

Aslanidis, E. (1985) Adolescents and mythology. In A. Doxiadi-Trip and E. Zacharopoulou (eds) *Adolescents and Families.* Athens: Vivliopoleio tis Estias. (In Greek)

Berkovitz, I. (1972) *Experiences in Adolescent Group Psychotherapy.* New York: Brunner/Mazel.

Blatner, A. (1973) *Acting In.* New York: Springer Publishing Co.

Chabrol, H. (1987) *Suicidal Tendencies in Adolescents.* Athens: Hadzinikoli.

Cherry, C. (1976) *Creative Play for the Developing Child*. Belmont, Ca.: Tearon Pitman.

Chetwynd, T. (1987) *A Dictionary of Symbols*. London: Paladin.

Courtney, R. (1974) *Play Drama and Thought*. London: Cassell.

—— (1980) *The Dramatic Curriculum*. London: Cassell.

Cramer, B. (1992) *Occupation: Baby*. Athens: T.G. Kastaniotis.

Davou, B. (1992) *Smoking in Adolescence*. Athens: Papazisis Editions. (In Greek)

Doxiadi-Trip, A. and Zacharopoulou, E. (eds) (1985) *Adolescents and Families*. Athens: Vivliopoleio tis Estias. (In Greek)

Dragona, T. (1992) Concepts of the self and psychosocial framework. In *Adolescence: expectations and investigations*. Athens, Child Research Institute: G. Papazisis Editions. (In Greek)

Erikson, E. (1965) *Childhood and Society*. London: Penguin.

Freud, S. (1932) The acquisition and control of fire. SE, vol. 13.

Hodgson, J. (ed.) (1982) *The Uses of Drama*. London: Methuen.

Jennings, S. (ed.) (1987) *Dramatherapy for Teachers and Clinicians*. London: Routledge.

—— (1994) The theatre of healing. In S. Jennings (ed.) *The Handbook of Dramatherapy*. London: Routledge.

Kakridis, F. (1986) *The Greek Mythology,* vol. 3. Athens: Ekdotike Athinon. (In Greek)

Klein, M. (1969) *The Psycho-Analysis of Children*. London: Hogarth Press..

Landy, R. (1994) *Persona and Performance*. London: Jessica Kingsley.

Lanffere, M. (1992) *Adolescence Disorders and Mental Breakdown*. Athens: T.G. Kastaniotis.

Mitchell, S. (1994) The theatre of self-expression. In S. Jennings (ed.) *The Handbook of Dramatherapy*. London: Routledge.

Panopoulou-Maratou, O. (1987) The psychoemotional development of babies and infants. In G. Kastaniotis *Contemporary Issues in Child Psychiatry*, vol. 1. Athens: T.G. Kastaniotis. (In Greek)

Polos, Y. (1989) Light and darkness in depression. Final essay in dramatherapy. Institute of Dramatherapy, PO Box 32, Stratford-upon-Avon, CV37 6GU, UK.

—— (1988) Theatre at an adolescent psychiatric unit. Paper given at 5th Panhellenic Psychiatric Congress.

Starr, A. (1979) *Psychodrama*. Chicago: Nelson-Hall.

Stefanatos, Y. (1987) Psychiatric services as institutions. In *Contemporary Issues in Child Psychiatry,* vol. 2. Athens: Kastaniotis.

Steinberg, D. (1986) *The Adolescent Unit*. London: John Wiley.

Townsend, S. (1984) *The Secret Diary of Adrian Mole*. London: Methuen.

Turner, V. (1967) *A Forest of Symbols*. Ithaca and London: Cornell University Press.

Way, B. (1968) *Development through Drama*. London: Longman.

Willett, J. (trans.) (1964) *Brecht on Theatre*. London: Methuen.

Winnicott, D. (1964) *The Children, the Family and the Outside World*. Harmondsworth, Middlesex: Penguin.

—— (1971) *Playing and Reality*. Harmondsworth, Middlesex: Penguin.

Name index

Ariel, S. 41–2
Arieti, S. 157
Aslanidis, E. 238
Aspy 201
Axline, Virginia M. 203

Bannister, Anne 3, 169–85, 198, 204
Baptiste, D.A. Jr 224
Bateson, G. 67, 213
Bax, M. 113
Bergman, A. 152
Bettelheim, B. 193
Blatner, H. 154–5, 185
Blos, P. 152, 153, 156, 164
Boeresma, F.J. 202
Boszormenyi-Nagy, I. 75, 77, 79, 81, 82, 86, 87–9
Bowen, M. 214
Bowlby, John 202
Brecht, B. 226, 240
Breger, L. 159
Brook, P. 216
Bruner, J. 67
Byng-Hall, J. 213, 214

Cade, B. 213, 228
Carroll, Lewis 7
Carter, Betty 229
Casement, Patrick 204
Cechin, C. 221
Courtney, R. 237
Crawley, R.J. 129

Dequine, E. 151
Dermody, Simon 3, 210–41

Eerenbeemt, E.M. van den 84, 86
Eichenbaum, L. 203, 205

Eicher, V. 151
Emunah, Renée 3, 150–67
Epston, D. 63, 67, 68, 69, 73, 226
Erickson, M. 213
Erikson, E. 147, 150, 151, 152, 153, 158
Esman, A. 152

Fairbairn, R.W.D. 192, 193, 202
Foucault, M. 67
Freud, A. 159
Freud, S. 192
Furman, L. 151

Garcia, A. 151
Gersie, A. 128, 151, 182
Gibran, K. 195, 201
Gilligan, C. 152
Grainger, Roger 196
Green, R.L. 7
Grimshaw, Di 3, 189–208
Guex, Germaine 191, 198
Guntrip, Harold 48, 202

Hanochi, N. 112
Hellendoorn, J. 183
Hersch, P. 153
Heusden, A. van 84, 86
Hillman, J. 8
Holmes, P. 185

Irwin, E. 218

Jampolsky, G.G. 114
Jennings, Sue 1–3, 41, 44, 58, 63, 90–106, 109, 126–8, 138, 148, 151, 182, 204, 211, 225, 236
Johnson, D.R. 151

Johnstone, K. 216
Jung, Carl 12, 23, 26, 207

Kellerman, P.F. 154, 185
Klein, M. 42, 48, 54, 192, 234
Kohlberg, L. 152
Kohut, H. 163
Kramer, S. 152, 164

Lahad, M. 114, 120, 124, 226
Landy, Robert J. 2, 7–27, 55, 158, 167, 211, 236
Lanffere, M. 240
Lee, D. 128
Liedloff, Jean 190–1

McBain, J.M. 35, 36
McGoldrick, Monica 229
Mahler, M. 14, 152
Malloy, E. 218
Marner, Torben 2, 63–73
Massey, D. 202
Mead, G.H. 15
Miller, Alice 199, 201, 205
Mills, J.C. 129
Minuchin, S. 213, 222
Mitchell, S. 236
Mond, Pamela 3, 109–48
Moreno, J.L. 151, 158, 169, 170, 185
Moskal, R. 202
Murray, G. 114

Newell, W.W. 34

Ogden, T.H. 40, 42–4, 48, 54, 57
Onderwaater, A. 76, 79
Opie, Iona 2, 28–39, 99
Orbach, S. 203, 205
Oren, Galila 2, 40–58
Ormont, L.R. 154

Palazzoli, M. 214
Papp, P. 230
Pearson-Davis, S. 151
Piaget, J. 8, 15, 151
Pine, F. 152

Pitzele, P. 151, 161, 167, 171
Polos, Yiorgos 3, 233–41

Roebuck, C. 201
Rogers, Carl 163, 201

Satir, V. 213
Scheff, T.J. 124, 218
Segal, E. 126
Selvini, M.P. 63
Shephard, Roger 2
Shuttleworth, R. 151, 211, 213, 228
Snoonit, M. 132
Spiegel, L.A. 153
Spitz, R.A. 191, 192, 193
Stanislavski, C. 154
Stern, D. 45
Sternberg, P. 151
Suttie, Ian D. 203

Tatham, P. 214
Thomas, K. 38
Turner, V. 238
Tustin, F. 45

Van Gennep, A. 67
Verschueren, R. 86

Walsh, S. 211
Watzlawick, P. 213, 215
Whelan, Peter 195
White, M. 63, 67, 69, 73, 226
Whitiker, Carl 213
Wijk, Jan-Berend van der 2, 75–89
Willis, S.T. 183
Winnicott, Donald W. 13, 26, 40, 41, 46, 48, 97, 164, 192, 202, 203, 205, 237
Wordsworth, W. 27

Yalom, I. 147, 154, 164
Yolen, J. 202
Young, E. 202

Zeider, Y. 111, 112

Subject index

abuse 196, 198
acceptance 164, 199, 203
Accrington Pals, The 195, 206
acting games 33–4
acting in/acting out *see* focusing
action techniques 169
adolescence 100, 104, 150–67; acting
    out to acting 154–5; adjustment
    reaction 150; breakdown 240;
    development 153; and dramatherapy
    109–85; expression and containment
    156–8; group collaboration and
    intimacy 164–5; role experimentation
    158–63; structuring therapy 240–1;
    themes 234–5; trauma 151–3
adoption 82, 83
adulthood 100
age-stages 104
aggression 21, 22, 23, 194–5, 201;
    fantasies 86–7; role 24
albinism 19
anger 147, 173–4, 176, 194, 196, 205
anorectic symptoms 79–80
anxiety fits 65, 66
art work 136, 137
'art–science–belief' 91, 92, 95
autism 110
autistic-contiguous mode 43–7, 57, 58

baby role 15–17, 20
behaviour 150
behavioural symptoms 201
behaviours, multiple high-risk 153
belief 93, 132
bibliotherapy 114–20, 130
birth: cultural 238–9, 240; second 238;
    see also self-birth
'Blind Man's Buff' 29

body image 90
'body–mind–spirit' 91
'Bogey' 31, 32
bonding process 192
bride and groom roles 11–12, 13, 14, 15
bullies/aggressors 194–5

Carnegie Council on Adolescent
    Development 153
cerebral palsy 110
chasing games 31
childhood 100; to adulthood transition
    99–101; trauma 157; *see also* 'inner-
    child'
children with difficulties 42–57;
    autistic-contiguous mode 43–7;
    depressive-mode 54–7; paranoid-
    schizoid mode 48–54
children's games, fear and tension in
    26–39
children's theatre 95
child's play 216
church 95; *see also* religion; theatre
circular questioning 221–2
client families 211, 213
'client-centred' 215
co-therapist 217–18
cocoon ritual 45–7
cognition 124
collage work 137–8
communication 157
companionship 193
conciliatory roles 21, 22, 23
conflict 122–3, 238; avoidance 224; *see
    also* dysfunction
consensual validation 164
consistency 203
containment 156–8; emotional 166

contiguous *see* autistic
Continuum Concept 190–1
contradictions, normalizing of 239–40
'controller' 170–1, 172–3
Cornelia de Langue syndrome 110, 144
countertransference *see* transference
court *see* justice image
creative: activities 77; arts therapy 153;
    Process Theory 77; Therapies Clinic
    231; therapy course 77; writing
    131–3, 134
crisis, normative 153
'Crusts and Crumbs' 30
cultural birth 238–9, 240

de-roling process 159
dead baby image 169, 174–7
death role 24–5
defence system 198
delinquent activity 150
denial 110, 131, 199
depressive mode 42, 43, 54–7, 58
depressive position 234
desensitization techniques 202
development: normal 41; *see also*
    dramatic development
developmentally delayed 110
dialectical relationship 57
dialogue, playful 58
diary-writing 133–5
'differentness' 164
difficulties, emotional 50
directive 66–7
disabilities, developmental 144
discipline, therapeutic 212
disguises 36
disloyalty 88, 89
dissociation 198–9
distance in therapy 126, 236
distortion, perceptual 90
doubling 160, 163, 165, 198, 199, 224
Down's syndrome 110, 142, 144
drama 95, 105, 161, 194
dramatherapist, role of 189
dramatherapy assessment 215–23;
    family change tactics 228–31; family
    puppet story 218–19; family
    spectograms 219–21; free play
    215–16; micro- and mini-sculpture
    221–3; stagecraft 216–18; *see also*
    symbolic dramatherapy methods
dramatherapy context 63–106

dramatic development 90–106;
    childhood to adulthood transition
    99–101; settling 101–4; theatre,
    medicine and religion 91–6
dramatization leading to diary-writing
    133–5
drawing 10, 73, 115–20; before and
    after 142–6; families 141–7, 225;
    figure 141–7; individual 141, 142;
    line/colour/shape 126, 136, 137
dyads 214, 215, 223, 225
dysfunction 156, 166; sexual 227–8; *see
    also* dysfunctional families
dysfunctional families 86–7, 88, 150,
    165, 213; *see also* families in
    distress

education 95
'Electra complex' 24
embodiment play 97, 204, 206
embodiment and projection 126–8
embodiment, projection and role theory
    (EPR) 58, 97
empathy 161–3, 165, 166–7, 201
enactment 154, 156, 213; families 226,
    228, 230; symbolic 154, 230; *see also*
    storytelling
encopresis 80, 81
envy themes 193
EPR *see* embodiment, projection and
    role theory
everyday reality 98, 99, 105, 148
evil 194; *see also* good and evil
expression 156–8; emotional 166
externalization 63, 64, 67–73, 81
extremism 159

failure 235
'false self' 192
families 147, 211, 213; change tactics
    228–31; client 211, 213;
    dramatherapy 112, 211–12; drawings
    109, 141–7; life cycle 229;
    mythology 214; organization 217;
    pattern 217; play 217; script 213–14;
    structure 217; as a system 214;
    therapy 64, 87, 88; therapy, systemic
    63; *see also* families in distress;
    stepfamilies
families in distress 210, 210–41;
    dramatherapy assessment 215–23;
    dramatherapy and play therapy

211–12; reasons for therapy 212–13; symbolic dramatherapy methods 223–8; theoretical framework 213–15; therapist 210–11
fantasy 88, 98, 170, 236, 237; aggressive 86–7; guided 136–7
father–son patterns 219, 222, 223
fear 147; image of 177–9; *see also* children's games 26–39
feelings: groups 200; inner 161; strong 154
fictional mode *see* scenarios, hypothetical
fictional scenes 151
figure drawings 141–7
'finding one's own space' 199
flexibility 141
focusing 166, 235–8, 240
foster parents 82
'Fox and Chickens' 34–5
framework, developmental 189–241
free play 215–16, 217
'French and English' 30
frightened, desire to be 30
fringe theatre 95
frustration 176

games 26–39, 99
genograms 219
genuineness 201
'getting-up story' 226–7
gifts 139
'good enough mothering' 205, 207
good and evil 36–7, 193, 205
'Grandmother's Footsteps' 99
greed themes 193
grief 173–4
group: collaboration and intimacy 164–5; dramatherapy 109; improvisations 140; process 182–4; psychotherapy 211; theory 211; therapy 153
gypsy role 10–11, 12

handicap and healthy siblings 109–48; development of work 127; home interview 114–25; results 141–7; role play 128–41; scene setting 110–13; work programme development 126–8
hate 147
healing metaphors 128–41; art work 136; collage work 137–8; creative

writing and drama 131–3; dramatization leading to diary-writing 133–5; group improvisations 140; improvisations 129–30; magic wishes and gifts 139; medal-presentation ceremony 141; poster presentations 138–9; puppetry 136, 139; secret writing 139–40; set induction and guided fantasy 136–7
'Healing Theatre' 95
Holland 77
home interview 114–25
hospital 95
'How Green You Are' 28–9
humiliation 195
'hunter-gatherers' 100, 101, 102, 103
hurt roles 21
hydrocephalus 110

idealized figures 160
identification 41–2
identity cohesion 159
images 169, 219; *see also* recurring images; self-image
imaginary: roles 205; scenes 156
imagination 90, 97, 98, 99, 102, 124, 222; *see also* make-believe
imaginative expression 207
improvisation 95, 114, 129–30, 147, 156; families 228; group 140
individual 147
individual therapy 75–89; contextual therapy 75–7; pitfalls 79, 88
individuation: phase 152; *see also* separation–individuation
induction, set 136–7
'inner child' 203–4, 205, 206, 207, 208
inner feelings 161
insecurity, emotional 191
integration: of dramatic processes of theatre art 105; of historical facts with dramatic 'as if' principle 94; of person 91; of person in relation to the world 92; of preventive and curative theatre through the mask 93; of society 92
intensive therapy 40
intention, positive 230
interview 194
intrapsychic drama 161
intrapsychic problems 81
invitation 65

isolation, emotional 205–7
Israel 40

jealousy 147
journey play 102
judgement day scenes *see* justice image
justice image 169, 172–3, 179–82

kidney disorder 110

labyrinth idea 233–41; adolescent
    themes 234–5; cultural birth and the
    meta-family 238–9; focusing 235–8;
    normalizing of contradictions
    239–40; structuring therapy 240–1
language: metaphorical 213; symbolic
    88, 211, 212, 213, 218, 221, 222
learning disabilities 50
linear chair sculpt 224
loneliness 193
love and hate 193
loyalty 81, 88–9, 193; horizontal/
    vertical 75–6; *see also* disloyalty;
    over-loyal; split-loyalty

make-believe 41–2, 49, 50, 51, 52, 53,
    54
Malaysia 90, 103
masks 93, 126; coping 171, 172;
    families 221, 224–5
maturational process 100
medal-presentation ceremony 141
medicine 93, 95, 105; *see also* theatre–
    medicine–religion
mental retardation 110
meta-family 238–9
metaphor 147, 207; therapeutic 128; *see
    also* healing
method acting 154
Milan Systemic Associates 63
mime 95
mistrust 196, 205
monster image *see* fear
morality games 36
mother–child relationship 189, 202,
    203, 207
mother-love 193–5
mothering 205, 207
moulding 161
mourning *see* grief
movement 126
myth synthesis 239

'mythopoetic process' 234

National Association for Young People
    in Care (NAYPIC) 184
needs, unmet 192, 193, 198
neglect, emotional 198
nightmares 72
nostalgia 236

Object Relations Theory 189, 192, 205
objectifying 63
objects, transitional 13–14, 97
'Old Man in the Well' 33
one-to-one *see* individual
outer projection 161
over-loyal 76
overconstriction 159
overdistancing technique 126
overprotectiveness 68, 202

paranoid-schizoid mode 42, 43, 48–54,
    56, 58
parents: biological 82, 194; role 12, 15,
    21; *see also* foster parents
partiality, multidirectional 77, 88, 89
'Peep bo' 30
peer interaction 165
personality disorders 111
personification 63, 71
phobias 201
play 102; developmental 189, 204;
    dramatic 90, 98, 99, 100; projective
    97, 204; symbolic 81, 84; therapy
    211–12; of young children 7–58; *see
    also* free play; spontaneous play
'play oneself' 156
playfulness 42
'Poison' 31
poster presentations 138–9
power themes 193
practical jokes 29–30
presenting behaviour 202
primary carer 190
Prophet, The 195
protective bars image 178, 179
protectiveness 68, 202
psycho-ecology 211, 219, 224
psycho-system 210, 223
psychodrama 156, 158, 165; *see also*
    sexual abuse
psychology, developmental 193
psychosis *see* adolescence breakdown

psychotherapy 163, 164, 211
puberty 152, 153
puppetry 126, 136, 139, 218–19

quarrelling 79–80
questioning, circular 221–2

realification 41
reality 54, 128, 170, 237; dramatic 98,
    99, 105, 128, 148; explicit 128;
    ground 90; see also everyday reality
rebelliousness 152
recurring images 174–82; dead baby
    174–7; fear 177–9; justice 179–82
recurring themes 223
referral 64
regression in peer group 238
regressive engulfment and
    dedifferentiation 152
rejection 30, 194, 198, 205
religion 94, 95, 96, 105; see also
    theatre–medicine–religion
rescue theme stories 129
respect 203
right and wrong 193
rituals 238–9; cocoon 45–7; obsessional
    68; physical 44; social 99;
    transitional 100
role: baby 15–17, 20; conciliatory 21,
    22, 23; confusion 90, 158; death
    24–5; experimentation 158–63; hurt
    21; imaginary 205; parents 12, 15,
    21; restriction 159, 166; sick 19–20;
    -taking 22, 26, 224; theory 12;
    transitional 19; types 12; see also
    role-play; role-reversal
role-play 63–73, 97, 114, 178, 204–5;
    children 7–27; externalization 67–73;
    families 221, 223–4, 228; handicap
    and healthy siblings 128–41;
    individual therapy 78, 80, 82–3, 85
role-reversal 67, 73, 155, 199; families
    224; sexual abuse 176, 177; young
    children 20–1, 22

'safe space' 190
safety, conditions of 182
scenarios, hypothetical 160
scene-work 151, 156
schizoid personality 202, 206; see also
    paranoid-schizoid mode
school failure 153

school-phobia 68, 79, 202
science–art–belief 91, 92, 95
sculpting 126, 199, 221–3, 224
secrets 111, 147; disclosure 165; see
    also writing
secure unit 197
self-birth 238
self-image 112, 235
sensory experience 44–5, 206
separation, mother and infant 191
separation–individuation 152, 164,
    218–19
settling 100, 102, 104
sexual abuse and psychodrama 165,
    169–85; benefits 171–4; coping
    170–1; group process 182–4;
    recurring images 174–82
sexual identity 234
sexuality 23
sexualized behaviour, inappropriate 201
sibling conflicts/rivalry 18, 80–2, 112,
    126, 141
'sick' role 19–20
singing games 33
singling out 28–9
skills, social 124
small objects/spectograms 124–5
Social and Cognitive Belief Systems
    132
social stigma 111
sociodramatic approach 151
'song-machine' 51, 52
spectograms 124–5, 219–21
split-loyalty 76, 85
spontaneous play 40–58, 215, 217;
    children with difficulties 42–57;
    make-believe play 41–2; operational
    framework 40–1
stagecraft 216–18
stepfamilies 225–6, 228
stepmother 193–5
stigma 111
'storm of puberty' 152, 153
story-making 120–4, 226
storytelling 9–18, 55–7, 73, 95, 175;
    alternative 226; families 221, 226–8
substance abuse 150
suicide/suicide attempts 84–6, 150
supernatural undertones 35
suspense-start chasing games 31
symbolic dramatherapy methods 223–8;

masks 224–5; role-play 223–4; storytelling 226–8
symbolism 55; sexual 176

team spirit 30
team work 217–18
Temiar tribe 90, 99, 103–4
tension *see* children's games 26–39
theatre 93, 99; art 96, 105, 106; children's 95; as entertainment 95, 96; fringe 95; group, therapeutic 103; as healing 95; -in-education 95; –medicine–religion 91–6
themes 122–3; greed 193; recurring 223; rescue 129
therapist–child relationship 203
therapy: of the absurd 213; bibliotherapy 114–20; co-therapist 217–18; contextual 75–7, 82, 89; distance 236; dramatherapy context 63–106; group 153; individual 147; intensive 40; play 211–12; psychotherapy 163, 164, 211; strategic 215; structuring 240–1; travel 101
threes *see* triangles
tolerance 203
Trade Descriptions Act 215
transference/countertransference 189–208

transformation 237, 240
transgenerational patterns 213, 219, 223, 224
trauma 157, 201
travel therapy 101
triangles 214, 215, 222, 223, 225
true self 237
trust 165, 197
twos *see* dyads

Unit for Intensive Therapy for Children 40

victim role 22, 23, 171, 173–4
victimization 180
video facilities 217

wandering 101, 102, 104, 105
warmth 201
welcome 64
'What's the Time, Mr Wolf?' 32
wishes, magic 139
witchcraft/witches 36, 38, 193–5
withdrawal 150, 201
witnessing 163, 224
work: physical 124, 126; physical-sensory 57; programme development 126–8
world view, dramatic 7–27
writing 178; secret 133–5, 139–40